Dear Reader,

Thank you for choosing *Microsoft Word 97 for Wind* [resource] for learning Word 97.

The material in this book is classroom tested and written by Logical Operations, one of the world's foremost computer training organizations. Every exercise and explanation has been adapted from a Logical Operations course specially designed for people just like you. Since we opened our door in Rochester, New York in 1982, we've taught more than 20,000 people annually how to master dozens of software programs.

Since you can't come to our classrooms, we've created the QuickStart series to bring the instructor to you. QuickStart books feature easy-to-learn, detailed step-by-step instructions and plain-English explanations to make learning complex software easier and faster.

Our research shows two things that are very important to get the most out of learning: practice and fun. You'll get the most out of this book if you have a computer with the software nearby so you can try things out as you learn them. And when you have completed the book, be sure to practice with the software as much as possible. The more you use the software, the more your learning will become permanent.

You'll also learn more if you make your learning experience as enjoyable as possible. Pick a time and place to read this book where you're comfortable and won't be distracted. The QuickStart series is designed to challenge any idea you may have about learning being a chore—with this book and a positive attitude, you'll have fun.

So, find a great spot, crack the cover of this book, relax, and enjoy learning Word 97.

Bill Rosenthal
President

Microsoft Word 97 for Windows

QUICKSTART

Microsoft Word 97 for Windows

QUICKSTART

JIM O'SHEA
FOR **Logical Operations®**

Ziff-Davis Press
An imprint of Macmillan Computer Publishing USA
Emeryville, California

Publisher	Stacy Hiquet
Writer	Jim O'Shea
Curriculum Development	Logical Operations
Acquisitions Editor	Lysa Lewallen
Copy Editor	Nicole Clausing
Proofreader	Timothy Loughman
Cover Illustration and Design	Megan Gandt
Book Design and Layout	Bruce Lundquist
Indexer	Valerie Robbins

Ziff-Davis Press imprint books are produced on a Macintosh computer system with the following applications: FrameMaker®, Microsoft® Word, QuarkXPress®, Adobe Illustrator®, Adobe Photoshop®, Adobe Streamline™, MacLink®Plus, Aldus® FreeHand™, Collage Plus™.

Ziff-Davis Press, an imprint of
Macmillan Computer Publishing USA
5903 Christie Avenue
Emeryville, CA 94608

ISBN 1-56276-471-3

Manufactured in the United States of America

10 9 8 7 6 5 4 3 2

CONTENTS AT A GLANCE

TABLE OF CONTENTS

INTRODUCTION

Welcome to *Microsoft Word 97 for Windows QuickStart*, a hands-on instruction book that will introduce you to Microsoft Word 97 for Windows while helping you attain a high level of Word for Windows fluency in the shortest time possible. And congratulations on choosing Microsoft Word 97 for Windows; you have much to look forward to. It's a powerful and feature-packed program that will greatly enhance your creation and editing of written documents.

We at Logical Operations believe this book to be a unique and welcome addition to the teeming ranks of "how to" computer publications. Our instructional approach stems directly from over a decade of successful teaching in a hands-on classroom environment. Throughout the book, we combine theory with practice by presenting new techniques and then applying them in hands-on activities. These activities use specially prepared sample files, which are stored on the enclosed data disk.

Unlike a class, this book allows you to proceed at your own pace. And, we'll be right there to guide you along every step of the way, providing landmarks to help chart your progress and hold to a steady course.

When you're done working your way through this book, you'll have a solid foundation of skills in:

- Creating, editing, printing, storing, and retrieving text documents
- Modifying a document's appearance (typestyles and sizes, page layout, and so on)
- Checking documents for spelling, grammar, style, and wording errors
- Creating, modifying, printing, storing, and retrieving AutoText entries (files that hold frequently used text you can insert in your documents without retyping)
- Creating, modifying, and enhancing tables
- Creating and modifying multicolumn text
- Inserting, sizing, moving, and modifying graphics (onscreen pictures)
- Creating and generating form letters
- Using templates and styles to simplify the creation of documents
- Creating outlines from existing documents
- Saving Word for Windows documents as HTML documents
- Accessing Word for Windows help on the Internet

This foundation will enable you to quickly and easily create sophisticated, professional-quality documents.

WHO THIS BOOK IS FOR

We wrote this book for the beginning to intermediate level Microsoft Word for Windows user. While experience with personal computers, word processors, and the Internet is certainly helpful, it is not required. You should know how to turn on your computer, monitor, and printer; how to use your keyboard and mouse; and how to connect to your network (if you're on one) and the Internet (if you have access). We'll explain everything beyond that.

HOW TO USE THIS BOOK

You can use this book as a learning guide, a review tool, and a quick reference.

AS A LEARNING GUIDE

Each chapter covers one broad topic or set of related topics. Chapters are arranged in order of increasing proficiency; skills you acquire in one chapter are used and elaborated on in later chapters. For this reason, you should work through the chapters in sequence.

Each chapter is organized into explanatory topics and step-by-step activities. Topics provide the theory you need to master Word for Windows; activities allow you to apply this theory to practical, hands-on examples.

You get to try out each new skill on a specially prepared sample file stored on the enclosed data disk. This saves you typing time and allows you to concentrate on the technique at hand. Through the use of sample files, hands-on activities, illustrations that give you feedback at crucial steps, and supporting background information, this book provides you with the foundation and structure to learn Word 97 for Windows quickly and easily.

AS A REVIEW TOOL

Any method of instruction is only as effective as the time and effort you are willing to invest in it. For this reason, we strongly encourage you to spend some time reviewing the book's more challenging topics and activities.

AS A QUICK REFERENCE

General procedures such as opening a document or italicizing selected text may be presented as a series of bulleted steps; you can find these bullets (•) easily by skimming through the book. Bulleted procedures can serve as a handy reference. At the end of every chapter, you'll find a quick reference table that lists the general procedure steps necessary to perform the techniques introduced in that chapter.

WHAT THIS BOOK CONTAINS

This book contains the following 14 chapters and 2 appendices:

Chapter 1:   Getting Started

Chapter 2:   Word Basics

Chapter 3:   Editing Text

Chapter 4:   Character Formatting

Chapter 5:   Paragraph Formatting

Chapter 6:   Page Formatting

Chapter 7:   Proofing Your Documents

Chapter 8:   Advanced Formatting and Editing Techniques

Chapter 9:   Storing Frequently Used Text With the AutoText Feature

Chapter 10:   Working with Tables

Chapter 11:   Newspaper-Style Columns and Graphics

Chapter 12:   Creating Form Letters

Chapter 13:   Using Templates and Styles to Automate Your Work

Chapter 14:   Introducing the Internet

Appendix A: Installation

Appendix B: Keystroke Reference

SPECIAL LEARNING FEATURES

The following features of this book will facilitate your learning:

- Carefully sequenced topics that build on the knowledge you've acquired from previous topics

- Frequent hands-on activities that sharpen your Microsoft Word 97 for Windows skills

- Numerous illustrations that show how your screen should look at key points during these activities

- The data disk, which contains all the files you will need to complete the activities (as explained in the next section)

- Easy-to-spot bulleted procedures that provide the general step-by-step instructions you'll need to perform Microsoft Word 97 for Windows tasks

- A quick reference at the end of each chapter, listing the mouse/keyboard actions needed to perform the techniques introduced in the chapter

THE DATA DISK

One of the most important learning features of this book is the data disk, the 3½-inch floppy disk that accompanies the book. This disk contains the sample files you'll retrieve and work on throughout the book.

To perform the activities in this book, you will first need to create a work folder on your hard disk, as explained in Chapter 1, "Getting Started." You'll then copy the files from the data disk to your work folder. This folder will also hold all the files that you will be creating, editing, and saving during the course of this book.

WHAT YOU NEED TO USE THIS BOOK

To run Word 97 for Windows and complete the activities in this book, you need a computer with a hard disk and at least one floppy-disk drive, a monitor, a keyboard, and a mouse (or compatible tracking device). Although you don't absolutely need a printer, we strongly recommend that you have one. If you plan to complete Chapter 14, you must also have a browser such as Microsoft Internet Explorer 3.0 and Internet access.

Windows 95 or Windows NT must be installed on your computer; if it is not, see your Windows 95 or Windows NT reference manuals for instructions. Word 97 for Windows must also be installed; for help see Appendix A.

COMPUTER AND MONITOR

You need an IBM or IBM-compatible personal computer and monitor that are capable of running Microsoft Windows (version 95 or higher). We recommend that you use a 486 or higher computer.

You need a hard disk with at least 80 megabytes of free storage space (if Word 97 for Windows is not yet installed) or 160 megabytes of free storage space if you plan to completely install Microsoft Office 97. If Microsoft Word or Office has been installed, you need 5 megabytes of free disk space.

Finally, you need an EGA or higher (VGA, SVGA, and so on) graphics card and monitor to display Windows and Word 97 at their intended screen resolution.

(**Note:** The Word for Windows screens shown in this book are taken from a VGA monitor. Depending on your monitor type, your screens may look slightly different.)

A SPECIAL NOTE

We created this book on the Windows 95 platform, using the custom installation option in Microsoft Office 97. If you are working on the Windows NT platform, or chose a different installation option, your screens might not match ours, and you might not be able to follow all of the steps as they are written in the book.

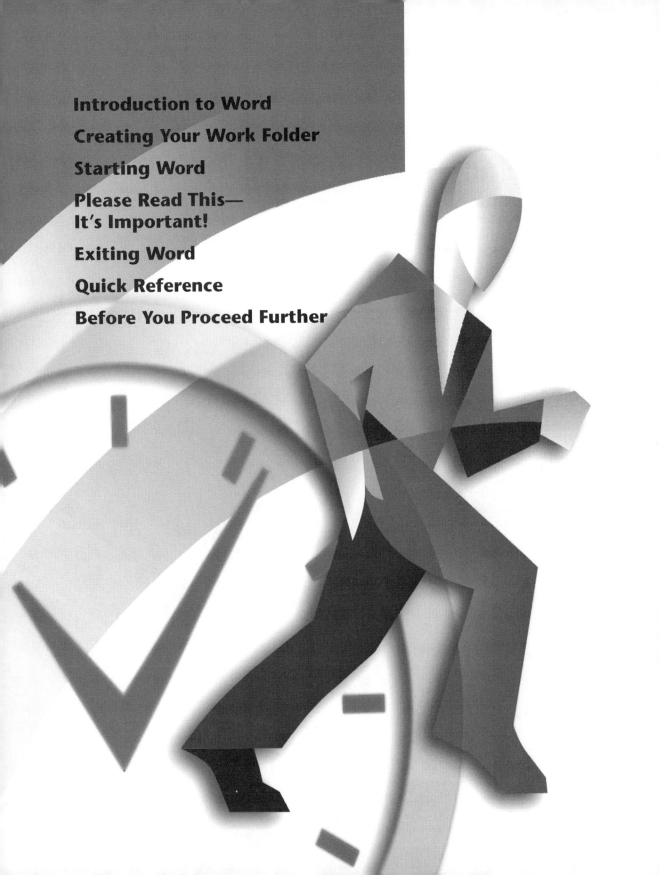

Chapter 1
Getting Started

Welcome to Word for Windows 8.0—from here on referred to simply as Word—and the exciting world of word processing! In this chapter, we'll get you up and running in Word and introduce you to the Word working environment. Then you'll learn how to exit the program.

When you're done working through this chapter, you will know

- How to use the mouse

- How to start Word

- How to exit Word

A QUICK REVIEW OF MOUSE SKILLS

You can use the *mouse* to select and deselect menu commands, and copy, move and delete text and graphical objects. Table 1.1 displays the various mousing techniques you'll need to know to complete the exercises in this book. Use this table as a quick reference, referring to it whenever you need to refresh your memory.

INTRODUCTION TO WORD

A *word processor* (such as Word) is a computer program that enables you to create, edit, print, and save documents for future retrieval and revision. You enter text into the computer by using a keyboard. As you type, your words are displayed on a monitor, or screen, and are stored temporarily in computer memory as you are creating the document (and permanently on disk once you save it) rather than on paper.

One of the chief advantages of a word processor over a conventional type-writer is that a word processor enables you to make changes to a document without retyping the entire document. For example, you can create a letter in a word processor and then, after you are finished, go back and change margins, add sentences, delete words, move paragraphs, correct spelling errors, and so on. You can do all of this without retyping the original text.

CREATING YOUR WORK FOLDER

Throughout this book, you'll be creating, editing, and saving a number of files. To keep these files in one place, you'll need to create a work folder for them on your hard disk. Your work folder will also hold the sample files contained on the enclosed data disk.

Note: Before you start Word, both Microsoft Windows 95 and Word for Windows 8.0 must be installed on your hard disk. If either of these programs is not installed, please install it now. For help installing Windows 95, see your Windows documentation. For help installing Word for Windows 8.0, see Appendix A of this book.

Table 1.1
Mousing Techniques

Technique	How to Do It
Point	Move the mouse until the tip of the mouse pointer is over the desired object. "Point to the word *File*" means "Move the mouse until the tip of the mouse pointer is over the word *File*."
Click	Press and release the left or right mouse button. When we want you to click the left mouse button, we'll simply say "click." For example, "Click on the word *File*" means "Point to the word *File* and then press and release the left mouse button." When we want you to click the right mouse button, we'll say so. For example, we'll either ask you to click the right mouse button or to right-click.
Double-click	Press and release the left mouse button twice in rapid succession. "Double-click on the *Preview 1 file*" means "Point to the file name *Preview 1* and then press and release the left mouse button twice in rapid succession."
Choose	Click on a menu command or a dialog-box button. "Choose File, Open" means "Click on the word *File* (in the menu bar), and then click on the word *Open* (in the File menu)."
Drag	Press and hold the left mouse button while moving the mouse. "Drag the scroll box upward" means "Point to the scroll box, press and hold the left mouse button, move the mouse upward, and then release the mouse button."
Scroll	Click on a scroll arrow or within a scroll bar, or drag a scroll box.
Select	Click on an object (to select the entire object), or drag over part of a text object (to select part of the text). "Select the Chapter 2 file" means "Click on the file name *Chapter 2*." "Select the first four letters of the title *Vision Office Products*" means "Drag over the letters *Visi*."
Check/Uncheck	Click on a check box to check (turn on) or uncheck (turn off) that option. "Check the Match Case option" means "Click on the Match Case check box to check it."

Let's create our work folder. First you must log onto Windows 95. If you are already logged on, skip directly to the paragraph following step 6.

1. If Windows 95 is not currently installed on your computer, please install it now, before proceeding.

2. If your computer is turned off, remove all floppy disks and turn it on.

3. The Logon Information dialog box appears. In the User name box, verify that the current name is yours; if not, type your username. In the Password box, type your password and click on **OK**. (If you don't have a password, leave the box blank and press **Esc**.)

4. If the Welcome to Windows 95 window appears, click on **Close** to close it.

Next you need to determine whether your local hard disk has enough free space for your new work folder:

1. Use your mouse to point to the **My Computer** icon. Double-click (press the left mouse button twice in rapid succession) on this icon to open the My Computer window.

2. In this window, point to the **icon representing the disk** on which you want to create your work folder. Click once on this icon to select it.

3. Click on the word **File** located near the top of the My Computer window. The drop-down File menu opens

4. In this menu, click on **Properties** to display the Properties dialog box for your selected hard disk, as shown in Figure 1.1.

Figure 1.1
The Properties dialog box

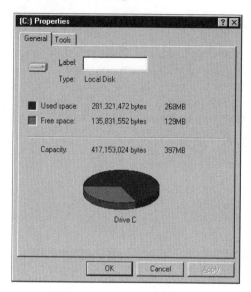

5. Observe the Free Space line in the middle of the dialog box; it shows the number of free bytes on your hard disk. Jot this number down.

6. Click on ⊠ (the **Close** button) in the upper-right corner of the Properties dialog box. The Close button appears in the upper-right corner of many windows and dialog boxes. Clicking on it always closes the open dialog box or window.

7. Observe the number of free bytes you jotted down in step 5. If it's 10,000,000 (10MB) or more, skip the rest of this step. If not, you'll have to delete (or move) enough files from your hard disk to increase its free byte total to 10,000,000. Otherwise, you won't be able to create your work folder and perform the hands-on activities in this book while still maintaining an adequate amount of free hard-disk space. Make sure to back up all important files before deleting them! (For help deleting and backing up, consult your local Windows 95 guru.)

Now that you're in the 10,000,000+ club, you can safely create your work folder:

1. Insert the data disk from the back of this book into the floppy-disk drive.

2. Click on the **Start** button to open the Start menu. (If your Start button is not visible, press **Ctrl+Esc** to open the Start menu.)

3. In this menu, click on **Run** to open the Run dialog box.

4. Type a command of the form

   ```
   fdrive:\install hdrive: Wordwork
   ```

   where f is the letter of the floppy-disk drive holding your data disk, and h is the letter of the hard-disk drive on which you want to create your work folder. (Make sure to type a backslash (\)—not a forward slash (/)—before *install*, and to type a space between *install*, *hdrive:*, and *Wordwork*.) For example, if your data disk is on drive A and you're creating your work folder on drive C, you'd enter

   ```
   a:\install c: Wordwork
   ```

5. Click on **OK** to enter your command. If all goes well, the message

   ```
   Work folder under construction.
   Please wait ......................
   ```

   will appear, followed by a list of files being copied. And when the procedure is complete, the message

   ```
   Work folder successfully completed!
   ```

   will appear, followed by a line reporting the name of your work folder (c:\Wordwork, for example) and the closing line

   ```
   Press any key to continue...
   ```

   If these messages appear, press **Enter** to return to Windows 95 and skip directly to the Note following the next step.

6. If all does not go so well, one of two error messages will appear. The first is

   ```
   ********************************************************
   ```

   Installation failed! c: drive does not exist.

   Reenter the INSTALL command using the correct drive.

   ```
   ********************************************************
   ```

   (Your drive letter may be different.) This message indicates that the hard drive you specified in your step 4 command does not exist on your computer. If you get this message, press Enter to return to Windows 95, and then repeat step 4, making sure to specify the correct letter of your hard drive.

The second error message is

****

Installation failed! c:\Wordwork folder already exists.

Reenter the INSTALL command using a new work folder name.

****

Press any key to continue...

(Your drive letter and/or folder name may be different.) This message indicates that a folder with the same name as your proposed work folder (Wordwork) already exists on your specified hard disk. If this happens, press Enter to return to Windows 95, and then repeat step 4, specifying a new work folder name of your choice instead of Wordwork.

Note: The hands-on activities in this book assume that your work folder is on drive C and is named Wordwork. If you specified a different hard-disk drive or a different folder name, please remember to substitute this drive and/or name whenever we mention drive C or Wordwork.

STARTING WORD

Before you start Word, both Microsoft Windows 95 and Word for Windows 8.0 must be installed on your hard disk. If either of these programs is not installed, please install it now. For help installing Windows 95, see your Windows documentation. For help installing Word for Windows 8.0, see Appendix A of this book.

You also need to have created a work folder on your hard disk and copied the files from the enclosed data disk to this folder. If you have not done this, please do so now; for instructions, see "Creating Your Work Folder" earlier in this chapter.

Note: In this book, we present two types of procedures: bulleted and numbered. A bulleted procedure—one whose steps are preceded by a bullet (•)— serves as a general reference; you should read its steps without actually performing them. A numbered procedure—one whose steps are preceded by numbers (1., 2., and so on)—is a specific hands-on activity; you should perform its steps as instructed.

To start Word:

* Turn on your computer.

* Enter your Windows 95 password.

* From the Start menu, open the *Programs* menu, and select *Microsoft Word*. If you have installed Microsoft Office, you might need to move

through additional layers of the Start menu to locate Word; for example, you might have to choose *Start, Programs, Microsoft Office, Microsoft Word*.

Note: To start Word, we must first locate the program in the Start menu. Because Windows 95 is a customizable program, we cannot know the details of your Windows 95 setup. So please bear with us as we search for your Microsoft Word program.

With Windows 95 already running, let's start Word:

1. Click on the **Start** button in the taskbar.

2. Highlight (point to) **Programs** to display the available programs (see Figure 1.2; your menu choices will vary). Depending on your Windows 95 setup, you might need to search through a few layers of menus to find Microsoft Word (or you might have created a shortcut to it). If Word was installed as part of Microsoft Office, then you will probably find it in the Microsoft Office menu.

Figure 1.2
The Start and Programs menus

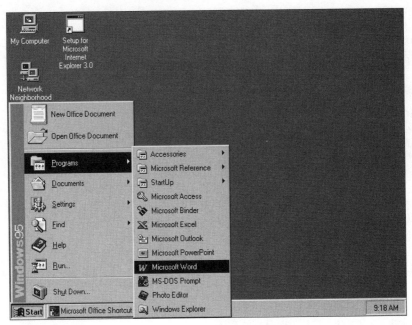

3. Click on the **Microsoft Word** choice to start the program. Your screen should match—or closely resemble—Figure 1.3. (**Note:** If this is the first time you are opening Word for Windows, press **Esc** to close the Office Assistant Help bubble. If necessary, enter your name and initials in the User Name box, and click on **OK**.)

Figure 1.3
Word 8.0, after start-up

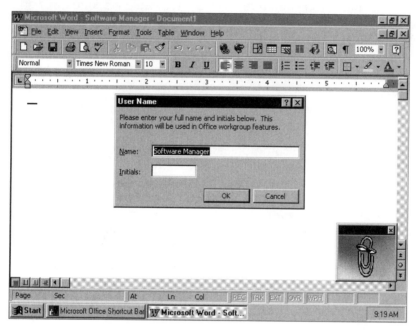

4. If necessary, click on ![Maximize button] (the **Maximize** button) in the upper-right corner of the screen.

Note: You only need to click on the Maximize button if your Word window does not fill the entire screen.

PLEASE READ THIS—IT'S IMPORTANT!

Like Windows 95, Word can be customized. Depending on how you (or perhaps a colleague) have set up your Word program, it may look very different from another user's Word setup, or from the Word setup used in this book.

To write this book for an "invisible" audience—with hundreds, if not thousands, of different Word setups—we had to assume that you are running Word with the same *default* (standard) settings that were automatically chosen when you first installed the application. Of course, this assumption may be false. You or a colleague may have customized your Word program to show additional toolbars, run in full-screen view, display onscreen text as 20-point Gargantuan Urdu, hide the formula and status bars, and so on.

Here's our recommendation: First of all, relax. Chances are your program settings are fine. But if you should run into a snag while working through this book—for example, if your screen displays differ markedly from ours, or if tools we ask you to use are missing from your screen—simply use your ever-increasing Word expertise to make the changes necessary to match your Word setup as closely as possible to ours.

THE WORD APPLICATION AND DOCUMENT WINDOWS

Word is built around a set of interactive *windows*—rectangular, onscreen boxes through which you communicate with the Word program and create your documents. When you start Word, two windows appear on the screen, one nestled snugly within the other. The larger of these, called the *application window*, frames the entire screen; you use it to communicate with the Word program. (The terms *program* and *application* are synonymous.) The smaller window, called the *document window*, fits seamlessly within the application window; you use it to create and edit your Word documents.

Table 1.2 and Figure 1.4 show the screen elements with which you need to be familiar when using Word.

Table 1.2
Screen Elements of Word

Term	Definition
Application window	Larger of two start-up windows; provides interface between user and Word
Document window	Smaller of two start-up windows; holds currently active Word document
Control-menu icons	Located in upper-left corner of screen; they control size and position of application window (upper box) and document window (lower box)

Table 1.2
Screen Elements of Word (Continued)

Title bar	Displays name of application (Microsoft Word) and active document (Document1, in this case)
Close buttons	Close the application window (upper button) and document window (lower button)
Maximize/Restore buttons	Control size of application window (upper button) and document window (lower button)
Minimize buttons	Reduce application and document windows
Menu bar	Lists Word menu options
Standard toolbar	Provides quick access to Word's most frequently used commands and utilities
Formatting toolbar	Provides quick access to Word's most frequently used formatting commands
Ruler	Provides ongoing page measurement as well as quick access to margins, tabs, and indents
Scroll bars	Used to display different areas of active document (each scroll bar contains pair of directional scroll arrows)
Navigation buttons	Used to move to different pages and areas of the document
View buttons	Used to change document display to Normal view (leftmost button), Page Layout view (middle button), and Outline view (rightmost button)
Status bar	Displays variety of details relating to active document
Office Assistant	Provides quick access to context-sensitive Office 97 help topics.

Figure 1.4
The Word application window

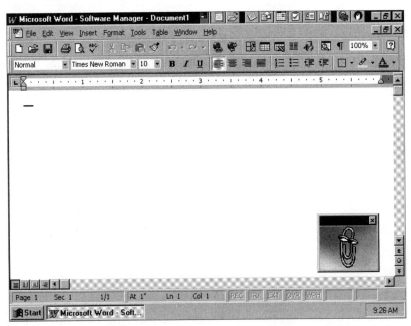

Let's take a closer look at some of these screen elements. (We'll discuss the remaining elements over the next few chapters.)

1. Click on ![W] (the application-window **Control-menu** icon) to open its drop-down menu. (Do not *double*-click on the Control-menu icon, as this would cause you to exit Word.) Note the Control-menu options: Restore, Move, Size, Minimize, and so on.

2. Click on the application-window **Control-menu** icon again to close its drop-down menu.

3. Now click on ![icon] (the document-window **Control-menu** icon). The document-window Control-menu opens. Note that its options are very similar to the application window Control-menu options you saw in the previous step.

4. Click on the document-window **Control-menu** icon again to close its drop-down menu.

5. Click on ![icon] (the application-window **Maximize/Restore** button). Word restores (shrinks) the application window. Note that the Maximize/Restore

button now contains the graphic of a single large window, indicating that its function is to maximize (rather than to restore) the window.

6. Click on the application-window **Maximize/Restore** button again to maximize the application window to fill the entire screen.

7. Now click on the document-window **Maximize/Restore** button (at the right edge of the menu bar) to restore the document window. Note that the Maximize/Restore button moves to the upper-right corner of the restored (shrunken) document window. Note also that when the document window is restored, it gets its own title bar (in this case, it reads *Document1*).

8. Click on the document-window **Maximize/Restore** button again to maximize the document window to fit snugly within the application window. Note that when the document window is maximized, it loses its title bar, and the document title (Document1) appears in the application-window title bar.

USING THE MENU BAR TO ISSUE COMMANDS

To perform a word processing task (such as retrieving a document from disk, formatting text, printing a document, and so on), you must issue the appropriate Word command. You can do this by:

- Using the mouse to choose the command from the menu bar
- Using the mouse to choose the command from one of the toolbars or the ruler
- Using the mouse to choose the command from a shortcut menu
- Using the keyboard to enter a keyboard shortcut

For example, to italicize text, you could

- Use the mouse to choose the *Font* command from the Format option in the menu bar, and then select the *Italic* option.
- Use the mouse to click on the *Italic* button on the Formatting toolbar.
- Use the mouse to choose the *Font* command from the shortcut menu, and then select the *Italic* option.
- Use the keyboard to press *Ctrl+I* (press and hold the **Ctrl** key, press and hold the **I** key, and then release both keys), the keyboard shortcut for italicizing text. Please do not perform any of these actions now.

Using the menu bar is the only method that allows you to issue every available Word command. The toolbars and ruler provide a subset of Word's most frequently used commands, as do the shortcut menus and the keyboard. For this reason, we'll begin our exploration of commands by using the menu-bar approach.

Let's issue some commands by using the menu bar:

1. Point to the **File** option (move the mouse pointer until its tip is over the word *File* in the menu bar). Click the left mouse button. The drop-down File menu opens, displaying a set of file-related commands: *New, Open, Close, Save, Save As,* and so on.

2. Move the mouse pointer down to highlight the **Save As** command and click the mouse button to open the Save As dialog box (see Figure 1.5). *Dialog boxes* prompt you to enter information relating to the selected command (File, Save As, in this case). You will work extensively with dialog boxes during the course of this book.

Figure 1.5
The Save As dialog box

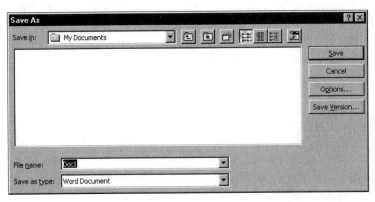

3. Click on the **Cancel** button in the upper-right corner of the Save As dialog box to close it without making any changes.

4. Click on the **Edit** option in the menu bar. The drop-down Edit menu opens, displaying Word's editing commands.

5. Observe that several Edit commands are dimmed (displayed in light letters): *Cut, Copy, Paste, Links,* and so on. Word dims menu commands to show that they are unavailable in the current context. For example,

the Copy command is dimmed because you have not selected any text to copy.

6. Observe also that several commands are followed by ellipses (*Find...*, *Replace...*, *Go To...*, and so on). When you choose a command with an ellipsis, Word displays a dialog box prompting you for further information; for example, when you choose *Find...*, Word displays a dialog box prompting you for the word(s) you want to find. When you choose a command without an ellipsis, Word simply carries out the command; for example, when you choose *Select All*, Word immediately (with no intervening dialog box) selects all the text in the current document. To keep this book easy to read, we chose not to print command ellipses. In step 2 of this activity, for example, we asked you to click on the Save As command, though *Save As...* is how the command actually appears on your screen.

7. Click on **Edit** again to close the Edit menu.

EXITING WORD

Earlier you learned that there are multiple ways to issue many of the commands available in Word. Exiting Word is no exception; for example, you could exit the program by using any one of the following techniques:

- Choose *File, Exit* from the menu.
- Click on the application-window *Control-menu* icon, and choose *Close*.
- Double-click on the application-window *Control-menu* icon.
- Click on the application-window *Close* box.

The method that you choose to issue any command is to some extent a matter of preference. For example, if you're one who computes by mouse alone, you might not want to learn any keyboard shortcuts; if, on the other hand, you're a dyed-in-the-wool keywhacker, you might be violently allergic to mouse pointers.

Let's exit Word:

1. Use one of the techniques described in the bulleted list above to exit from Word. (Remember, if you use the Close button, the top Close button closes the application. The document window has a Close button of its own, which allows you to close the document without exiting Word.)

QUICK REFERENCE

In this chapter, you learned how to start and exit Word, and you've been introduced to the Word environment.

Here's a quick reference guide to the Word features introduced in this chapter:

Desired Result	How to Do It
Start Word	Start Windows. Choose *Start, Programs.* Locate and click on *Microsoft Word* choice.
Exit Word	Click on the application-window *Close* box, or Choose *File, Exit*, or Click on the application-window *Control-menu* icon and click on *Close*, or, Double-click on the application-window *Control-menu* icon.

In the next chapter, we'll show you the basics of using Word: how to enter and edit text, how to save the text in a file, how to create a new document, how to print a document, and how to navigate in Word. You'll also learn how to obtain helpful Word tips, open a file, display different portions of a document, search for text in a document, control document magnification, and obtain online help.

BEFORE YOU PROCEED FURTHER

The activities within each remaining chapter proceed sequentially. In many cases, you cannot perform an activity until you've performed one or more of the activities preceding it. For this reason, we recommend that you allot enough time to work through an entire chapter in one continuous session. Feel free to take as many breaks as you need: Stand up, stretch, take a stroll, do some wrist and hand exercises, drink some hot chocolate, tell a joke. Don't try to absorb too much information at any one time. Studies show that people assimilate and retain information most effectively when it is presented in digestible chunks and followed by a liberal amount of hands-on practice.

If you wish to stop here, please feel free to do so now. If you feel energetic and wish to press onward, please proceed directly to the next chapter.

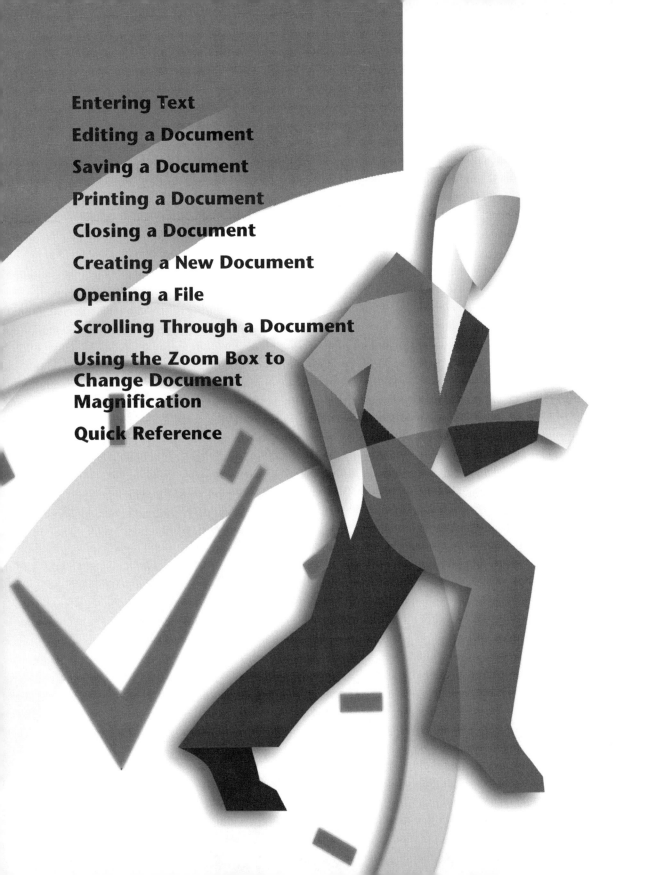

Chapter 2
Word Basics

In this chapter, we'll lead you through one complete Word work session: You'll start the Word program, create and edit a document, save and print the document, create and save a new document, and learn some important navigation techniques. This, in a nutshell, is the procedure you will use in your day-to-day word processing work with Word.

You'll also learn how to use the mouse *and* the keyboard to navigate through a multipage document. It's essential for you to master these navigational techniques as early as possible in your Word career. The more comfortable you feel moving around within a document, the more you'll be able to concentrate on the contents of the document itself.

When you're done working through this chapter, you will know

- How to enter text
- How to insert, delete, and replace text
- How to save and name a document
- How to print and close a document
- How to create a new document
- How to open a file
- How to use the mouse to scroll through a document
- How to use the keyboard and menus to move through a document
- How to use the Find command to search for text
- How to use the Zoom Control box to change the document magnification
- How to use Word Help to obtain online help

ENTERING TEXT

Word is a WYSIWYG (What You See Is What You Get) program; that is, the screen shows you (more or less) exactly how your document will look when you print it. WYSIWYG programs are not subject to the arcane codes and inaccurate page layouts that plague non-WYSIWYG programs. Word's "WYSIWYG-ness" encourages you to work in a visual-intuitive style in which you treat the word processor as a computerized extension of a typewriter.

Over the next several sections, we'll discuss the basics of entering text in a Word document.

THE TEXT AREA

When you start Word, a new document window automatically opens, providing you with a blank text area in which you can type your desired text. Word automatically selects a whole slew of critical document settings, including margins, font and font size, line spacing, tab stops, page dimensions, and many other document attributes. Because Word preselects these settings—which are called defaults—you can start to type immediately, without first having to specify any of the settings yourself.

The characters you type are inserted in front of a blinking vertical bar called the insertion point. To move the insertion point—and thus change where your typing appears in the document—you simply move the mouse pointer and click at the desired new place in the text.

If you are not running Word, please start it now (for help, see "Starting Word" in Chapter 1). Let's examine Word's text area (see Figure 2.1):

1. Observe the *insertion point* (the blinking vertical bar). Its location determines where the next character you type will be entered into your document. Note that the insertion point of a new document always appears in the upper-left corner (that is, at the beginning) of the document window.

2. Observe the *end mark*. This is the broad horizontal line that indicates the end of the document. The end mark cannot be formatted or deleted (erased), and you cannot place the insertion point beyond it.

3. Observe the *mouse pointer*. The pointer becomes an *I-beam* (as shown in Figure 2.1) when it is within the text area. When you move it outside the text area, it becomes an arrow. Take a moment to verify this.

Figure 2.1
The text area

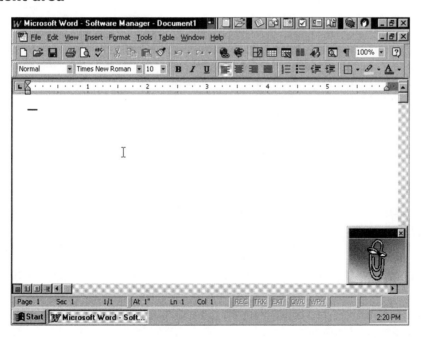

USING CAPS LOCK TO TYPE CAPITAL LETTERS

When the Caps Lock key is active, you don't have to press Shift to type uppercase letters. In fact, if you press Shift while typing in Caps Lock mode, Word will display lowercase letters. To use the Caps Lock key to type uppercase letters, simply press it. Pressing the key again turns off Caps Lock mode.

WORD-WRAP AND THE ENTER KEY

The Enter key on your keyboard is similar to—but not exactly the same as—the Return key on a typewriter. On a typewriter, you need to hit the Return key whenever you want to end a line. In Word, when a word does not fit on a line, it automatically flows to the beginning of the next line. This feature is called *word-wrap*. However, you do need to press Enter to:

- End a short line (one that doesn't reach the right margin)

- End a paragraph

- Create a blank line

Let's type some text in our new document window and practice using the Caps Lock key and the Enter key. (We'll demonstrate word-wrap in "Using the Backspace Key to Delete Text" later in this chapter.)

1. Observe the status bar. The vertical page position measurement (*At*) and the line number (*Ln*) reflect the current position of the insertion point.

2. Press the **Caps Lock** key to turn on Caps Lock mode.

3. Type **INTEROFFICE MEMO** to enter the characters at the insertion point, and press **Enter** to end the line. Note that the status bar At and Ln numbers show the new insertion point position.

4. Press **Enter** to create a blank line.

5. Press **Caps Lock** to turn off the Caps Lock key.

NONPRINTING CHARACTERS

You can choose to have Word display a number of special characters on the screen that show the places in the text where you pressed the spacebar, or the Enter and Tab keys. These *nonprinting* characters (so called because they do not appear on paper when you print the document) are often useful to see. This is particularly true when you are working with heavily formatted documents and need to keep track of your tabs, spaces, blank lines, and so on.

To display Word's nonprinting characters, you click on the Show/Hide button in the Standard toolbar.

Let's display the nonprinting characters of our active document:

1. Examine the screen. Each line of text is short, not reaching the right margin. Note that there are no characters marking the ends of these lines.

2. Click on ¶ (the **Show/Hide** button) to display Word's special format-ting characters.

3. Examine the screen. Each time you pressed Enter in the previous activity, Word placed a paragraph mark (¶) in the document. Each time you pressed the spacebar, Word placed a space mark (·) in the document. These non-printing characters only appear on the screen when the Show/Hide button is depressed; they will not appear in your printed document.

4. Click on the **Show/Hide** button again to hide the nonprinting characters. Clicking on this button *toggles* the display between its Show and Hide modes.

5. Click on the **Show/Hide** button again to display the nonprinting characters.

USING THE TAB KEY TO ALIGN TEXT HORIZONTALLY

Tabs enable you to align text horizontally. These lines are properly aligned:

   Line 1 ....

   Line 2 ....

These are not:

Line 1 ....

 Line 2 ....

Pressing the Tab key moves the insertion point to the next tab stop to the right. *Tab stops* are fixed horizontal positions within a line. By default, Word's tab stops are set at 1/2-inch increments. Pressing Tab once moves the inser-tion point 1/2-inch to the right; pressing Tab again moves it another 1/2-inch, for a total of one inch from the left margin; and so on. (We created the prop-erly aligned example just shown by pressing Tab once at the beginning of each line. We created the improperly aligned example by using the spacebar to insert blank spaces at the beginning of each line.)

USING THE BACKSPACE KEY TO DELETE TEXT

You can use the Backspace key to delete text one character at a time. Simply press Backspace to delete the single character immediately to the left of the in-sertion point.

Let's experiment with Word's Tab, Backspace, and word-wrap features:

1. Type **To:**

2. Press **Tab** to insert a tab after the text. This moves the insertion point to the first tab stop, 1/2-inch to the right. Note that Word displays the tab

mark (‹), since the Show/Hide button is still depressed from our last exercise. As with the paragraph and space marks, this tab mark will not appear on the printed page.

3. Press **Tab** again to insert another tab. This moves the insertion point to the second tab stop, one inch from the left margin.

4. Press **Backspace** to remove the second tab character.

5. Type **Syriana Sarkis**. Then press **Enter** twice to move to the next line and insert a blank line. Notice that Word has placed a wavy, red line beneath *Syriana* and *Sarkis*, suggesting that these words might be misspelled. This is because the *Spell As You Type* option (on the Spelling and Grammar tab of the Options dialog box) is turned on by default. Later in this chapter, we'll turn this option off until we're ready to take a closer look at it in Chapter 7. For now, let's continue creating our memo.

6. Type **From:**, press **Tab**, and then type **Erin Brabant**.

7. Press **Enter** twice to end the line and create a blank line.

INSERTING THE CURRENT DATE

With Word for Windows' *Insert, Date and Time* command, you can automatically insert the current date. If you check the Update Automatically option at the bottom of the Date And Time dialog box, Word automatically updates the date each time you open or print the document.

Let's insert the current date and finish the memo.

1. Type **Date:**, press **Tab**, and choose **Insert, Date and Time** to open the Date and Time dialog box. You can insert the date or the date and time in any of the available formats.

2. Click on **OK** to insert the date and close the dialog box. Then, press **Enter** twice to end the date line and create a blank line.

3. Type **Re:**, press **Tab**, type **Car Rentals**, and press **Enter** twice.

4. Type **Cyndi, The planning calendars that you ordered from Marshall's Business Products are temporarily out of stock.** (Include the period.)

5. Observe the screen. Note that the text automatically wraps (moves) to the next line, even though you did not press Enter. This is an example of word-wrap.

PRACTICE YOUR SKILLS

Complete the memo as shown below:

INTEROFFICE·MEMO¶
¶
To: →   Syriana·Sarkis¶
¶
From: → Erin·Brabant¶
¶
Date: → 10/10/96¶
¶
RE: →   Car·Rentals¶
¶
Cyndi,·The·planning·calendars·that·you·ordered·from·Marshall's·Business·Products·are·temporarily·out·of·
stock.·We·will·let·you·know·as·soon·as·they·come·here.¶
¶

EDITING A DOCUMENT

As mentioned in the introduction to this chapter, one of the strongest arguments for switching from a typewriter to a word processor is the greatly increased ease of editing your documents. In the time it would take you just to pencil in your desired changes to a typewritten document (without actually retyping it), you could incorporate these changes into a word-processed document, print it, and save it on a hard or floppy disk for future revision.

In the next several sections, we'll discuss the basics of text editing in Word.

INSERTING TEXT

By default, Word runs in *insert* mode: As you type, text to the right of the insertion point is pushed further to the right to make room for your new text. To insert text in a document, perform these two steps:

• Place the insertion point (use the mouse to position the I-beam and click) where you want to insert your new text.

• Type the new text.

Using Overtype Mode

Word gives you the option of turning off insert mode and turning on overtype mode. Instead of pushing text to the right as you type, overtype mode replaces existing text, one character at a time.

You can turn on overtype mode by double-clicking on OVR on the status bar or by pressing the Insert key on the keyboard. If you accidentally turn on overtype mode, you can double-click on OVR or press the Insert key to turn it off.

Let's practice inserting text in a document:

1. Point to the left of the *p* in *planning* (located in the paragraph beginning with *Cyndi,*). Click the mouse button to place the insertion point directly before the *p* in *planning*. (Do not place the insertion point before the space preceding the *p*.) This is where you will insert your new text.

2. Type **monthly** and press the **spacebar**. Note that the existing text is pushed to the right of the inserted text.

SELECTING TEXT

At times, you'll find it more convenient to work with a block of text than with a single character. For example, if you needed to underline a sentence in a paragraph, you would not want to underline each character separately (a multistep, tedious task); rather, you would want to underline the entire sentence at once (a single-step, straightforward task).

To work with a block of text, you must first select it. In the next activity (in the section "Deleting Text") you'll select text by using the following method:

- Point to the first (or final) character of the text to be selected.
- Press and hold the left mouse button.
- Drag across the text to the final (or first) character to be selected.
- Release the mouse button.

Note: As just indicated, you can select text downward (from the first to the last character) or upward (from the last to the first character). Both methods are effective; use whichever you feel more comfortable with.

DELETING TEXT

As you know, pressing Backspace deletes the character to the left of the insertion point. To delete the character immediately to the right of the insertion point, press the Delete key (on the cursor-movement keypad of an enhanced keyboard) or the Del key (on the numeric keypad).

Note: If you use the Del key on the numeric keypad, make sure that Num Lock is off. (To turn Num Lock on/off, press the Num Lock key.) If Num Lock is on, Del functions as a decimal point key; when you press it, Word displays a period (.) on the screen instead of performing the deletion.

To delete a block of selected text:

- Select the text.

- Press *Del* (or *Delete*).

Let's begin by deleting text one character at a time:

1. Place the insertion point directly to the left of the *C* in *Car Rentals*, which is located in the *Re:* line of the memo.

2. Press **Del** (or **Delete**) eleven times to delete the words *Car Rental*. (To keep things simple, we'll only mention the Del key from here on. Feel free, however, to use the Delete key instead, if you wish.)

3. Type **Calendar order**.

4. Place the insertion point to the right of the *e* in *here*, at the end of the second sentence in the memo text, and press **Backspace** four times to delete the word *here*.

5. Type **in**.

Now let's delete a block (in this case, a single word) of selected text:

1. Point to the left of the *t* in *temporarily* in the first sentence of the memo text.

2. Press and hold the (left) mouse button. Then drag over *temporarily* (don't worry about selecting the space after temporarily; when you delete a word, Word automatically deletes the trailing space too) to select the text. Release the mouse button.

3. Press **Del** to delete the selected text.

REPLACING TEXT

You already learned how to insert new text within a document. At times, however, you may want to replace existing text with new text. For example, you may want to replace the standard letter salutation "Dear Sir or Madam" with "To Whom It May Concern." One way you can do this is by inserting the new text and then deleting the old text. This, however, doubles your work and can grow very tiresome, particularly when you are replacing many blocks of text. Fortunately, Word provides a more convenient solution.

To replace existing text with new text:

- Select the text to be replaced.
- Type the new text.

Let's use this technique to replace some text in our letter:

1. Select the name **Syriana Sarkis** in the *To:* line of the memo.

2. Type **Cyndi Wood** to replace *Syriana Sarkis* with *Cyndi Wood*.

PRACTICE YOUR SKILLS

Make the following additional corrections to your letter:

1. Delete *out of stock* (in the first sentence of the memo text) and replace it with **back ordered**.

2. Delete *We* (in the next sentence) and replace it with **I**.

3. Compare your memo to the one shown below:

```
INTEROFFICE·MEMO¶
¶
To:  →  Cyndi·Wood¶
¶
From: →Erin·Brabant¶
¶
Date: →  10/10/96¶
¶
RE:  →  Calendar·order¶
¶
Cyndi,·The·monthly·planning·calendars·that·you·ordered·from·Marshall's·Business·Products·back·ordered.·
I·will·let·you·know·as·soon·as·they·come·in.¶
¶
```

SAVING A DOCUMENT

Before you save it, a document exists only in computer memory, a temporary storage area. For permanent storage, you must save the document as a file on a hard or floppy disk. Word provides two commands you can use to save your documents: File, Save As; and File, Save. Let's explore the differences between these commands.

THE FILE, SAVE AS COMMAND

You use the *File, Save As* command to save a document for the first time, to save a document with a new name, or to save a document in a different location (on another disk or in another folder).

To save a document using File, Save As:

- Choose *File, Save As* to open the Save As dialog box.

- Select the location (drive and folder) in which you wish to save the document, if this location is not already selected.

- In the File Name box, type the name of the file.

- Click on *Save*.

THE SAVE COMMAND

You use the *Save* command (rather than Save As) to save a document with its current name and in its current location. Save updates a saved document; it replaces the last-saved version of the document with the new version of the document on your screen. For example, let's say you'd used Save As to save a business report to your reports folder as *Report 1,* and then you'd gone back and revised the report by adding an extra closing paragraph. If you then issued the Save command, the new (extra paragraph) report version would replace the last-saved (no extra paragraph) version on the disk. Once you've used Save As to name and save a document, you should generally use Save for all subsequent updates of that document. However, if you later want to rename it or save it in a different location (while retaining a copy of the original file in the current location), you should use Save As.

Saving Guidelines

You should save your active documents frequently; every 10 to 15 minutes is a good rule of thumb. That way, if something happens to your computer memory (for example, a power failure, which erases the contents of memory), you will have a recent copy of the document safely stored on disk. This precaution will keep your eventual retyping to a minimum.

Word provides an automatic save option. When this option is turned on, Word automatically saves all your active documents at a specified time interval (for example, every 10 minutes), making it unnecessary for you to save your documents manually (by issuing Save commands). This feature is a godsend for those who just can't seem to remember to save as often as they should.

Let's take a moment to make sure that your automatic save option is turned on:

1. Choose **Tools, Options** (click on **Tools**, and click on **Options**) to open the Options dialog box.

2. Click on the **Save** tab to display the available Save options.

3. Observe the Save AutoRecover Info Every ____ Minutes option. If this option is unchecked—that is, if the square box preceding *Save* is empty—check it (turn it on) by clicking on the square box to fill it with an X.

4. If the rectangular box between *Every* and *Minutes* does not contain the value *10*, select its current value (by dragging over it), and then type **10**.

5. Your option should now read *Save AutoRecover Info Every 10 Minutes*. This means that Word will automatically save all your active documents every ten minutes. Compare your screen to Figure 2.2.

Figure 2.2
The Save panel in the Options dialog box

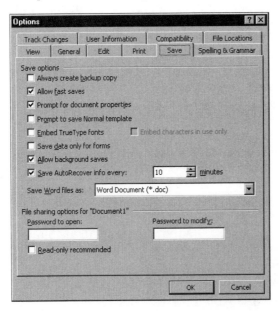

While the Options dialog box is open, let's turn off the automatic spelling and grammar options. You'll learn more about these features in Chapter 7, but until then, we won't use them.

1. Click on **Spelling & Grammar** to display the Spelling & Grammar panel of the Options dialog box.

2. In the Spelling section, uncheck (click on) the **Check Spelling As You Type** option.

3. In the Grammar section, uncheck (click on) the **Check Grammar As You Type** and **Check Grammar With Spelling** options. Your screen should match that shown in Figure 2.3.

Figure 2.3
Turning off Spelling and Grammar options

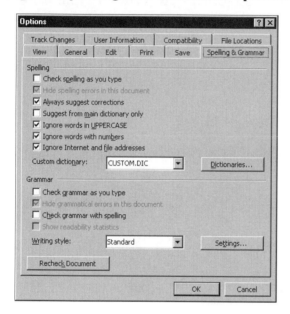

4. Click on **OK** to close the Options dialog box.

Naming a Document

When you save a document for the first time, you must name it. Follow these guidelines when naming documents:

- A file name can contain from 1 to 255 letters (uppercase and/or lowercase), numbers, spaces, or the following special characters: ! @ # $ % ( ) - _ { } ' ~

- A file name should be descriptive so that you can remember the file's contents (for example, *My Essay on Life* rather than *X117-A*).

Let's save our new document:

1. Choose **File, Save As** to open the Save As dialog box. Since our document is new (unsaved, as of yet) we're using Save As—rather than Save—to save it. In the Save In box, the My Documents folder is currently displayed.

2. Click on 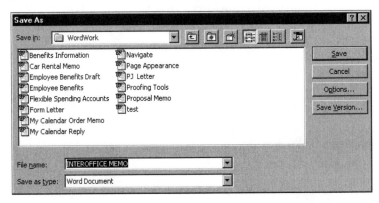 (the **Up One Level** button). Word displays the contents of the folder up one level. Repeat this procedure, as necessary, until drive C (or whatever drive your hard disk is) is displayed. The drive's contents are displayed in the large box below the Save In box.

3. If necessary, use the horizontal scroll bar to display the WordWork folder. This is the work folder we created in Chapter 1; here you will store and retrieve all of the documents you work with in this book.

4. Double-click on the **WordWork** folder to display its contents (see Figure 2.4).

Figure 2.4
Saving the new file in the WordWork folder

5. Select (drag over) the contents of the File Name box. Notice that Word has quite sensibly used information in our document to suggest a descriptive file name; however, we'll make up our own name.

6. Type **My Calendar Order Memo** to name the document, and click on **Save** to save the document as a disk file in your WordWork folder.

7. Observe the title bar. Note that it has changed to display the document's name, *My Calendar Order Memo*.

DOCUMENT PROPERTIES

Word provides an option called Prompt For Document Properties. By default, this option is disabled. When this option is turned on, the first time you save a new document, Word displays the Summary panel of the Document Properties dialog box. This box prompts you for supplementary information about the document, including the subject, author, keywords, comments, and a descriptive title. This option allows for quite a bit of detail in describing a document. You can also choose to skip any, or all, of these categories. The Document Properties option is especially useful for keeping track of author names and for storing comments and notes related to a document.

To enable/disable the Document Properties feature:

- Choose *Tools, Options*.
- Click on the *Save* tab.
- Check/Uncheck (click on) *the Prompt For Document Properties* option.
- Click on *OK*.

PRINTING A DOCUMENT

By default, Word prints one copy of the entire active document. You can, however, choose to print the current page only, multiple pages, multiple copies, or selected text. You can also print to a document rather than to a printer. (We'll discuss these print options in Chapter 6.)

To print the active document:

- Choose *File, Print*.
- Select the desired options from the Print dialog box.
- Click on *OK*.

Now let's print our document:

1. Choose **File, Print** to open the Print dialog box (see Figure 2.5). Notice that this dialog box contains a number of options for printing your documents.

2. Click on **OK** to print the document. (Or, if you do not have a printer, click on **Cancel** to cancel the Print command and return to your document.)

3. If your document failed to print, make sure your printer is online, then try again. If it still won't print, refer to Appendix A for help selecting your printer.

Note: You can print one copy of the entire document by clicking on the Print button on the Standard toolbar.

Figure 2.5
The Print dialog box

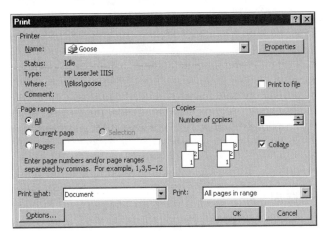

CLOSING A DOCUMENT

When you're finished working with a document—that is, after you've completed, saved, and (if desired) printed it—you should close the document window. You can do this by clicking on the document-window Close box, or by choosing File, Close.

Let's close our document, since we've saved and printed it:

1. Click on the document-window **Close box** (the one below its application-window counterpart) to close the document and remove it from memory.

2. Observe the screen. Word remains loaded, but there is no active document. The title bar displays only *Microsoft Word* and the user name, and the ruler and scroll bars have disappeared.

CREATING A NEW DOCUMENT

After you've closed the active document, you're ready—if you choose—to create a new document. To do this:

• Click on the *New* button in the Standard toolbar.

• Word will open a new, blank document window.

Let's create a new document and then save it:

1. Click on [image] (the **New** button). Word opens a new, blank document window. Notice that the title bar reads *Document2*.

2. Type **Thanks for the update on my calendar order**.

3. Choose **File, Save As** to open the Save As dialog box.

4. Select (drag over) the text in the File Name box, and type **My Calendar Reply** to name the document. Note that the WordWork folder is still selected; Word remembered it from the last time we selected it, earlier in this chapter.

5. Observe that the Save button (in the dialog box) has a border that is somewhat darker than the other buttons in the dialog box. This means that Save is the default button. To choose a default button, you simply press Enter.

6. Press **Enter** to choose **Save** instead of clicking on the button with the mouse.

7. Close the new document (click on the document-window **Close** box).

OPENING A FILE

Opening (retrieving) a *file* (a document that is stored on a disk) enables you to revise previously saved documents and then reprint and resave them.

Note: The terms *file* and *document* are two different ways of looking at the same thing. When referring to a text object on your screen, we call it a document; when referring to this same text object stored on a disk, we call it a file.

To open a file:

- Click on the *Open* button in the toolbar to display the Open dialog box.

- Select the desired drive and folder, if necessary.

- In the list of files, double-click on the desired file (or click on the file, and then click on *Open*).

When you open a file, Word places a copy of the file in a document window on your screen. Because this is a *copy* of the file, and not the original, you can revise it to your heart's content without changing the original document stored on your disk. You will, however, change the original document if you save your revised document as a file with the same name, and in the same location, as the original. For this reason, if you want to preserve the original document, make sure to give your revised file a new name.

Word also provides a convenient file-opening shortcut; it keeps track of the last four files that you worked on and displays their names at the bottom of the drop-down File menu. To open one of these documents, simply choose File and click on the desired document name.

Let's begin by opening a file that's stored in our WordWork folder:

1. Click on 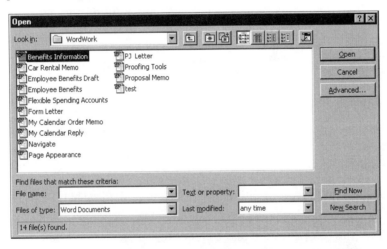 (the **Open** button) in the toolbar. The Open dialog box appears (see Figure 2.6). The contents of your WordWork folder should be displayed; notice the folder name in the Look In box.

Figure 2.6
The Open dialog box

2. In the list of files, double-click on the **Navigate** file. A copy of the file appears in an active document window. Notice that the title bar reads *Microsoft Word - User Name - Navigate*.

Now let's try the shortcut method for opening this same file. First we'll close it:

1. Click on the **document-window** (*not* the application-window) **Close** box to close the Navigate file.

2. Open the **File** menu (click once on **File** in the menu bar). Notice that *Navigate* appears in the recently accessed files section at the bottom of the menu.

3. Choose (click on) **1 Navigate** to open the file.

SCROLLING THROUGH A DOCUMENT

At normal (100 percent) magnification, a Word document window can only display about half of a standard business-size (8 1/2- by 11-inch) page on the screen. To view the remainder of the page (or other pages within the document), you can use the mouse in conjunction with the vertical and horizontal scroll bars to *scroll* through the document. The vertical scroll bar controls up-down scrolling; the horizontal scroll bar controls side-to-side scrolling.

Scrolling through a document changes the document display, but does *not* change the position of the insertion point. For example, if the insertion point is at the top of page 2 and you use the vertical scroll bar to scroll down to page 8, the contents of page 8 will be displayed on the screen, but the insertion point will still be at the top of page 2. If you then begin to type, your text is entered at the insertion point on page 2, not on page 8. (You'll learn how to change both the document display *and* the insertion point position in the next section.)

Table 2.1 lists Word's vertical and horizontal scrolling options and how to perform them. Figure 2.7 identifies screen elements used for scrolling.

Table 2.1
Vertical and Horizontal Scrolling Options

To Scroll	Do This
Up or down one line at a time	Click on up or down scroll arrow
To top, bottom, or middle of document	Drag vertical scroll box to top, bottom, or middle of scroll bar
Up or down one screen at a time	Click in shaded area above or below vertical scroll box
Left or right one character at a time	Click on left or right scroll arrow
To left edge, right edge, or middle of document	Drag horizontal scroll box to left, right, or middle of scroll bar
Left or right one screen at a time	Click in shaded area to left or right of horizontal scroll box

Figure 2.7
Scrolling terminology

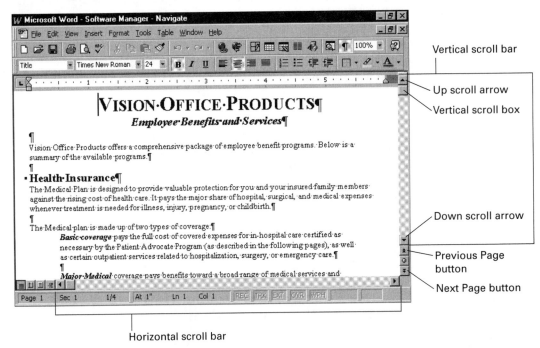

Vertical scroll bar

Up scroll arrow

Vertical scroll box

Down scroll arrow

Previous Page button

Next Page button

Horizontal scroll bar

Let's practice scrolling through the active document, Navigation:

1. Use the techniques described in Table 2.1 to practice scrolling through the document. Note that the insertion point does not move when you scroll through a document.

Note: See Figure 2.7 to locate the screen elements used for scrolling.

Let's take a moment to observe a common scrolling mistake. Assume you wanted to enter your initials at the end of the active document:

1. Drag the **vertical scroll** box to the bottom of the scroll bar to display the end of the document.

2. Type your initials. The text is inserted at the top of the document (where your insertion point is located), not at the end (where you scrolled to). Notice that Word automatically repositions the document to display the inserted text. To avoid making such a mistake, remember these two facts:

• Text that you type is always inserted at the insertion point.

- The insertion point does not move when you use the mouse to scroll through your document.

3. Use **Backspace** to erase your initials.

MOVING THROUGH A DOCUMENT

When you *scroll* through a document, you change the document display but not the insertion point. When you *move* through a document, you change both the document display *and* the insertion point. For this reason, you should scroll when you just want to view different parts of a document, and you should move when you want to view and modify a document.

Table 2.2 lists several ways to move through a document by using the keyboard and the mouse.

Table 2.2
Movement Techniques

To Move	Do This
Up one screen	Press *PgUp* (or *Page Up* on enhanced keyboards)
Down one screen	Press *PgDn* (or *Page Down*)
To top of document	Press *Ctrl+Home*
To end of document	Press *Ctrl+End*
To beginning of line	Press *Home*
To end of line	Press *End*
To the top of the previous page	Click on the *Previous Page* button (below the vertical scroll bar)
To the top of the next page	Click on the *Next Page* button (below the vertical scroll bar)

Now let's practice moving—rather than scrolling—through a document.

Note: If you intend to use the PgDn and PgUp keys on the numeric keypad, make sure that Num Lock is off.

1. Press **PgDn** (or **Page Down**) twice to move two screen lengths down through the document. Notice that the insertion point has moved along with the document display.

2. Press **PgUp** (or **Page Up**) twice to move two screen lengths up through the document. Notice that the insertion point has moved.

3. Press **Ctrl+End** (press and hold down the **Ctrl** key, press the **End** key, and then release both keys) to move to the end of the document.

4. Click on [↥] (the **Previous Page** button). Word moves the insertion point and the screen display to the top of page 3.

5. Click on [↧] (the **Next Page** button).

6. Press **Ctrl+Home** (press **Ctrl**, press **Home**, and then release both) to move to the beginning of the document.

Let's redo our initial-writing task, this time using the correct method:

1. Press **Ctrl+End** to move to the end of the document.

2. Type your initials. They now appear in the desired location, because you used Ctrl+End (not the scroll bar) to move the insertion point along with the document display.

USING *GO TO* TO MOVE TO A PAGE

You can use the Go To command to move to the top of a specified page in the active document. This technique is particularly useful when you are moving through a long (multipage) document.

To move to the top of a page:

- Press *F5* (or choose *Edit, Go To*).

- Type the page number and then click on *Go To* (or press *Enter*).

- To move to a different page, repeat the previous step.

- When you're finished using Go To, click on the *Close* box (or click on the *Close* button).

Let's use the Go To command to move through a document:

1. Press **F5** to open the Go To panel of the Find and Replace dialog box.

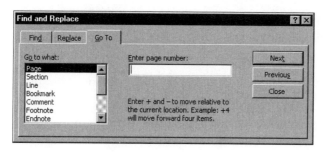

2. In the Enter Page Number text box, type **2** to specify the destination page. Then click on **Go To** to move (the document display and the insertion point) to the top of page 2. Notice that your current page number is displayed in the status bar. The Go To dialog box remains on the screen, allowing you to move to another page.

3. *Enter* **1**—that is, type **1** and then press **Enter**—to move to the top of page 1. (From here on, we'll use "enter text" to mean "type *text* and then press *Enter*.")

4. Click on the **Close** box to close the Go To dialog box.

PRACTICE YOUR SKILLS

1. Use **Go To** to move to the top of page 3.

2. Use **Go To** to move to the top of page 1, and then attempt to move to the top of page 5. Since this document does not have a page 5, Word moves you to the top of the final page (4).

3. Click on **Close** or press **Esc** to close the dialog box.

USING FIND TO SEARCH FOR TEXT

One of Word's most powerful features is its ability to locate a specific word or phrase in a document. You can use this feature to move rapidly to any desired document location. For example, you can move to the sentence containing the phrase "We would like to establish...," even if you have no idea on which page this sentence appears.

To use Edit, Find to search for text within a document:

- Choose *Edit, Find* or press *Ctrl+F* to open the Find panel.

- In the Find What text box, type the *search text* (the text that you want to find).

- Click on *More* and select any desired search options (as explained in the paragraph following this bulleted procedure).

- Click on *Find Next* (or press *Enter*); Word finds and highlights the first occurrence of your search text.

Repeat the previous step as many times as necessary until you have searched through the entire document (or cancel your search at any time by clicking on *Cancel*).

- When Word has finished searching the document, it displays a message informing you so. Click on *OK* (or press *Enter*) to close this message box.

- If desired, perform another search by repeating the previous five steps.

- When you are finished searching, close the Find and Replace dialog box.

Edit, Find provides several options that allow you to refine your text searches. When you first open the Find and Replace dialog box, you can't see these additional options because the entire dialog box is not displayed. To display the entire dialog box, click on the More button. Once all of the options are available, you can check (turn on) the *Match Case* option to locate only words that exactly match the case (capitalization) of your search text. If you check the *Find Whole Words Only* option, you tell Find to locate only whole words that match your search text. By default, Word searches your entire document; however, you can choose Up or Down from the Search drop-down list to search the entire document from the insertion point upward or from the insertion point downward.

Let's experiment with the Edit, Find command:

1. Your insertion point should be at the top of page 3. If it is not, use **Go To** to move it there.

2. Choose **Edit, Find** to open the Find panel of the Find and Replace dialog box.

3. In the Find What box, type **Vacation**. This is the word we're going to search for. Before we actually perform the search, we need to verify that the search options are correctly set.

4. Click on the **More** button to display the entire Find panel (see Figure 2.8).

Figure 2.8
The Find panel with options displayed

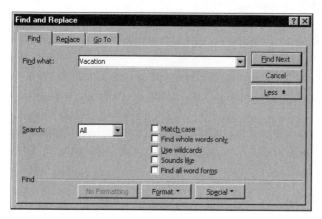

5. Uncheck all of the following options: **Match Case**, **Find Whole Words Only**, **Use Wildcards**, **Sounds Like**, and **Find All Word Forms**. Verify that the Search list box is set to *All* (if not, select this option by clicking on the **down arrow** next to the Search list box and then clicking on **All**); this option tells Word to search the entire document. If the **No Formatting** button is active—that is, if it is not dimmed—click on it; this tells Word to ignore the formatting (font, style, and so on) of your search word (*Vacation*).

6. Click on **Less** to close the options portion of the Find panel.

7. Click on **Find Next** until a *message box* appears, informing you that Word has finished searching the document. Pause each time to examine the found word; when a word is found, it is highlighted in the document. Word finds several occurrences of *vacation* in the following forms:

   • Vacation

   • vacation

   • vacations

   Word found V*acation* because it exactly matches your search text (*Vacation*). It found v*acation* because by unchecking the Match Case option, you told it to ignore capitalization. It found v*acations* because by unchecking the Find Whole Words Only option, you told it to find not just *Vacation*, but to find all words that contain *vacation* (*vacations* contains *vacation*).

8. Click on **OK** (or press **Enter**) to close this message box.

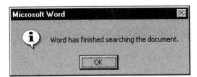

9. Click on **Cancel** (or press **Esc**) to close the Find And Replace dialog box.

Now let's refine our search by using the Match Case and Find Whole Words Only options:

1. With the insertion point at the top of page 3, press **Ctrl+F** (you do not need to capitalize shortcut-key letters) to open the Find dialog box.

2. Display the Find options (click on **More**).

3. Check the **Find Whole Words Only** option.

4. Click on **Find Next** (or press **Enter**), pausing to examine each found word until the end-of-document message box is displayed. This time, Word finds only *Vacation* and *vacation*. *vacations* is not found, because you told Word to find only whole-word matches of *vacation*.

5. Click on **OK** (or press **Enter**) to close the message box, but do not close the Find dialog box.

6. Check the **Match Case** option; both Match Case and Find Whole Words Only should now be checked. Click on **Find Next** (or press **Enter**) until Word is finished searching. Only *Vacation* is found. *vacation* is not found, because you told Word to find only case-matching occurrences of *Vacation*.

7. Click on **OK** to close the search-finished message box.

PRACTICE YOUR SKILLS

1. Uncheck the **Match Case** and **Find Whole Words Only** options, and search your entire active document for *benefits*. There are nine matches.

2. Close the **Find** dialog box.

USING THE ZOOM BOX TO CHANGE DOCUMENT MAGNIFICATION

Word allows you to change the level of magnification at which your documents are displayed on the screen. By default, documents are displayed at 100 percent magnification (where the screen display matches the actual document size), but you can adjust this magnification to anywhere from 10 percent to 500 percent.

Lower magnifications (from 99 percent to 10 percent) shrink the onscreen document, allowing you to view more of a page at once. Higher magnifications (from 101 percent to 500 percent) enlarge the onscreen document, allowing you to view text and graphics close up to perform detail work.

To change the magnification of the active document:

- Click on the *down arrow* to the right of the percentage displayed in the *Zoom Control* box to open a drop-down list of magnification options.

- Click on your desired magnification. Clicking on the *Page Width* option shrinks a page so that its extra-wide text lines fit onscreen.

Let's change the magnification of our document:

1. Move the insertion point to the top of the document.

2. Observe the Zoom Control box. Notice that it reads *100%*, meaning that the active document is displayed at 100 percent (actual-size) magnification.

3. Click on the **down arrow** to the right of the percentage in the Zoom Control box to open its drop-down list of magnification options.

4. Click on the **50%** option to shrink the document to half its actual size.

5. Using the technique outlined in the previous two steps, change the magnification to **150%** (see Figure 2.9). Note how much less of the text fits onscreen.

6. Change the magnification back to **100%**.

7. Close the document. (Click on the Document window's **Close** button.)

Figure 2.9
The document at 150% magnification

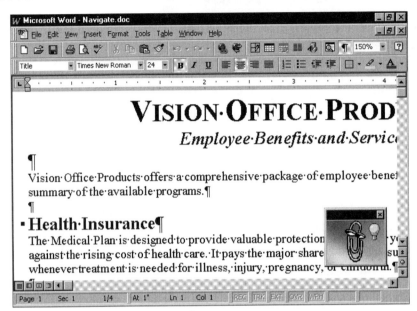

QUICK REFERENCE

In this chapter, you learned the basics of the document creation-revision-saving-printing cycle, a procedure you'll use frequently in your daily word processing work. You now know how to enter, insert, delete, and replace text; how to save, name, print, and close a document; and how to create a new document. You also learned how to navigate in Word. You now know how to obtain Word tips, open a file, scroll and move through a document, search for text, and control document magnification. Congratulations! You're well on your way to mastering Word.

Here's a quick reference guide to the Word features introduced in this chapter:

Desired Result	How to Do It
End paragraph or short line	Press *Enter.*
Create blank line	Press *Enter.*
Display/hide nonprinting characters	Click on *Show/Hide* button.
Align text horizontally	Use *Tab* key.

Desired Result	How to Do It
Delete character to left of insertion point	Press *Backspace*.
Select text	Point to first (or final) character of text; press and hold mouse button. Drag across text to final (or first) character; release mouse button.
Delete character to right of insertion point	Press *Del*.
Delete selected text	Select text; press *Del*.
Replace selected text	Select text; type replacement text.
Save document for first time	Choose *File, Save As*.
Rename document or save it to new location	Choose *File, Save As*.
Save previously saved document under same name/location	Click on *Save* button.
Turn on automatic save option	Choose *Tools, Options*. Click on *Save* tab. Check *Save AutoRecover Info Every* _____ *Minutes* option; if desired, change number of minutes between auto-saving. Click on *OK*.
Print active document	Choose *File, Print*.
Close active document	Click on document-window *Close* box, or choose *File, Close*.
Create new document	Click on *New* button.
Open file	Click on *Open* button. Select drive and folder; double-click on file name.
Open recently used document	Choose *File*; click on document name at bottom of File menu.
Scroll up or down one line	Click on *up* or *down* scroll arrow.

Desired Result	How to Do It
Scroll to top, bottom, or middle of document	Drag *vertical scroll* box to top, bottom, or middle of scroll bar.
Scroll up or down one screen	Click in *vertical scroll* bar above or below scroll box.
Scroll left or right one column	Click on *left* or *right scroll* arrow.
Scroll to left edge, right edge, or middle of document	Drag *horizontal scroll* box to left, right, or middle of scroll bar.
Scroll left or right one screen	Click in *horizontal scroll* bar to left or right of scroll box.
Move up one screen	Press *PgUp*.
Move down one screen	Press *PgDn*.
Move to beginning of document	Press *Ctrl+Home*.
Move to end of document	Press *Ctrl+End*.
Move to beginning of line	Press *Home*.
Move to end of line	Press *End*.
Move to top of previous page	Click on *Previous Page* button.
Move to top of next page	Click on *Next Page* button.
Use Browse button to open Go To panel	Click on *Browse* button; click on *Go To*.
Move to top of page	Press *F5*. Type page number and click on *OK*; repeat previous step, if desired. Click on *Close*.
Use the Browse button to open Find tab	Click on *Browse* button. Click on *Find* button.

Desired Result	How to Do It
Search for text	Choose *Edit, Find* (or press *Ctrl+F*). Type search text. Click on *More*; select desired search options. Click on *Less*. Click on *Find Next* (or press *Enter*); if desired, perform another search. Click on *Close*.
Change document magnification	Open *Zoom Control* box; click on desired magnification option.

In the next chapter, you'll learn how to edit text. The editing process includes replacing found text, moving text, and copying text. You'll also be introduced to a handy way to undo an action when you change your mind about an editing decision.

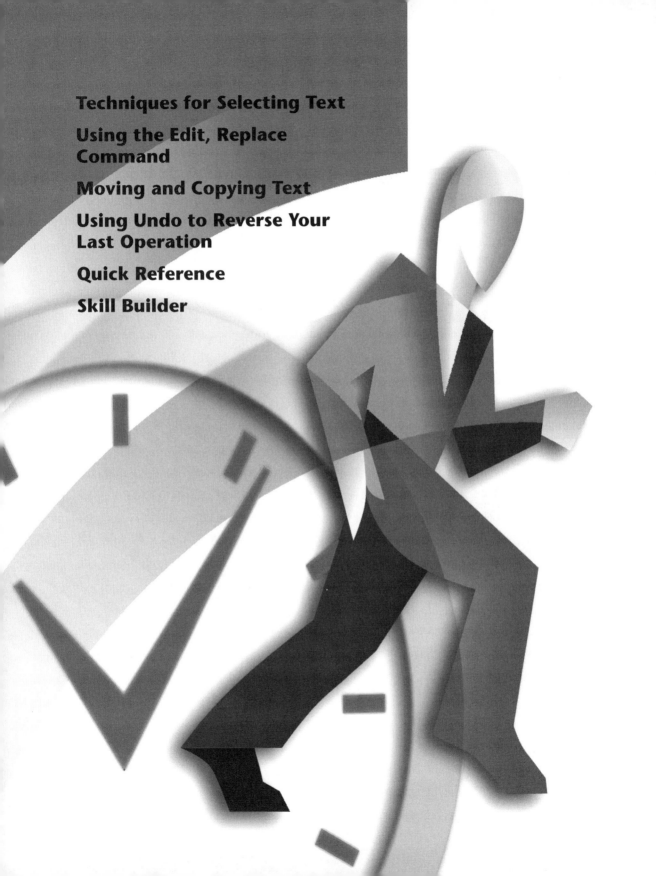

Techniques for Selecting Text

Using the Edit, Replace Command

Moving and Copying Text

Using Undo to Reverse Your Last Operation

Quick Reference

Skill Builder

Chapter 3
Editing Text

In Chapter 2, you learned the basics of editing—how to insert, select, replace, and delete text. In this chapter we'll introduce you to some of Word's more advanced editing techniques. You'll learn sophisticated ways to select text and then move and copy this text to other locations in your document. You'll find out how to use the Replace command (Find's more powerful cousin) to find text and replace it with new text of your choice. Finally, we'll show you how to use the Undo command to rescue yourself from a potentially catastrophic word processing mistake.

When you're done working through this chapter, you will know:

- How to use the mouse, the keyboard, and menus to select text
- How to use the Replace command to replace found text
- How to move and copy text
- How to use the Undo command to reverse your last operation

TECHNIQUES FOR SELECTING TEXT

Before you can move or copy text, you must select it. You can do this by using the mouse, keyboard, or menus. Table 3.1 lists Word's text selection techniques.

If you are not running Word, please start it now (for help, see "Starting Word" in Chapter 1). Let's begin this chapter's activities by opening a new document file and then using the mouse-dragging method to select text:

1. Click on the ⬚ **Open** button. The Open dialog box is displayed.

2. If your **WordWork** folder is not already selected, select it now.

3. In the list of files, double-click on **PJ Letter** to open the document file.

4. Point to the left of the *P* in *Paris,* in the fourth line of the document. Press and hold the mouse button.

5. Drag to the right to select **Paris,** and the trailing space.

6. Release the mouse button. Your screen should resemble Figure 3.1.

Figure 3.1
Dragging the mouse to select

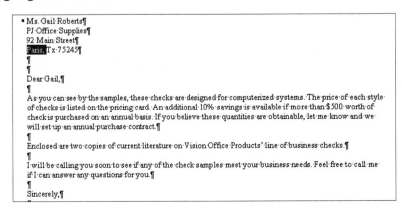

Table 3.1
Text Selection Techniques

Selection Technique	How to Do It
Dragging	Point at one end of the text you want to select. Press and hold the mouse button. Move (drag) the mouse pointer to the other end of the text. Release the mouse button. All text between the ends is selected.
Using Shift	Place the insertion point at one end of the text. Press and hold *Shift.* Click at the other end of the text you want to select (do not drag). Release *Shift.* All text between the ends is selected.
Selecting a word	Point anywhere inside a word and double-click the mouse button. The trailing space is automatically selected along with the word.
Selecting a sentence	Point anywhere inside a sentence. Press and hold the *Ctrl* key, then click the mouse button. Release *Ctrl*—the sentence is selected, along with the punctuation and trailing space.
Selecting a line	Point in the *selection bar* area (the blank vertical bar on the left side of the text area) next to the line. Click the mouse button—all the text on that line is selected.
Selecting multiple lines	Point in the selection bar next to the first or last line of the text you want to select. Press and hold the mouse button, then drag down or up. Release the mouse button—all the lines you "dragged" are selected.
Selecting a paragraph	Point in the selection bar next to a paragraph. Double-click the mouse button. The ending paragraph mark is selected along with the paragraph.

Table 3.1
Text Selection Techniques (Continued)

Selecting the entire document	Choose *Edit, Select All*, or, point anywhere in the selection bar. Press and hold the *Ctrl* button. Click the mouse button; and then release *Ctrl*.
Extending an existing selection	While holding *Shift*, click beyond the existing selection. The selection extends to that point.
Shortening an existing selection	While holding *Shift*, click inside the existing selection. The selection shortens to that point.
Deselecting an existing selection	Make another selection, or, click the mouse button in the text area anywhere outside the existing selection.

Now let's use the whole-word selection technique:

1. Point to the word *Enclosed* in the second paragraph in the body of the letter.

2. Double-click the mouse button to select the entire word **Enclosed**. Note that selecting *Enclosed* deselects *Paris,*.

3. Examine the selected text. The trailing space after *Enclosed* is also selected.

Now let's use the selection bar to select text:

1. Move the mouse pointer into the selection bar—the blank vertical bar to the left of the document text (see Figure 3.2). Note that the pointer changes from an I-beam into a right-pointing arrow.

2. Point in the selection bar next to the line beginning with *I will be calling*. Click on the mouse button to select the entire line.

3. Point in the selection bar next to the paragraph that begins with *As you can see*. Double-click the mouse button to select the entire paragraph.

Figure 3.2
The selection bar

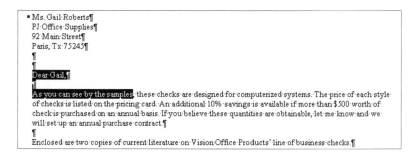

4. Point in the selection bar next to the paragraph that begins with *Enclosed are two copies.* Press and hold the mouse button, and then drag down to the paragraph mark before *Sincerely* to select multiple lines of text. Release the mouse button

Let's use the Shift key to select a block of text and then extend and shorten this selection:

1. Place the insertion point before the *D* in *Dear Gail* in the seventh line of the document.

2. Press and hold **Shift**; then click the mouse pointer in the space after *samples* (located two lines down) to select all the text from *Dear* to *samples.* Release **Shift** (see Figure 3.3).

Figure 3.3
Selecting text with the mouse and the Shift key

3. Point to the end of the word *systems* on the same line (but do *not* click). Press and hold **Shift**; then click the mouse button to extend the selection to the end of *systems*. Release **Shift**.

4. Point to the word *designed*. Note that the pointer appears as an arrow (instead of an insertion point) when you point to selected text. Press and hold **Shift**; then click the mouse button to shorten the selection. Release **Shift**.

Finally, let's use the menu to select the entire document:

1. Choose **Edit, Select All** to select the entire document.

2. Click anywhere within the text area to *deselect*.

PRACTICE YOUR SKILLS

1. Select the first sentence of the paragraph beginning with *I will be calling you,* using the mouse-dragging technique.

2. Deselect.

3. Select the same sentence as in step 1, this time using the mouse in conjunction with **Ctrl** to select the entire sentence without dragging. (For help, refer to Table 3.1, earlier in this chapter.)

4. Use the double-clicking technique to select each of the following words in the first paragraph in the body of the letter: *samples, checks, designed, computerized,* and *systems.* Note that double-clicking selects the trailing space after a word, but not the trailing comma (as in *samples,*) or period (as in *systems.*).

5. Use the selection-bar technique to select the first line of the document. Extend the selection to include the first five lines. Shorten the selection to include the first two lines.

6. Place the insertion point at the top of the document.

USING THE EDIT, REPLACE COMMAND

In Chapter 2, you learned how to use Find to search for text in a document. Here you'll learn how to use the Replace command to search for text and replace it with new text of your choice.

Replace is one of Word's most powerful commands. Let's say you typed a 100-page document that made frequent reference to a man named *Pablo Sitauskus* and then you found out that the correct spelling was *Sitauskis*. Normally, you'd have to find each occurrence of *Sitauskus* and correct it—an ugly task considering the length of the document. Using Edit, Replace, you could issue a single command that would automatically (and rapidly) replace every occurrence of *Sitauskus* with *Sitauskis*.

To use Replace to search and replace found text in a document:

- Choose *Edit, Replace* to open the Find and Replace dialog box with the Replace tab selected.

- In the Find What text box, type the *search text* (the text you wish to find).

- In the Replace With text box, type the *replace text* (the text you wish to replace the search text with).

- If necessary, click on the *More* button and check your desired search option(s)—*Match Case, Find Whole Words Only, Wildcards, Sounds Like,* or *Find All Word Forms.*

- If necessary, click on the *Search* list box and select *Down* (to search from the insertion point to the end of the document), *Up* (to search from the insertion point to the beginning of the document), or *All* (to search the entire document).

- If necessary, click on the *Less* button to hide the search options and to reduce the size of the dialog box.

- Click on *Find Next* (or press *Enter*); Word highlights the first occurrence of your search text.

- Click on either *Replace* (to replace the found text and search for the next occurrence), *Find Next* (to leave the found text unchanged and search for the next occurrence), or *Replace All* (to replace all occurrences of the search text throughout the rest of the document).

- Repeat the previous step as many times as necessary until you have searched through the entire document, or cancel your search at any time by clicking on *Cancel.*

- Close the Find and Replace dialog box.

Let's use the procedures just described to find and replace some text:

1. Click on the **Open** button and double-click on **Employee Benefits** to open the document. Note that both *PJ Letter* and *Employee Benefits* are open in Word.

2. Choose **Edit, Replace** to open the Find and Replace dialog box with the Replace tab selected (see Figure 3.4).

Figure 3.4
The Find and Replace dialog box

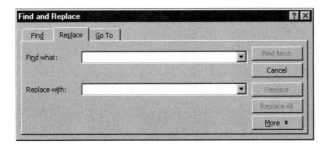

3. In the Find What box, type **programs**. This is the text we will search for and replace.

4. Press **Tab** to move the insertion point into the Replace With text box and then type **options**. This is the text that will replace the search text (*programs*).

5. Click on the **More** button. Uncheck (deselect)the **Match Case** option, if necessary.

6. If necessary, select **All** from the Search list drop-down list box to search the entire document. Click on the **Less** button.

7. Click on **Find Next** to find the first occurrence of *programs* in the first sentence of the document.

8. Click on **Replace** to replace *programs* with *options* and to search for the next occurrence of *programs*.

9. Repeat step 8.

10. Click on **Find Next** to leave *Weight Reduction Programs* unchanged and search for the next occurrence of *programs*. The message "Word has finished searching the document" is displayed.

11. Click on **OK** to remove the message. Because there are no more occurrences of *programs*, the insertion point moves back to where it was in the document when you began the search.

12. Click on **Close** to close the Find and Replace dialog box.

You'll have a chance to use the Replace All command in the "Skill Builder" section at the end of this chapter.

Creating a Sub-Folder

In addition to saving files, you can use the Save As dialog box to create a new folder. To create a new folder (or a sub-folder) from the Save As dialog box:

• Choose *File, Save As*.

• In the Save As dialog box, click on the *Create New Folder* button to open the New Folder dialog box.

• In the Name text box, type the name of the new folder.

• Click on *OK*.

The new folder can be created inside an existing folder. (In this case, the new folder will be a sub-folder to WordWork.)

Let's create a sub-folder and save My Employee Benefits in the new folder:

1. With Employee Benefits open, choose **File, Save As** to open the Save As dialog box.

2. Click on the **Create New Folder** button (use ToolTips to locate the button) to open the New Folder dialog box. Note that the current path reads "C:\WordWork." The new folder will be created inside WordWork (as a sub-folder).

3. In the Name text box, type **My Folder** and click on **OK** to create the new folder and return to the Save As dialog box.

4. In the file Name text box, type **My Employee Benefits**.

5. Double-click on **My Folder** (if necessary) and click on **Save**.

MOVING AND COPYING TEXT

Another of Word's powerful editing features is its ability to move and copy text within a document. You can, for example, quickly and easily move a table of numbers from the top of the fifth page of a business report to the bottom of the 11th page, or copy a four-line address to several locations within the body of a letter.

THE CLIPBOARD

Windows provides a temporary storage area called the *Clipboard* for those times when you move or copy text. When selected text is *cut* (removed) or copied, it is placed on the Clipboard. *Pasting* inserts a copy of the Clipboard contents before the insertion point. You'll notice that the Paste button on the toolbar resembles a clipboard. An entry remains on the Clipboard, either until you cut or copy another entry to it, or until you exit Windows.

MOVING TEXT

To move text within a document:

- Select the text to be moved.

- Click on the *Cut* button in the toolbar to cut the selected text from the document and place it on the *Clipboard*.

- Place the insertion point where you want to move this text.

- Click on the *Paste* button to paste the cut text before the insertion point.

Let's practice moving text from one location to another within a document:

1. Choose **Window,** 2. **PJ Letter** to select the document. Drag in the selection bar to select the paragraph beginning with *As you can see* and the blank line below it.

2. Click on ✂ (the **Cut** button).

3. The selected text is removed from the document and placed on the Windows Clipboard.

4. Place the insertion point before the paragraph that begins *I will be calling.*

5. Click on 📋 (the **Paste** button).

6. A copy of the Clipboard contents is then pasted before the insertion point (see Figure 3.5).

Figure 3.5
PJ Letter, after pasting

```
▪ Ms. Gail Roberts¶
  PJ Office Supplies¶
  92 Main Street¶
  Paris, Tx 75245¶
  ¶
  ¶
  Dear Gail,¶
  ¶
  Enclosed are two copies of current literature on Vision Office Products' line of business checks.¶
  ¶
  As you can see by the samples, these checks are designed for computerized systems. The price of each style
  of checks is listed on the pricing card. An additional 10% savings is available if more than $500 worth of
  check is purchased on an annual basis. If you believe these quantities are obtainable, let me know and we
  will set up an annual purchase contract.¶
  ¶
  I will be calling you soon to see if any of the check samples meet your business needs. Feel free to call me
  if I can answer any questions for you.¶
  ¶
  Sincerely,¶
```

7. Save the document as **My PJ Letter** to the WordWork folder (click on the Up One Level button if necessary) and close it. (The document *My Employee Benefits* is open.)

COPY TEXT

To copy text within a document:

- Select the text to be copied.

- Click on the *Copy* button in the toolbar to copy the selected text to the Clipboard.

- Place the insertion point where you want to copy this text.

- Click on the *Paste* button to paste the Clipboard text before the insertion point.

Now let's practice copying text within a document:

1. Verify that the document **My Employee Benefits** is open.

2. Select the first three lines of the document (the two-line page heading and the blank line below it).

3. Click on [icon] (the **Copy** button).

4. A copy of the selected text is placed on the Clipboard. Note that the selected text is not removed from the document, as it was when you used Cut.

5. Click on the **Select Browse Object** button (under the vertical scroll bar) and select **Browse by Page**. Word automatically moves to page 2. Note that the insertion point is at the top of page 2.

6. Click on the **Paste** button to paste a copy of the Clipboard contents before the insertion point (see Figure 3.6).

Figure 3.6
Page 2 of My Employee Benefits, after pasting

Vision·Office·Products¶
Employee·Benefits·and·Services¶
¶
Your·disability·benefits·are·made·up·of·two·types·of·coverage:¶
¶
Short·Term·Disability·Plan·coverage·continues·50%·or·all·of·your·pay·for·up·to·26·weeks,·based·on·your·
length·of·service.¶
¶
Long·Term·Disability·Plan·coverage·continues·60%·of·your·pay·after·you·have·been·disabled·for·26·weeks·
and·throughout·your·disability — generally·up·to·age·65.¶
¶
Profit·Sharing·and·Retirement¶
The·Company·Profit·Sharing·Retirement·Plan·lets·you·share·directly·in·the·Company's·growth·and·success,·
contributing·to·your·financial·security·for·the·future.·You·become·a·Plan·participant·after·you·have·
completed·one·year·of·service·(minimum·1000·hours)·with·the·Company.¶
¶
Company·Contributions¶
Once·you·become·a·Plan·participant,·the·Company·automatically·begins·making·annual·basic·contributions·
to·the·Plan·on·your·behalf·equal·to·6%·of·your·annual·pay,·up·to·$15,000·each·year·(or·a·maximum·Basic·

PRACTICE YOUR SKILLS

1. Use the **Next Page** arrow (located at the bottom of the vertical scroll bar) to place the insertion point at the top of page 3.

2. Paste the contents of the Clipboard at the insertion point. Because a copy of the text is still on the Clipboard, you do not need to copy the text again before pasting.

3. Paste the contents of the Clipboard at the top of page 4.

4. Save the document.

USING UNDO TO REVERSE YOUR LAST OPERATION

Word provides an Undo command that allows you to reverse (undo) one or more of the most recent operations that you have performed.

Use either of the following Undo methods to reverse your last operation:

• Click on the *Undo* button in the toolbar.

• Choose *Edit, Undo*.

You can also repeat an action that you've canceled (with Undo) by using the Redo command. (This is the equivalent of choosing the Repeat option from the Edit menu.) To repeat an action that you've undone, click on the Redo button in the toolbar or choose Edit, Redo.

Note: It is possible to Undo or Redo any of several actions, not just the most recent one. To list several of the most recent procedures that you've performed or undone, click on the down arrow button immediately to the right of either the Undo or Redo button, respectively. Then drag to select the operation that you wish to undo or redo.

Let's delete a block of text from My Employee Benefits and then use the Undo feature to undelete this text:

1. Move to the top of the document. Select the heading **Health Insurance**.

2. Press **Del** to delete the text. (Because you used Del rather than Cut or Copy, the text has not been placed on the Clipboard.)

3. Click on **Edit** to display the Edit drop-down menu. Observe the Undo option at the top; it reads *Undo Clear*. The Edit, Undo option changes to reflect the operation to be undone. Close the Edit menu.

4. Click on [⤺▾] (the **Undo** button).

5. The deleted text is restored.

Now let's use the undo button to reverse a potentially catastrophic text-replacement mistake:

1. Select the entire document. (Choose **Edit, Select All**.)

2. Type your first initial. (This is similar to "accidentally" pressing a key while the whole document is selected.) Surprise! All that's left in the text area is a single letter. This could be a very serious error.

3. Click on the **Undo** button to restore the original text. All is well.

4. Deselect to avoid deleting the entire document again.

5. Click on the **Save** button to update the document—that is, to save it with the same name and in the same location.

6. Close the document.

QUICK REFERENCE

In this chapter, you learned how to use the mouse, keyboard, and menus to select text; how to use the Edit, Replace command to replace found text; how to move and copy text; and how to use the Undo command to reverse one or more of your most recent operations.

Here's a quick reference guide to the Word features introduced in the chapter:

Selection Technique	How to Do It
Select text by dragging	Point at one end of the text you want to select. Press and hold the mouse button. Drag the mouse pointer to the other end of the text. Release the mouse button.
Select text by using Shift	Place insertion point at one end of the text. Press and hold *Shift*; click at other end of the text. Release *Shift*.
Select a word	Point anywhere inside a word and double-click.
Select a sentence	Point anywhere inside a sentence. Press and hold the *Ctrl* key. Click the mouse button; release *Ctrl*.
Select a line	Point in the *selection bar* next to the line. Click the mouse button.
Select multiple lines	Point in the selection bar next to the first or last line of text to be selected. Press and hold the mouse button. Drag down or up. Release the mouse button.
Select a paragraph	Point in the selection bar next to a paragraph. Double-click the mouse button.
Select the entire document	Choose *Edit, Select All*, or point anywhere in the selection bar. Press and hold *Ctrl*. Click the mouse button; and then release *Ctrl*.

Selection Technique	How to Do It
Extend an existing selection	While holding *Shift*, click beyond the existing selection.
Shorten an existing selection	While holding *Shift*, click inside the existing selection.
Deselect an existing selection	Make another selection, or click in the text area anywhere outside the existing selection.
Replace found text in document	Choose *Edit, Replace*; type the search text in the Find What text box. Type the replace text in the Replace With text box. Click on *More* and select the desired search options. Click on the *Less* button. Click on *Find Next* (or press *Enter*) to find the first occurrence. Click on either *Replace, Find Next*, or *Replace All*. Repeat previous step as many times as necessary until you have searched through entire document (or cancel search at any time by clicking on *Cancel*). Close the *Find and Replace* dialog box.
Move text within document	Select the text to be moved. Click on the *Cut* button. Place the insertion point where you want to move the text. Click on the *Paste* button.
Copy text within document	Select the text to be copied. Click on the *Copy* button. Place the insertion point where you want to copy the text. Click on the *Paste* button.
Undo last operation	Click on the *Undo* button.
Undo multiple operations	Click on the down arrow next to the Undo button. Select the operations you want to undo.
Redo the last Undo	Click on the *Redo* button.

In the next chapter, you'll learn the basics of character formatting—how to apply and remove character styles (such as bold and italic) and how to change fonts (typestyles) and point sizes of your text.

SKILL BUILDER

In Chapters 2 and 3, you've learned how to navigate within a document and how to select, replace, move, and copy text. The following two Skill Builder activities give you the opportunity to apply these techniques to realistic word processing situations.

Follow these steps to produce the final document shown in Figures 3.7 and 3.8 from the original document Practice 3A.

1. Open **Practice 3A** (Chapter 2).

2. Replace all occurrences of *Mayco* with **Macco**. (**Hint:** Click on **Replace All** in the Replace dialog box.)

3. On page 1, move the paragraph that begins with *Congratulations to all*, and the blank line below it, to before the paragraph that begins with *As we expected*.

4. Copy the three-line heading, and the blank line below it at the top of page 1, to the top of page 2.

5. Save the document as **My Practice 3A** (Chapter 2).

6. Print the document and compare it to Figures 3.7 and 3.8 (Chapter 2).

7. Close the document (Chapter 2).

Figure 3.7
Page 1 of My Practice 3A

Macco·Plastics·Inc.¶
Quarterly·Sales·Report¶
First·Quarter¶
¶
1.·Introduction¶
¶
Congratulations·to·all·of·you!·An·initial·review·of·the·sales·figures·for·the·nation·reveals·a·surge·in·sales·in·all·of·Macco's·sales·areas.·Major·new·clients·have·been·added·and·many·new·products·are·on·the·way.¶
¶
As·we·expected·when·we·entered·the·field,·computer-related·products,·such·as·keyboard·housings·and·protective·carrying·cases,·are·accounting·for·a·major·portion·of·this·upswing.¶
¶
2.·Regional·Updates¶
¶
Midwestern·Territory¶
¶
After·several·years·of·falling·sales·due·to·the·slump·in·the·auto·industry,·Blair·Williams·and·his·folks·have·something·to·celebrate.·The·recent·boom·in·auto·manufacturing·has·led·to·renewed·demand·of·Macco·Products·in·Detroit.¶

Figure 3.8
Page 2 of My Practice 3A

```
Macco·Plastics·Inc.¶
Quarterly·Sales·Report¶
First·Quarter¶
¶
4.·Quarterly·Meeting¶
¶
The·quarterly·meeting·will·take·place·in·Memphis·this·time.··You·will·find·the·agenda·attached·to·this·report.¶
¶
5.·Conclusion¶
¶
If·the·recovery·continues·at·the·current·pace,·this·year·should·be·a·banner·year·for·all·of·us·at·Macco.·We·
want·to·thank·all·of·you·for·the·outstanding·jobs·you·have·done·and,·most·important,·for·standing·by·Macco·
in·hard·times.·Keep·up·the·good·work!¶
¶
John·Smith¶
Regional·Coordinator¶
Macco·Plastics·Inc.¶
¶
```

Follow these steps to produce the final document shown in Figures 3.9 and 3.10 from the original document Practice 3B:

1. Open **Practice 3B** (Chapter 2).

2. Replace all case-matching occurrences of *Territory* with **Region**.

3. Move the heading *3. Computer Study* and the subsequent paragraph and paragraph marks (located on the bottom of page 1) to before the heading *2. Regional Updates*.

4. Change *3. Computer Study* to **2. Computer Study** (Chapter 2).

5. Change *2. Regional Updates* to **3. Regional Updates** (Chapter 2).

6. Add the current date as a fourth line to the three-line heading on the top of page 1 (Chapter 2).

7. Copy the entire date line from the heading on page 1 to the heading on page 2.

8. Save the document as **My Practice 3B** (Chapter 2).

9. Print the document and compare it to Figures 3.9 and 3.10 (Chapter 2).

10. Close the document (Chapter 2).

Figure 3.9
Page 1 of My Practice 3B

Macco·Plastics·Inc.¶
Quarterly·Sales·Report¶
First·Quarter¶
(today's·date)¶
¶
1.·Introduction¶
¶
Congratulations·to·all·of·you!·An·initial·review·of·the·sales·figures·for·the·nation·reveals·a·surge·in·sales·in·
all·of·Macco's·sales·regions.·Major·new·clients·have·been·added·and·many·new·products·are·on·the·way.¶
¶
As·we·expected·when·we·entered·the·field,·computer-related·products,·such·as·keyboard·housings·and·
protective·carrying·cases,·are·accounting·for·a·major·portion·of·this·upswing.¶
¶
2.·Computer·Study¶
¶
A·companywide·study·will·begin·in·March,·under·the·direction·of·Cathy·Donaldson·and·Bill·Schuster·in·data·
processing,·to·determine·how·to·most·effectively·implement·automation·in·our·firm.·We·will·be·making·a·
large·commitment·to·productivity·gains·via·computerization·sometime·late·this·year.¶
¶

Figure 3.10
Page 2 of My Practice 3B

Macco·Plastics·Inc.¶
Quarterly·Sales·Report¶
First·Quarter¶
(today's·date)¶
¶
4.·Quarterly·Meeting¶
¶
The·quarterly·meeting·will·take·place·in·Memphis·this·time.·You·will·find·the·agenda·attached·to·this·report.¶
¶
5.·Conclusion¶
¶
If·the·recovery·continues·at·the·current·pace,·this·year·should·be·a·banner·year·for·all·of·us·at·Macco.·We·
want·to·thank·all·of·you·for·the·outstanding·jobs·you·have·done·and,·most·important,·for·standing·by·Macco·
in·hard·times.·Keep·up·the·good·work!¶
¶
John·Smith¶
Regional·Coordinator¶
Macco·Plastics·Inc.¶

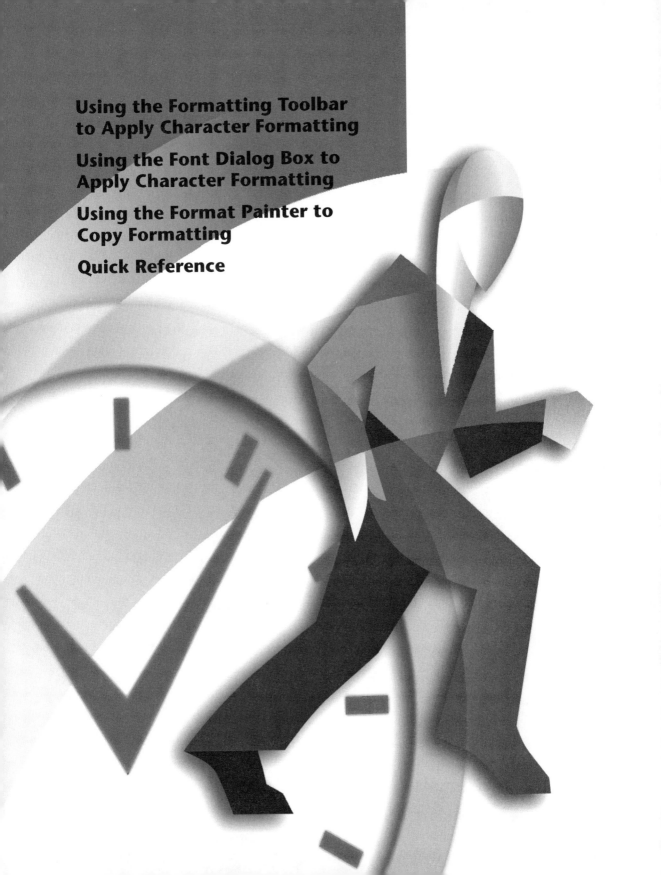

Using the Formatting Toolbar to Apply Character Formatting

Using the Font Dialog Box to Apply Character Formatting

Using the Format Painter to Copy Formatting

Quick Reference

Chapter 4
Character Formatting

The overall effectiveness of a document is directly related to the way it looks. A brilliantly written business report, for example, can be severely undermined by an inappropriate typestyle, print too small to read comfortably, a dizzying barrage of italics or underlining, tables whose columns don't line up, an overbusy page layout, and so on. These next three chapters are devoted to *formatting*--controlling the way your documents look. We'll proceed logically: This chapter covers Word's smallest formatting units, *characters*; Chapter 5 covers its intermediate units, *paragraphs*; and Chapter 6 covers its largest units, *pages*.

When you're done working through this chapter, you will know

- How to use the Formatting toolbar to apply character formats
- How to use the Font dialog box to apply character formats
- How to copy character formats

USING THE FORMATTING TOOLBAR TO APPLY CHARACTER FORMATTING

You can enhance the appearance of your documents and emphasize selected text through the application of font styles (bold and italic) and fonts and font sizes. In this book, for example, we chose to bold certain headings (such as **Desired Result** and **How to Do It**, which appear in each chapter's Quick Reference section), and to italicize new terms (such as *font styles*).

Located just below the Standard toolbar, the Formatting toolbar provides quick access to font styles, fonts, and font sizes.

APPLYING FONT STYLES

You can use the bold, italic, and underline buttons on the Formatting toolbar to apply (you guessed it) bold, italic, and underline to selected text. All you have to do is select the text you want to format and click on the appropriate font style button.

If you decide to remove the font style, select the text and click on the font style button again. This is simple enough if you've only applied one font style to the text. But, say you've applied bold and italic and want to remove them both, you can press Ctrl+Spacebar. This is the keyboard shortcut to remove all formatting from selected text.

Let's practice using the Formatting toolbar to apply font and remove font styles:

1. Open **Benefits Information** from your WordWork folder (Click on the **Open** button and double-click on **Benefits Information**).

2. Select the text **Health Insurance** (select the text, not the entire line) near the top of page 1.

3. Click on [*I*] (the **Italic** button).

4. **Deselect** the text and notice that both words appear in italics. Note that the Italic button now appears to be pushed in.

5. Select **Health Insurance**.

6. Click on ☐ (the **Underline** button).

7. The selected text is underlined.

8. Click on the **Italic** button to remove italics from the selected text.

9. Click on ☐ (the **Bold** button).

10. Along with the underline, bold formatting is applied to the selected text.

Now let's apply multiple font styles and use the Ctrl+Spacebar technique to re-move them from your selected text:

1. Select the entire document and click on the **Italic** and **Bold** buttons to apply italics and boldface to the entire document.

2. With the entire document still selected, press **Ctrl+Spacebar** to remove all font styles (bold and italic) from the selected text.

PRACTICE YOUR SKILLS

1. Apply **bold** to the Health Insurance heading.

2. Apply the **bold** font style to the text **Plan Costs** (near the middle of page 1).

3. Save the file in your WordWork folder as **My Benefits Information**.

APPLYING FONTS AND FONT SIZES

You can change the shape and size of your selected text by changing the text's *font* and *font size*. The font determines the shape (typestyle) of the text; the point size determines the size of the font (one point equals 1/72 of an inch). The sentence you are reading, for example, is printed in 10-point Univers font. You can use the Font dialog box or the Formatting toolbar to apply fonts and point sizes.

Note: The specific fonts and point sizes that Word makes available for your use are dependent upon your currently selected printer. PostScript-type laser printers, for example, offer a large variety of fonts and point sizes, whereas low-end dot-matrix printers offer a much more limited selection.

You can use the Font and Font Size buttons on the Formatting toolbar to apply fonts and font sizes to selected text. Click on the down arrow of the Font or

Font Size buttons (respectively, the second and third boxes from the left in the Formatting toolbar) and select the font or font size you want.

Let's use the Formatting toolbar to change the font and font size:

1. Select the first line of the document, *Vision Office Products*, and observe the Font drop-down list box. The font "Times New Roman" is selected.

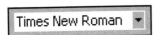

2. Click on the Font button's **down arrow** to display a list of available fonts similar to the one shown below. The fonts available depend upon the printer you have selected.

3. From the Font drop-down list box, select **Arial** to format the selected text with the Arial font. Arial is a *sans serif* font and stands out when you use it to format a document heading.

4. Observe the Font Size drop-down list box. Currently, the font size is set to 10. Since you want the document heading to stand out, you'll probably want to increase the font size.

5. From the Font Size drop-down list, select **18** to increase the font size to 18 points. (To display the Font Size drop-down list, click on the **Font Size button's drop-down arrow**.)

PRACTICE YOUR SKILLS

1. Apply the **bold** font style to the heading *Vision Office Products* at the top of page 1.

2. Format the second line of the heading *Employee Benefits and Services* as **Arial, 12 point, bold**.

3. Save the file.

USING THE FONT DIALOG BOX TO APPLY CHARACTER FORMATTING

Now you know how to use the Formatting toolbar to apply some common character formats, but what if you want to do something a little more unusual, something for which there is no button on the Formatting toolbar. The Font dialog box is your one-stop shopping center for character formatting. Every character format that you can apply to selected text is available through the Font dialog box. The Font dialog box consists of three panels:

- **Font** contains all the font formatting options. You can use the Font panel to apply the font, font style, font size, color, effects, and underline options to selected text (see Figure 4.1).

Figure 4.1
The Font panel of the Font dialog box

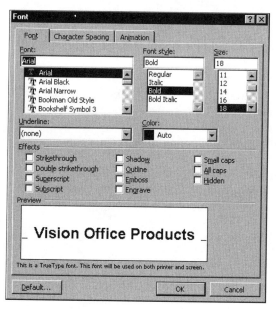

- **Character Spacing** contains all the options for changing the spacing between characters and the position of those characters in relation to the baseline.

- **Animation** contains options for animating selected text. When you animate text, the effects appear on screen, but do not print.

The Preview box at the bottom of the dialog box shows you how the character formatting you've selected will appear on your screen.

The Font panel in the Font dialog box contains additional formats that are not available on the Formatting toolbar, such as Double Underline, Small Caps, Subscript, Superscript, Strikethrough, and Outline.

Underlining Options

In addition to Underline and Double Underline, Word enables you to format text with the following underline options: Words Only, Dotted, Thick, Dash, Dot Dash, Dot Dot Dash, and Wave. To apply one of the various underline options:

- Select the text.

- Choose *Format, Font* to display the Font dialog box.

- In the Underline drop-down list box, select an underline type.

- Click on *OK*.

Let's use the Font dialog box to apply some character formats:

1. Select the first line of the heading at the top of page 1 (*Vision Office Products*).

2. Choose **Format, Font** to open the Font dialog box. If necessary, click on the **Font** tab to display the Font panel. You can use the Font panel to apply fonts, font sizes, font styles, underline styles, color, and special effects (such as strikethrough or all caps) to selected text.

3. Observe the Font dialog box. The font for the selected text *Vision Office Products* is set to Arial, 18 point, and the Font Style is set to Bold. Let's add some more formatting.

4. From the Underline drop-down list box, select **Double** to apply a double underline to the selected text.

5. Under Effects, check **Small Caps** to apply small caps to the selected text.

6. Observe the Preview box. The Preview box displays the selected text with the character formats you've applied. That double-underline looks awful. Let's get rid of it.

7. From the Underline drop-down list box, select **(none)** to remove the underline format from the text.

8. Click on **OK** to close the Font dialog box and apply the selected formats to *Vision Office Products*. Note that the selected text is formatted with Arial, 18 point, Bold, and Small Caps.

VISION·OFFICE·PRODUCTS¶

PRACTICE YOUR SKILLS

1. Use the Font dialog box to apply the Small Caps format to *Health Insurance*.

2. Save the file.

REPEATING CHARACTER FORMATTING

Once you have applied one or more character formats to your selected text, you can easily reapply (repeat) these styles to newly selected text. To do this:

* Select the new text.

* Choose *Edit, Repeat Font Formatting,* or press the *F4* (Repeat) shortcut key.

Note: If you wish to use the technique just described to repeat multiple font styles (for example, bold and italic), you must have applied these font styles through the Font dialog box. If you attempt to repeat multiple font styles that you applied by using the Formatting toolbar, only the last font style will be repeated.

1. Select the heading **Plan Costs** near the middle of page 1.

2. Choose **Edit, Repeat Font Formatting** to repeat the formatting.

3. Select the heading **The Patient Advocate Program** (below *Plan Costs*) and press **F4** to repeat the character formatting.

PRACTICE YOUR SKILLS

Repeat the character formatting for the following headings:

- Dental Insurance
- Disability Plans
- Profit Sharing and Retirement
- Company Contributions
- Wellness Program

APPLYING ANIMATION TO SELECTED TEXT

Suppose you want a particular section of text to really stand out. Word has several cool animation effects you can add to selected text. The animation will draw the reader's eye to that text. Animation effects are only visible onscreen. They do not print.

One last word of warning: Animation effects can be very distracting, especially if you use too many on one page or in one document. Use them sparingly.

Let's apply animation to Health Insurance:

1. Select the text **Health Insurance** (near the top of page 1) and choose **Format, Font** to open the Font dialog box.

2. Click on the **Animation** tab to display the Animation panel (see Figure 4.2).

3. Select the animation option of your choice. You can only apply one animation option at a time. You can use the **Preview** box to see how the animated text will appear on screen.

Figure 4.2
The Animation panel of the Font dialog box

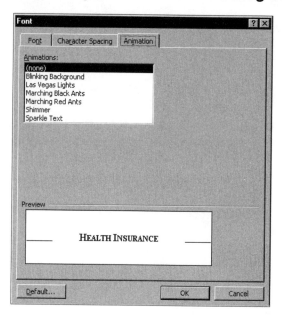

4. When you have an animation option that you like, click on **OK** to close the Font dialog box.

5. **Deselect** the text and observe the animation effect. Wow, that's cool!

6. Save the file.

USING THE FORMAT PAINTER TO COPY FORMATTING

Once you have applied one or more character formats to your text, you can easily use the Format Painter to copy these formats to newly selected text. Format Painter enables you to copy character or paragraph formats from a character or paragraph and apply them to any other character or paragraph in your document.

To copy character formats with Format painter:

• Place the insertion point in (or select) the text that is the desired format.

• Click (or double-click) on the *Format Painter* button in the Formatting toolbar.

- Select the text to which you wish to apply the copied format. If you double-clicked on the Format Painter button, you can *repeat* this step on as many text selections as you wish.

- Click on the *Format Painter* button again to turn off the feature.

Let's use the Format Painter button to copy character formatting:

1. Select **Vision Office Products** (the first line of the document).

2. Click on (the **Format Painter** button). The character formatting applied to the selected text is "copied."

3. Observe the mouse pointer.

4. It changes to an I-beam with a paintbrush.

5. Scroll to the top of page 2. (Use the **scroll bar**; any other method of navigating will deactivate the Format Painter feature.)

6. Drag to select the first line of page 2 (**Vision Office Products**) and observe the text. The character formatting copied from the text on page 1 is applied to the selected text on page 2. Note that the mouse pointer is just an I-beam again. The paintbrush is gone.

7. When you click once on the **Format Painter** button, Word will copy the character formatting once. If you want to copy the same character formatting to more than one piece of text, you must **double-click** on the **Format Painter** button.

Let's copy the formatting from the second line of the heading on page 1 to the second line of the heading on pages 2 and 3.

1. Move to the top of the document (press **Ctrl+Home**) and select the second line, *Employee Benefits and Services*.

2. Double-click on the **Format Painter** button to keep the Format Painter active for more than one copy.

3. Move to the top of Page 2 and drag to select the second line of text, *Employee Benefits and Services*. The character formatting is copied to the selected text and the mouse pointer is still an I-beam with the paintbrush.

4. Move to the top of page 3 and drag to select the second line of text, *Employee Benefits and Services*. Note that the mouse pointer is still an I-beam with a paintbrush. When you double-click on the Format Painter, it remains active until you turn it off.

5. Click on the **Format Painter** button to turn off the Format Painter.

PRACTICE YOUR SKILLS

1. Use the Format Painter to copy the formatting from the first two lines of the heading on page 1 (*Vision Office Products* and *Employee Benefits and Services*) to the headings on pages 3 and 4.

2. Save and close the document.

QUICK REFERENCE

In this chapter, you learned the basics of character formatting. You now know how to use the Formatting toolbar and the Font dialog box to apply and re-move font styles, as well as how to change fonts and font sizes. You also know how to repeat and copy character formatting.

Here's a quick reference guide to the Word features introduced in this chapter:

Desired Result	How to Do It
Use the Font dialog box to apply font styles	Select the desired text. Choose *Format, Font*. Select your desired font style options. Click on *OK* (or press *Enter*).
Use the Font dialog box to remove font styles	Follow the procedure just described and choose the *Regular* font style.
Use the Formatting toolbar to apply font styles	Select the desired text. Click on the desired font style button.
Use the Formatting toolbar to remove font styles	Select the desired text. Click on the button of the font style you wish to remove.
Remove all font styles from your selected text	Press *Ctrl+Spacebar*.

Desired Result	How to Do It
Repeat character formatting	Select the new text. Choose *Edit*, *Repeat Font Formatting* (or press *F4*).
Use the Font dialog box to apply fonts and point sizes	Select the desired text. Choose *Format*, *Font*. Select your desired font and/or point size. Click on *OK* (or press *Enter*).
Use the Formatting toolbar to apply fonts and point sizes	Select the desired text. Click on the *down arrow* of the Font or Size boxes. Select your desired font or point size.
Copy character formatting	Select the text that is the desired format. Click on the *Format Painter* button. Select the text to which you wish to apply the copied format.
Copy character formatting more than once	Follow the steps above, but double-click on the *Format Painter* button.
Turn off the Format Painter	Click on the *Format Painter* button.

In the next chapter, you will learn the basics of paragraph formatting. You'll find out how to work with tab stops and paragraph indents, create new lines within a paragraph, align paragraphs, and set line spacing.

Setting Paragraph Alignment

Setting Indents and Line Breaks

Using Shift+Enter to Create a New Line

Setting Line Spacing

Working With Tabs

Quick Reference

Skill Builder

Chapter 5
Paragraph Formatting

In Chapter 4, you learned the basics of character formatting. In this chapter, we'll move on to Word's intermediate unit of formatting: the paragraph. Many important document layout features are controlled at the paragraph level, including text alignment, indents, line spacing, and tab stops. Mastering paragraph formatting will greatly assist you in presenting professionally laid out, attractive documents.

When you're done working through this chapter, you will know

- How to align paragraphs

- How to set and repeat paragraph indents

- How to create new lines within a paragraph

- How to set line spacing

- How to set, change, and clear tab stops

SETTING PARAGRAPH ALIGNMENT

Paragraph alignment determines how text is positioned between the left and right margins. *Margins* define the upper, lower, left, and right page boundaries of an entire document. (See "Setting Margins" in Chapter 6 for details on this Word feature.)

SELECTING PARAGRAPHS FOR PARAGRAPH FORMATTING

Before you apply paragraph alignment, you must first select the desired paragraph or paragraphs. As you learned in the last chapter, when you select a paragraph for character formatting (character styles, font, point size, and so on), you must select the entire paragraph. However, when you select a paragraph for *paragraph formatting* (alignment, indents, line spacing, and so on), you *do not* have to select the entire paragraph. To select a *single* paragraph for paragraph formatting, place the insertion point anywhere in the paragraph. You do not have to select (highlight) any characters. To select *multiple* paragraphs for paragraph formatting, select (highlight) a portion of each paragraph.

The techniques just described are paragraph selection shortcuts. If you feel more comfortable selecting entire paragraphs for paragraph formatting, please do so.

PARAGRAPH ALIGNMENT TYPES

Word provides four types of paragraph alignment. Figure 5.1 illustrates how the four different paragraph alignments appear on your computer screen, and Table 5.1 defines each type of paragraph alignment.

To set paragraph alignment:

- Select the desired paragraph(s).

- Click on the appropriate alignment button in the Formatting toolbar (see Figure 5.1).

If you are not running Word, please start it now.

Figure 5.1
Paragraph alignment types

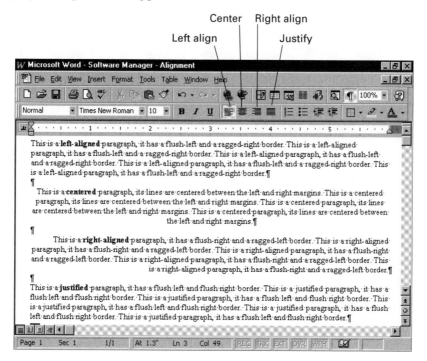

Table 5.1
The Four Paragraph Alignment Types

Type	Alignment
Left-aligned	Lines of text are *flush-left* (aligned evenly along the left margin) and *ragged-right* (aligned unevenly along the right margin). Left-aligned is the default paragraph-alignment setting.
Centered	Lines of text are centered between the margins. Both the left and right sides of a centered paragraph are ragged.
Right-aligned	Lines of text are flush-right and ragged-left, the opposite of left-aligned.
Justified	Lines of text are both flush-left and flush-right. In a justified paragraph, Word adjusts the spacing between words and characters so that they stretch from the left margin to the right margin.

Note: The further you progress in this book, the more succinct our activity in-structions tend to be. For example, instead of saying "Click on the Open but-ton, select the WordWork folder, and then double-click on VOP Benefits to open it," we now simply say "Open VOP Benefits from your WorkWord folder." If you are unsure of how to perform a certain Word task, use the Index, the end-of-chapter Quick Reference guides, or Word Help to jog your memory.

Let's open a document and begin our exploration of paragraph formatting by centering some paragraphs:

1. Open **VOP Benefits** from your WORK FILES folder.

2. Verify that the insertion point is at the top of the document in the first line, *Vision Office Products*. Observe the text-alignment buttons (located on the Formatting toolbar). The Left-Aligned text button is selected.

3. Click on [≡] (the **Center** button).

4. The paragraph is centered between the left and right margins. In this ex-ample, the paragraph contains only one line.

5. Select the second line, the heading, *Employee Benefits and Services*.

6. Click on the **Center** button to center the paragraph.

7. Deselect and compare your screen with Figure 5.2.

Now let's try the other paragraph alignments:

1. Place the insertion point in the paragraph beginning with *The medical plan is designed* (located under the *Health Insurance* heading). Observe the last word in each line of the selected paragraph: Because the para-graph is left-aligned, text does not always reach the right margin before wrapping to the next line.

2. Click on [≡] (the **Justify** button).

3. Observe the last word in each line: Word increases the spacing between words in the selected paragraph to fill each line (except the last line, which is too short) so that the text is even with both the left and right margins.

Figure 5.2
Centering paragraphs

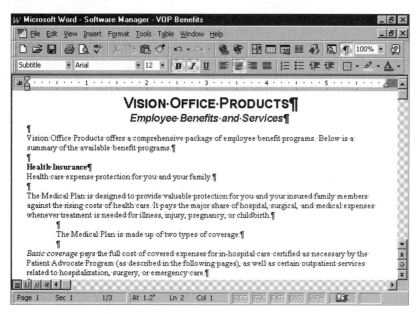

4. Click on [ ] (the **Align Right** button).

5. Observe the text: Text in the current paragraph now aligns only with the right margin.

6. Click on [ ] (the **Align Left** button).

7. The paragraph is now back to its original alignment.

PRACTICE YOUR SKILLS

1. Center both lines of the heading on the top of page 2 (select at least a portion of both paragraphs).

2. Repeat step 1 for the heading on the top of page 3.

3. Save the file as **My VOP Benefits** (use **File, Save As**).

SETTING INDENTS AND LINE BREAKS

Indents define the left and right boundaries of selected paragraphs within a document.

By default, a paragraph's left and right indents are set equal to the document's left and right margins. However, you can modify a paragraph's left and/or right indents without changing the document's margins. Figure 5.3 illustrates the relationship between margins and indents.

Figure 5.3
Margins and indents

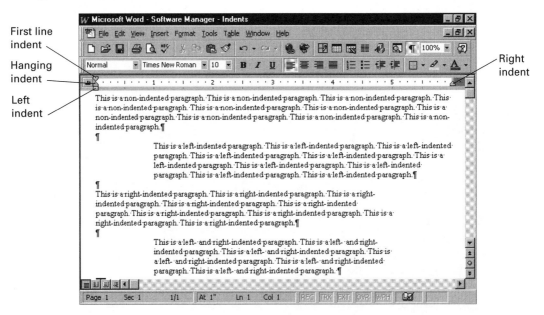

INDENT MARKERS

The ruler provides *indent markers* (see Figure 5.3) that you can use to control the positions of a selected paragraph's indents. There are four types of indent markers as shown in Figure 5.3. You can also you ToolTips to identify them.

Indent Marker Type	Location and Function
First-line indent	The upper-left triangle on the ruler. It controls the left boundary for only the first line of a paragraph.
Hanging indent	The lower-left triangle on the ruler. It controls the left boundary of every line in a paragraph except the first.

Indent Marker Type	Location and Function
Left indent	The small box below the hanging-indent marker. It controls both the first-line indent and hanging-indent markers.
Right indent	The triangle on the right end of the ruler. It controls the right boundary for every line in a paragraph.

SETTING INDENTS

Word allows you to quickly and easily set indents. To do this:

- Place the insertion point in the paragraph, or select a portion of each paragraph you wish to indent.

- Drag the appropriate indent marker to your desired new position on the ruler.

By default, if you drag the hanging-indent marker, the first-line-indent marker does not move along with it. To left-indent every line of a paragraph, move both these markers by dragging the small box, called the Left-indent, below the hanging-indent marker.

THE INCREASE INDENT AND DECREASE INDENT BUTTONS

If you wish to increase or decrease the left indentation of a paragraph one half-inch at a time, you can use the Increase Indent and Decrease Indent buttons in the Formatting toolbar (see Figure 5.3). To do so:

- Select the paragraph(s) you wish to affect.

- To increase the left indent by one half-inch, click on the *Increase Indent* button. To decrease the left-indent to the previous location, click on the *Decrease Indent* button.

REPEATING PARAGRAPH FORMATTING

In the last chapter, you learned how to repeat character formatting. Word also allows you to repeat paragraph formatting. To do this:

- Format a paragraph (such as align, indenting, and so on).

- Select a new paragraph.

- Choose *Edit, Repeat Formatting* (or press *F4*).

Let's set some indents and then repeat them:

1. Move to the top of page 1.

2. Place the insertion point in the paragraph that begins with *The Medical Plan is made up of two types of coverage*. This paragraph is indented one half-inch from the left margin.

3. Observe the ruler. The first-line indent, hanging indent, and left-indent markers (the lower and upper triangles and small box near the left end of the ruler, respectively) are together at the 0.5" mark.

4. Place the insertion point in the paragraph beginning with *Basic coverage*. This paragraph is not indented. Observe the ruler: The indent markers are set even with the margins.

5. Point the tip of the mouse pointer at the **hanging-indent** marker (use Tool-Tips to verify that you are selecting the correct marker). Drag the **hanging-indent** marker to **0.75"** to move the left boundary of every line in the paragraph except for the first line. (Use the measurement marks in the center of the ruler as a guide.)

6. Now, drag the **first-line indent** marker (use ToolTips) to **0.75"** to move the first line of the paragraph. The entire paragraph now has a left indent of 0.75".

7. Drag the **right-indent** marker—the triangle at the right end of the ruler—to **5.5"**. A right indent creates a different right boundary for the selected paragraph.

Now let's repeat our indent formatting:

1. Place the insertion point in the paragraph beginning with *Major Medical* (scroll down to just below the *Basic coverage* paragraph).

2. Choose **Edit, Repeat Formatting** (or press **F4**) to repeat the last formatting function you completed. Observe the new right indent.

3. Place the mouse pointer on the **left-indent** marker (use ToolTips), and drag it to the **0.75"** mark on the ruler.

4. Observe the ruler: The left-indent marker moved the first-line indent and hanging-indent markers together.

PRACTICE YOUR SKILLS

1. Move to the middle of page 2.

2. Format the paragraph beginning with *Short Term Disability Plan* with first-line and hanging-indents at **0.75"** and a right indent at **5.5"**.

3. Repeat the formats to the paragraph beginning with *Long Term Disability Plan*.

4. Compare your screen to Figure 5.4.

Figure 5.4
Page 2 of My VOP Benefits, after indent formatting

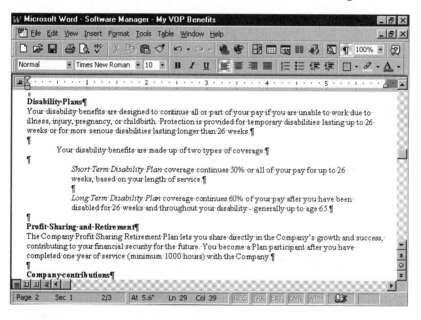

SETTING HANGING INDENTS

The term *hanging indent* is used to describe a format in which a paragraph's first line is left-indented less than all of its subsequent lines. In effect, the first line *hangs* over the rest. Hanging indents are most commonly used in bulleted or numbered lists, such as the list of bulleted instructions that appears next or the lists of numbered instructions in the activities throughout this book.

To create a hanging indent:

* Select the desired paragraph(s).

* If necessary, drag the *first-line indent* marker (the upper-left triangle) to the desired position.

* Drag only the *hanging-indent* marker (the lower-left triangle—not the small box below it) to the desired position (to the right of the first-line-indent marker).

Now let's set some hanging indents and then repeat them:

1. Move to the middle of page 3 (the *Time for yourself* heading should be at the top of the screen).

2. Place the insertion point in the paragraph beginning with *1. Vacation Plan*.

3. Drag the **hanging-indent** marker to the **0.25"** mark on the ruler. Observe your hanging indent: The second line is indented to one-quarter of an inch, while the first line remains at the left margin—that is, unindented.

PRACTICE YOUR SKILLS

1. Repeat a **one quarter-inch** hanging indent for the paragraphs from *2. Holidays* to *7. Study Time*. (**Hint:** Use **F4**.)

2. Deselect and compare your screen to Figure 5.5.

USING THE PARAGRAPH DIALOG BOX TO MANAGE YOUR INDENTS

We've shown you how to use the ruler to manage your indents. This is generally the preferred method because it is quick, easy, and provides immediate visual feedback. You can, however, perform all of the same indent-management tasks already presented in this chapter by using the Paragraph dialog box. (You may want to view the section on the Tabs dialog box, near the end of this chapter.)

We recommend that you use the ruler for managing your indents, except in those instances when you need to set an exact indent position that you cannot choose with the mouse and the ruler.

To use the Paragraph dialog box to manage your indents:

* Select the desired paragraph(s).

Figure 5.5
Setting hanging indents

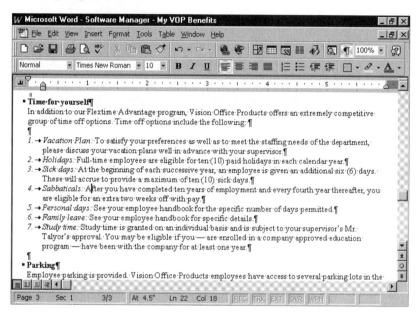

- Choose *Format, Paragraph* to open the Paragraph dialog box.

- Enter your desired indent settings.

- Click on *OK* (or press *Enter*).

USING SHIFT+ENTER TO CREATE A NEW LINE

When you press Enter to create a new line in a document, you also create a new paragraph. At times, this may be undesirable. For example, let's say that you wanted to insert a new line in the middle of a list within a hanging-indent paragraph. If you pressed Enter to create the new line, you would lose your indent. (Remember, pressing Enter creates a new first-line paragraph, and the first line of a hanging-indent paragraph is not indented.) To remedy this problem, Word allows you to use Shift+Enter to create a new line without creating a new paragraph. To do so:

- Place the insertion point where you want to end the current line and create a new line.

- Press *Shift+Enter*; Word inserts a *newline character* (⏎) and creates a new line (without creating a new paragraph).

Let's take a moment to observe the difference between new paragraphs and new lines:

1. In the paragraph beginning with *7. Study Time*, place the insertion point to the left of the hyphen (-) in — *are enrolled*.

2. Press **Shift+Enter** to create a new line without creating a new paragraph. Your hanging indent is maintained. Note that pressing Shift+Enter ends the line with a newline character (↵) instead of with the usual paragraph mark (see Figure 5.6).

**Figure 5.6
Inserting a newline character**

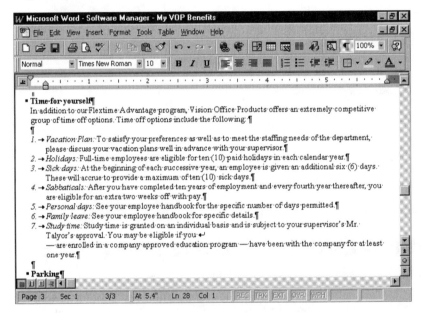

3. Place the insertion point to the left of the second hyphen (-) in the same paragraph, — *have been with*.

4. Press **Shift+Enter** to create a new line.

SETTING LINE SPACING

Line spacing is the vertical distance between lines of text. Word provides six line-spacing options:

- *Single* (the default setting) sets the line spacing to one single line; Single always maintains a minimum of 12-point (1/6") spacing.

- *1.5 lines* sets the line spacing to a line-and-a-half.

- *Double* sets the line spacing to two lines.

- *At Least* allows you to specify a custom minimum line spacing.

- *Exactly* allows you to specify exact line spacing that will not adjust according to font size.

- *Multiple* sets the line spacing to accommodate more than one line; the default is three lines.

To set line spacing:

- Select the desired paragraph(s).

- Choose *Format, Paragraph* to open the Paragraph dialog box; you cannot set line spacing by using the Standard toolbar, Formatting toolbar, or ruler.

- Display the *Indents and Spacing* panel (click on its tab), if necessary.

- Select your desired line-spacing setting from the *Line Spacing* drop-down list box.

- Click on *OK* (or press *Enter*).

Let's use the above procedure to change the line spacing of My VOP Benefits:

1. Select the entire document (place the mouse pointer in the selection bar and, **Ctrl+Click**).

2. Choose **Format, Paragraph**. Examine the Paragraph dialog box (click on the Indents and Spacing tab to display it, if necessary). Unlike the Formatting toolbar and ruler, the Paragraph dialog box provides access to *all* paragraph-formatting options and allows you to type in exact measurements.

3. Click on the **down arrow** of the **Line Spacing** list box to open the box and display the line-spacing choices.

4. Select **1.5 Lines** and then click on **OK** (or press **Enter**). Observe the text. The line spacing has changed from 1 to 1.5 lines (see Figure 5.7).

Figure 5.7
Changing the line spacing to 1.5 lines

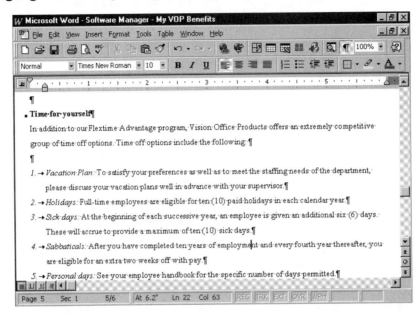

5. Choose **Format, Paragraph** and then open the **Line Spacing** list box (click on its **down arrow**).

6. Select **Double** and then click on **OK** (or press **Enter**). Observe the text: The line spacing has changed to 2 lines from its previous value of 1.5 lines.

7. Choose **Format, Paragraph** and then open the **Line Spacing** list box.

8. Select **Single** and then click on **OK** (or press **Enter**). Observe the text: The line spacing has returned to its original value of 1 line.

9. Deselect the text to avoid inadvertently deleting the entire document.

Up to now, you've always saved the changes you made to your active document before closing it. However, you can close a document without saving the changes. Let's see how:

1. Choose **File, Close**. Word prompts:

   ```
   Do you want to save changes to My VOP Benefits?
   ```

2. Click on **No** to save the document without saving the changes.

WORKING WITH TABS

As you learned in Chapter 1, you use tabs to align text at preset tab stops across the page. This type of alignment is particularly important in tables, where several categories of information must line up in precise columns. In this part of the chapter, you'll learn how to set, change, and clear custom tab stops.

TAB TYPES

There are four types of tab stops available in Word. Figure 5.8 illustrates how tab stops align on your computer screen, and Table 5.2 defines each tab type.

Figure 5.8
Tab stop types

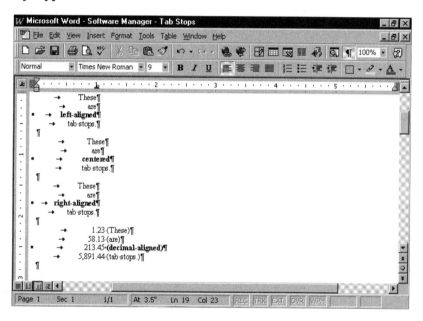

Table 5.2
The Four Tab Types

Type	How Tab Affects Text
Left-aligned	Text flows to the right of the tab stop
Centered	Text is centered on the tab stop
Right-aligned	Text flows to the left of the tab stop
Decimal-aligned	Text aligns on the decimal point (used for numbers)

Note: By default, left-aligned tab stops are set at one-half inch increments between the margins (0.5", 1", 1.5", and so on). These default tab stops are displayed as small vertical lines at the bottom of the ruler.

SETTING CUSTOM TAB STOPS

Word allows you to create your own custom tab stops, and in doing so, to clear its default tab stops. To set custom tab stops:

- Select the desired paragraph(s).

- Click on the *Tab Alignment* button at the left of the ruler until the desired tab type is displayed (see Figure 5.9).

Figure 5.9
The four tab indicators

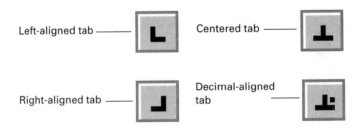

Left-aligned tab ——— **L**   Centered tab ——— **⊥**

Right-aligned tab ——— **⌐**   Decimal-aligned tab ——— **⊥·**

- Point at the desired tab-stop position in the ruler, and click the mouse button.

Your custom tab stop is set and all default tab stops to the left of your custom stop are automatically cleared.

As you click on the Tab Alignment button, it changes to indicate the type of tab: *left-aligned, centered, right-aligned,* or *decimal-aligned.* This is illustrated in Figure 5.9.

Let's open a new document and begin our exploration of tabs:

1. Open **Proposal Memo** from your WordWork folder.

2. Place the insertion point after the text **To:**. Press **Tab** to move to the first default tab stop (0.5" to the right) and type **Gill Bates**.

3. Move the insertion point after **From:**. Press **Tab** and type *Your Name*.

4. Move the insertion point after **Date:**. Press **Tab** and type in *Today's Date* (or choose **Insert, Date and Time**).

5. Move the insertion point after **Subject:**. Press **Tab** and type in **New contract** (The space between *Subject:* and *New contract* is very small.) Compare your screen to Figure 5.10.

Figure 5.10
Adding text to the Memorandum

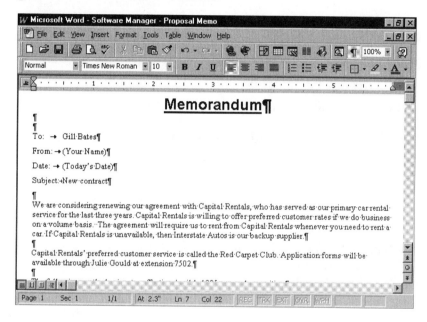

6. Using the selection bar, select the paragraphs from **To:** to **New contract**.

Now let's set some new tab stops to adjust the space between the text separated by tabs:

1. Verify that the text is selected. Observe the ruler: Word's default tab stops are set every half inch (0.5").

2. Observe that the Tab Alignment button is currently set to create a left-aligned tab (see Figure 5.9). Text flows to the right of a left-aligned tab stop. The Tab Alignment button determines the alignment of the *next* tab stop that you set; a left-aligned tab stop is the default.

3. Point directly at the **1"** tick mark on the ruler. Click the mouse button to set a left-aligned tab stop at 1". Note that the default tab stop to the left of 1" has automatically been cleared.

4. Deselect and observe the text. The second column in the selected text is now 1" from the left margin.

CHANGING THE POSITIONS OF CUSTOM TAB STOPS

Word allows you to quickly and easily change the positions of your custom tab stops. To do this:

- Select the desired paragraph(s).
- In the ruler, drag the custom tab stop to a new position.

CLEARING CUSTOM TAB STOPS

Word also allows you to quickly clear (delete) your custom tab stops. To do this:

- Select the desired paragraph(s).
- Drag the custom tab stop down into the text area.

Now let's adjust the Proposed Memo by changing and clearing tabs:

1. Select the four lines of tabbed text.

2. Point to the left-aligned tab stop at the **1"** mark with the tip of the mouse point until the ToolTip is displayed.

3. Press and hold the mouse button, and then drag the tab stop to the **1.5"** mark. Observe the text: The second column of the selected text is now one and one-half inches from the left margin.

4. Point to the tab stop at the **1.5"** mark and drag it down off the ruler into the text area, and then release the mouse button to clear the tab stop.

5. Deselect and observe the text: The second column of the selected text has moved back to the default tap stop at one half-inch.

6. Save the file as **My Proposal Memo** (use **File, Save As**).

SETTING DIFFERENT TYPES OF TABS

As mentioned in the previous section, Word provides four types of tab stops: left-aligned, centered, right-aligned, and decimal-aligned. Let's use the ruler and the tab buttons to experiment with these:

1. Select the four lines of the tabbed text.

2. Click once on the **Tab Alignment** button. It is now set to insert a centered tab (see Figure 5.9). Click a second time; it is now set to insert a right-aligned tab. Click a third time; it is set to insert a decimal-aligned tab.

Click once again; the Tab Alignment button cycles back to the left-alignment setting.

3. Click twice on the **Tab Alignment** button to right-align the next tab stop you set.

4. Set a right-aligned tab stop at **2.5"**. Observe the text: The selected text is flush right at the tab stop.

5. Drag the **right-aligned** tab stop off the ruler to delete it. Click on the **Tab Alignment** button three times to select the **center-aligned** tab stop.

6. Set a centered tab stop at **3.0"**. Note that the text is centered on the 3.0"mark.

7. Scroll down to the tabbed table and select five lines of text from **Subcompact** to **7.5%** (under the three column headings).

8. Set a centered align tab stop at **2.0"**. Observe the selected text: The second column is centered at the 2.0" mark under the *Rate Per Day* column heading.

9. Click on the **Tab Alignment** button to decimal-align the next tab stop you set. Notice the decimal point in the button's icon. Decimal tabs are used to align numbers containing decimals.

10. Set a decimal tab stop at **3.5"**. Notice that the tab markers on the ruler reflect the type of tab set at each location. (See Figure 5.11)

PRACTICE YOUR SKILLS

1. Move back to the top of the document. Select the tabbed text **To:** to **New contract**.

2. Remove the centered tab stop at **3.0"**.

3. Set a left-aligned tab stop at **1"**.

4. Deselect and compare the text to Figure 5.12.

5. Save and close the document.

Figure 5.11
A tabbed table with a decimal tab stop

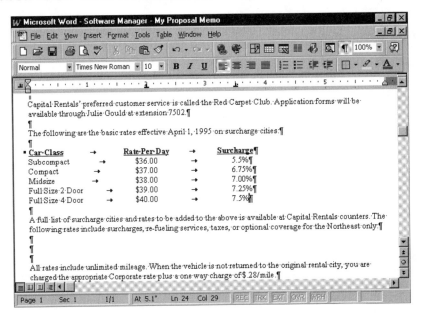

Figure 5.12
Using the left-aligned tab stop

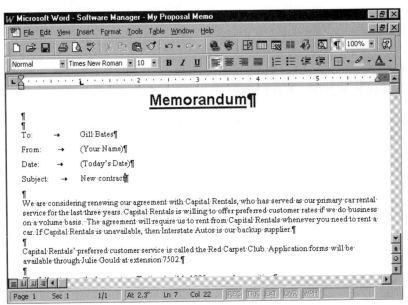

USING THE TABS DIALOG BOX TO MANAGE YOUR CUSTOM TAB STOPS

We've shown you how to use the ruler to manage your custom tab stops. This is generally the preferred method of tab management because it is quick, easy, and provides immediate visual feedback. You can, however, perform all of the tab-management tasks already presented in this chapter (setting, changing, and clearing tab stops) by using the Tabs dialog box (see Figure 5.13).

Figure 5.13
The Tabs dialog box

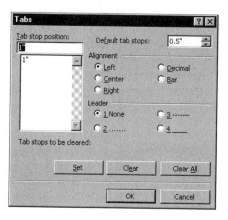

The advantage of using the Tabs dialog box is that you can specify exact tab-stop positions that you couldn't choose by using the mouse and ruler (for example, 3.12" or 6.78"). The disadvantages are that you must type in your tab-stop positions and that you only see how your tab-stop settings affect the selected paragraph(s) when you exit the Tabs dialog box.

To use the Tabs dialog box for managing your custom tab stops:

- Select the desired paragraph(s).

- Choose *Format, Tabs* to open the Tabs dialog box.

Note: The Tabs dialog box in Figure 5.13 reflects the settings for the tabbed text beginning with *To:*.

- Enter your desired settings to change or clear tab stops.

- Click on *OK* (or press *Enter*).

Note: We recommend that you use the ruler for managing your custom tab stops, except in those rare instances when you need to set an exact tab-stop position that you cannot choose with the mouse and the ruler.

QUICK REFERENCE

In this chapter, you learned the basics of paragraph formatting. You now know how to align paragraphs; how to set and repeat paragraph indents; how to create new lines within a paragraph; how to set line spacing; and how to set, change, and clear tab stops.

Here's a quick reference guide to the Word features introduced in this chapter:

Desired Result	How to Do It
Select a single paragraph for paragraph formatting	Place the insertion point anywhere in the paragraph.
Select multiple paragraphs for paragraph formatting	Select (highlight) at least a portion of each paragraph.
Set paragraph alignment	Select the desired paragraph(s). Click on the appropriate alignment button in the Formatting toolbar.
Set indents	Select the paragraph(s) you wish to indent. Drag the appropriate indent marker to your desired new position on the ruler.
Repeat paragraph formatting	Format paragraph(s). Select new paragraph(s). Choose *Edit, Repeat Formatting* or press *F4*.
Create a hanging indent	Select the desired paragraph(s). If necessary drag the *first-line-indent* marker to the desired position. Drag only the *hanging-indent* marker to the desired position.
Use the Paragraph dialog box to manage your indents	Select the desired paragraph(s). Choose *Format, Paragraph* to open the Paragraph dialog box. Click on the *Indents and Spacing* tab, if necessary. Enter your desired indent settings. Click on *OK* (or press *Enter*).
Create a new line without creating a new paragraph	Place the insertion point where you want to end the current line and create a new line. Press *Shift+Enter*.

Desired Result	How to Do It
Set line spacing	Select the desired paragraph(s). Choose *Format, Paragraph* to open the Paragraph dialog box. In the Indents and Spacing folder, select your desired line-spacing setting. Click on *OK* (or press *Enter*).
Create a custom tab stop	Select the desired paragraph(s). Select the desired type of tab stop by clicking on the *Tab Alignment* button until the desired tab type appears. Point at the desired tab-stop position on the ruler. Click the mouse button.
Change the position of a custom tab stop	Select the desired paragraph(s). Drag the custom tab stop (on the ruler) to a new position.
Clear (delete) a custom tab stop	Select the desired paragraph(s). Drag the custom tab stop down into the text area.
Use the Tabs dialog box to manage custom tab stops	Select the desired paragraph(s). Choose *Format, Tabs* to open the Tabs dialog box. Enter your desired settings to set, change, or clear tab stops. Click on *OK* (or press *Enter*).

In the next chapter, you will learn the basics of page formatting. You'll find out how to work with headers and footers, how to use Print Preview to preview a printed document, how to set margins, how to use page breaks to paginate a document, how to work in Page Layout view, how to hyphenate text, and how to control the printing of your documents.

IF YOU'RE STOPPING HERE

If you need to break off here, please exit Word. If you want to proceed directly to the next chapter, please do so now.

SKILL BUILDER

In Chapters 4 and 5, you learned the basics of character and paragraph formatting. The following two activities give you the opportunity to apply these formatting techniques to realistic word-processing situations.

Follow these steps to produce the final document shown in Figure 5.14 from the original document Practice 5a:

1. Open **Practice 5a** (Chapter 2).

2. Select the entire document and remove all of its character formats (Chapters 3 and 4). (**Hint:** Use the **Ctrl+Spacebar** shortcut.)

3. Bold the following headings (Chapter 4):

   1. Introduction

   2. Computer Study

   3. Regional Updates

   4. Quarterly Meeting

   5. Conclusion

4. Using the Font dialog box, change the font and point size of the three-line heading on the top of page 2 to **Arial, 12 point** (Chapter 4).

5. **Repeat** the formatting in step 4 for the three-line heading on the top of page 1 (Chapter 4).

6. Scroll to the bottom of page 1 (Chapter 2).

7. In the paragraph beginning with *After several years,* set left and first-line indents at **0.5"** and a right indent at **5.5"**.

8. **Repeat** the indents in step 7 for the paragraphs beginning with *John Martinson* and *Mark Daley.*

9. **Center** the three-line heading on the top of pages 1 and 2.

10. Save the disk file as **My Practice 5a** (Chapter 2).

11. Print the document and compare it to Figure 5.14 (Chapter 1).

12. **Close** the document (Chapter 1).

Figure 5.14
The completed document My Practice 5a

Macco Plastics Inc.
Quarterly Sales Report
First Quarter

1. Introduction

Congratulations to all of you! An initial review of the sales figures for the nation reveals a surge in sales in all of Macco's sales regions. Major new clients have been added and many new products are on the way.

As we expected when we entered the field, computer-related products, such as keyboard housings and protective carrying cases, are accounting for a major portion of this upswing.

2. Computer Study

A companywide study will begin in March, under the direction of Cathy Donaldson and Bill Schuster in data processing, to determine how to most effectively implement automation in our firm. We will be making a large commitment to productivity gains via computerization sometime late this year.

3. Regional Updates

Midwestern Region

After several years of falling sales due to the slump in the auto industry, Blair Williams and his folks have something to celebrate. The recent boom in auto manufacturing has led to renewed demand of Macco Products in Detroit.

Northeastern Region

John Martinson and his group are doing a great job in Nashua. They have secured major contracts for a wide range of new and existing products. Much of this business is coming from Computer Equipment Corporation, a major client of Macco's.

Southern Region

Mark Daley and his group have done a fine job of maintaining relations with Becker's Product Development Division in Boca Raton. They have been working closely with Becker to decrease manufacturing costs.

Figure 5.14
The completed document My Practice 5a (Continued)

Macco Plastics Inc.
Quarterly Sales Report
First Quarter

4. Quarterly Meeting

The quarterly meeting will take place in Memphis this time. You will find the agenda attached to this report.

5. Conclusion

The following items will be discussed at the next managers' meeting:

A.   Marketing and sales strategies for the introduction of the new System 400 and System 500 product lines.

B.   Current available positions resulting from the early retirement program and normal attrition of personnel.

C.   Development of the new expense form to facilitate the prompt payment of - travel reimbursements - other out-of-pocket expenses and - commissions.

If the recovery continues at the current pace, this year should be a banner year for all of us at Macco. We want to thank all of you for the outstanding jobs you have done and, most important, for standing by Macco in hard times. Keep up the good work!

John Smith
Regional Coordinator
Macco Plastics Inc.

Follow these steps to produce the final document shown in Figure 5.15 from the original document Practice 5b:

1. Open **Practice 5b** (Chapter 2).

2. Using the Font dialog box, **italicize** the first line on page 1, *Macco Plastics Inc.*, and change the point size to **24** (Chapter 4).

3. **Repeat** the formatting in step 2 for the first line on page 2 (Chapter 4).

4. Single-**underline** the following subheadings (near the bottom of page 1) (Chapter 4):

   • Midwestern Region

   • Northeastern Region

   • Southern Region

5. **Clear** (delete) the 2" **left-aligned tab** stop from the paragraph that begins with *B. Current available positions* (near the top of page 2).

6. Set a **0.5"** hanging indent for the paragraph beginning with *A. Marketing and sales.*

7. **Repeat** the 0.5" hanging indent for the paragraphs beginning with *B. Current available positions* and *C. Development of the* (this chapter).

8. In the paragraph beginning with *C. Development of the*, create new lines for:

   - travel reimbursements

   - other out-of-pocket expenses and

   - commissions.

9. Save the disk file as **My Practice 5b** (Chapter 1).

10. Print the document and compare it to Figure 5.15 (Chapter 1).

11. Close the document (Chapter 1).

Figure 5.15
The completed document My Practice 5b

Macco Plastics Inc.

Quarterly Sales Report
First Quarter

1. Introduction

Congratulations to all of you! An initial review of the sales figures for the nation reveals a surge in sales in all of Macco's sales regions. Major new clients have been added and many new products are on the way.

As we expected when we entered the field, computer-related products, such as keyboard housings and protective carrying cases, are accounting for a major portion of this upswing.

2. Computer Study

A companywide study will begin in March, under the direction of Cathy Donaldson and Bill Schuster in data processing, to determine how to most effectively implement automation in our firm. We will be making a large commitment to productivity gains via computerization sometime late this year.

3. Regional Updates

Midwestern Region

After several years of falling sales due to the slump in the auto industry, Blair Williams and his folks have something to celebrate. The recent boom in auto manufacturing has led to renewed demand of Macco Products in Detroit.

Northeastern Region

John Martinson and his group are doing a great job in Nashua. They have secured major contracts for a wide range of new and existing products. Much of this business is coming from Computer Equipment Corporation, a major client of Macco's.

Southern Region

Mark Daley and his group have done a fine job of maintaining relations with Becker's Product Development Division in Boca Raton. They have been working closely with Becker to decrease manufacturing costs.

Figure 5.15
The completed document My Practice 5b (Continued)

Macco Plastics Inc.
Quarterly Sales Report
First Quarter

4. Quarterly Meeting

The quarterly meeting will take place in Memphis this time. You will find the agenda attached to this report.

5. Conclusion

The following items will be discussed at the next managers' meeting:

A.   Marketing and sales strategies for the introduction of the new System 400 and System 500 product lines.

B.   Current available positions resulting from the early retirement program and normal attrition of personnel.

C.   Development of the new expense form to facilitate the prompt payment of

- travel reimbursements

- other out-of-pocket expenses and

- commissions.

If the recovery continues at the current pace, this year should be a banner year for all of us at Macco. We want to thank all of you for the outstanding jobs you have done and, most important, for standing by Macco in hard times. Keep up the good work!

John Smith
Regional Coordinator
Macco Plastics Inc.

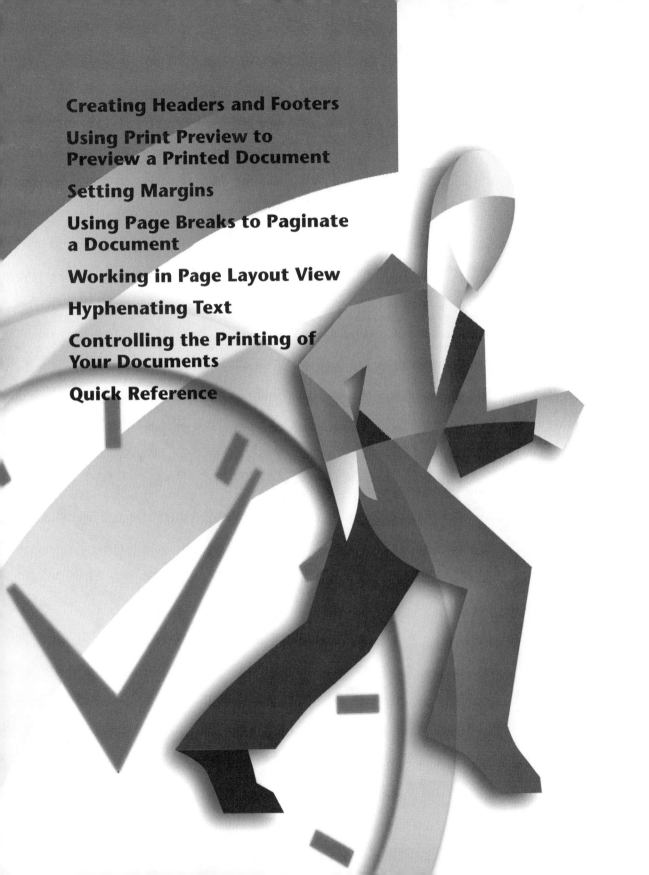

Chapter 6
Page Formatting

In Chapters 4 and 5, you learned how to format your documents at the character and paragraph levels. In this chapter, we'll introduce Word's final level of formatting—*page formatting*. Many powerful formatting features are controlled at the page level, including headers and footers, margins, page breaks, hyphenation, and advanced printing options.

We'll also present two new methods for displaying your documents—*Print Preview* and *Page Layout view*—both of which are well-suited for page-level formatting tasks.

When you're done working through this chapter, you will know

- How to create, edit, and view headers and footers

- How to use Print Preview to preview a printed document

- How to set margins

- How to use page breaks to paginate a document

- How to work in Page Layout view

- How to hyphenate text

- How to control the printing of your documents

CREATING HEADERS AND FOOTERS

A *header* is text that is automatically printed at the top of every page in a document, and a *footer* is text that is automatically printed at the bottom of every page. Headers and footers are used extensively in word processing to do such things as number each page in a document, place the current date on each page, print the document title and/or author name on each page, and so on.

To create a header or footer, choose *Header and Footer* from the View menu. Word automatically switches to Page Layout view, opens the Header area, and displays the Header and Footer toolbar (see Figure 6.1). You'll learn about Page Layout view later in this chapter.

To open the Footer area from the Header area and vice versa, click on the *Switch Between Header and Footer* button (see Figure 6.1).

To enter header/footer information:

- In the Header or Footer area, type your desired header or footer text, using the Header and Footer toolbar buttons as desired (these buttons are discussed in the next section).

- Click on *Close* to accept the header or footer and close the Header or Footer area.

To delete a header or footer:

- Follow the previous procedure to open the Header or Footer area.

- Choose *Edit, Select All* to select the entire contents of the Header or Footer area.

- Press *Del* to delete these contents.

- Click on *Close* to close the Header or Footer area.

Figure 6.1
The Header area and Header and Footer toolbar

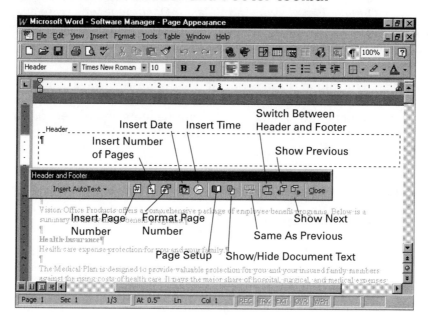

THE HEADER AND FOOTER TOOLBAR

You can use the Header and Footer toolbar buttons to insert the page number, the current date, or the current time into your header or footer (see Figure 6.1). When using the Date and Time buttons, keep in mind that your printout will reflect the date and time when you *print* the document, rather than the date and time when you first *created* the document.

The Show Previous, Show Next, and Same as Previous buttons are sometimes used in long documents that consist of more than one section, and in which each section has more than one header and/or footer. (You'll learn about sections in Chapter 11.) The Page Setup button opens the Page Setup dialog box, in which you can control, for example, your document's margins and the size of its pages. The Show/Hide Document Text button allows you to display the document text dimmed in the background (as in Figure 6.1) or to remove it from the screen display. The Insert Number of Pages button enables you to display the total number of pages in the document. For example, you might have a footer that says Page 1 of 3. The Format Page Number button opens the Page Number Format dialog box where you can select the format for your page numbers.

VIEWING HEADERS AND FOOTERS

Word provides six *views* (screen representations) for your documents: *Normal*, *Online*, *Outline*, *Page Layout*, and *Master Document*, which are available through the View menu; and *Print Preview*, which is located in the File menu. The three views we'll use in this chapter are Normal, Page Layout, and Print Preview.

When you are working in Normal view (the view we've always used up to now), your headers and footers are not shown onscreen, though they will still appear if you print the document. To see your headers and footers onscreen, you must be in Print Preview or Page Layout view. These views will be discussed later in this chapter.

If you are not running Word, please start it now. Let's begin this chapter's activities by opening a document and creating a header for it:

1. Open **Page Appearance** from your WordWork directory.

2. Choose **View, Header and Footer** to open the Header area and display the Header and Footer toolbar (see Figure 6.1). Word automatically switches to Page Layout view. Notice the following:

   - A vertical ruler is displayed along the left edge of the document.

   - The margin area is visible at the top of the page.

   - The header placeholder appears at the top of the window.

   - The document is grayed out.

3. Observe the Header area. Text entered here will automatically appear at the top of every page of your document.

4. Without clicking on any of the buttons, move the mouse pointer to each button. As in the main (Standard) and Formatting toolbars, the name of each button is displayed when you point to it.

5. Type **Vision Office Products**. Press **Tab** twice and then type **Employee Benefits**.

6. Observe the header text. Note that *Employee Benefits* is right-aligned. Observe the ruler. As long as the Header area is open, the ruler refers to the header, *not* to the document. Word has automatically set a centered tab stop at three inches (halfway between the left and right margins) and a right-aligned tab stop at six inches (at the right margin). These preset tab stops enable you to quickly and easily use tabs to center your header text or to align it with the right margin. (To align it with the left margin, you

would simply begin typing without pressing Tab, as you did with *Vision Office Products.*)

7. Click on **Close** in the Header and Footer toolbar to accept your header and close the Header area. Note that the ruler now refers to the document, not to the header. Note also that the header you just created is not displayed on the screen. As mentioned earlier in this section, headers and footers are only visible in Print Preview and Page Layout views.

8. Save the file as **My Page Appearance**.

Now let's create a footer:

1. Choose **View, Header and Footer**. The header you just created is again visible in the Header area.

2. Click on the **Switch Between Header and Footer** button (see Figure 6.1) to open the footer area.

3. Examine the Footer area. It is identical to the Header area. However, the text you type here will be displayed at the *bottom* of every page, instead of at the top.

4. Click on the **Insert Date** button (see Figure 6.1) to insert the current date.

5. Press **Tab** twice to move to the right margin.

6. Type **Page** and then press the **Spacebar**.

7. Click on the **Insert Page Numbers** button (see Figure 6.1) to insert automatic page numbering into the footer text.

8. Close the Footer area (click on **Close**) to accept your footer and return to the document.

USING PRINT PREVIEW TO PREVIEW A PRINTED DOCUMENT

Print Preview provides a miniature view of how a document will look when it is printed. You can use Print Preview to examine and adjust the layout of a document before you actually print it.

In Print Preview, you can edit text and control the placement of text on the page by changing the margins. You also can print the active document and view two or more pages at one time.

To use the Print Preview option:

● Choose *File*, *Print Preview* to open the Print Preview window.

● To print the document, click on the *Print* button in the Print Preview option bar (see Figure 6.2).

Figure 6.2
The Print Preview window

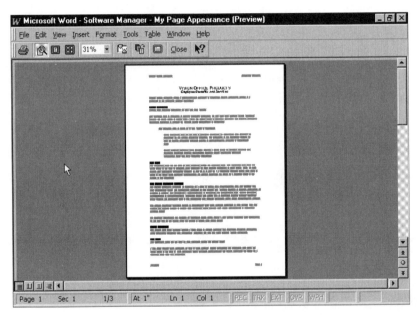

● To change the magnification of the document, click on the Zoom Control button.

● To view more than one page at a time, click on the *Multiple Pages* button in the Print Preview option bar, and then drag over the grid to select the desired number of pages and their configuration (see the next exercise); to return to single-page view, click on the *One Page* button.

● To close the window, click on the *Close* button in the Print Preview option bar.

Let's use Print Preview to examine our header and footer:

1. Choose **File**, **Print Preview** to open the Print Preview window (see Figure 6.2). Print Preview provides a miniature display of your document as it will print, including headers and footers.

2. Click on [icon] (the **View Ruler** button). Notice that, in addition to the horizontal ruler displayed above the document page, a vertical ruler at the left of the Print Preview window is displayed.

3. Click on [icon] (the **Multiple Pages** button).

The Multiple Pages grid is displayed.

4. Click in the third cell of the first row to display a single row of (all) three pages of the document at one time. Compare your screen to Figure 6.3. Notice that the horizontal ruler, which functions in the same manner as the one in Normal document view, appears above the page that currently contains the insertion point (page 1).

Figure 6.3
Print Preview in Multiple Pages view

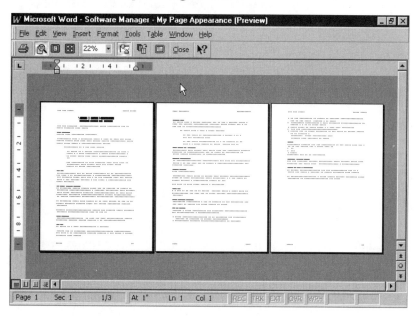

5. Click on [icon] (the **One Page** button).

The document returns to single-page view.

6. Click on the **bottom scroll** arrow (see Figure 6.2) to display page 2 of the document; then click again on the **bottom scroll** arrow to display page 3. In Print Preview, each click scrolls one full page. Notice that the headers and footers appear on every page. My Page Appearance is a three-page document. Click once again on the **bottom scroll** arrow to verify this; your computer may beep, and the screen display does not change, since there are no more pages to scroll to.

7. Click on the **top scroll** arrow (see Figure 6.2) twice to return to page 1 and move the mouse pointer onto the header. The mouse pointer changes into a magnifying glass with a plus sign.

8. Click the mouse button. The view zooms to 100 percent, displaying the header. Notice that the mouse pointer now displays a minus sign in the magnifying glass.

9. Click the mouse button again to zoom out and view the entire page.

10. Click on **Close** to close the Print Preview window and return to Normal view.

SETTING MARGINS

Margins determine the space between the four edges of the page and the text of the document. Figure 6.4 shows a Print Preview of a sample document with Word's default margin settings—the top and bottom margins are set to one inch; the left and right margins are set to one and one-quarter inches. Figure 6.5 shows the same document with custom margins set to twice the default values—the top and bottom are set to two inches; the left and right are set to two and one-half inches.

You can set a document's margins either from the Print Preview window (by dragging the margin boundaries) or in any view by using the Page Setup dialog box.

Use the following methods to adjust margins in Print Preview:

- To change the left and right margins, place the mouse pointer over the left margin boundary on the horizontal ruler (between the left-indent and first-line-indent markers) to change the left margin, or over the right margin boundary (directly above the right-indent marker) to change the right margin. When the mouse pointer becomes a left- and right-pointing arrow, drag the margin to the desired position.

- To change the top and bottom margins, place the mouse pointer in the vertical ruler, at the top margin boundary to change the top margin, or the bottom boundary to change the bottom margin, until the mouse pointer

Figure 6.4
A sample document with default margins

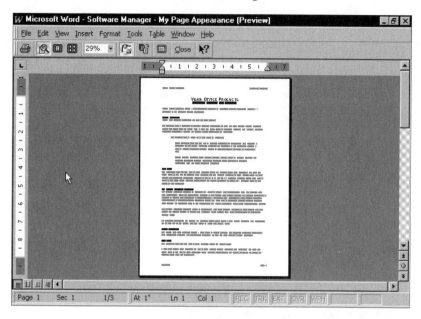

Figure 6.5
A sample document with custom margins

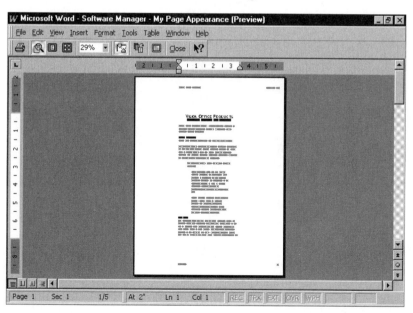

becomes an up- and down-pointing arrow. Then drag the margin to the desired position.

To set margins by using the Page Setup dialog box:

- Choose *File, Page Setup* to open the Page Setup dialog box.
- Display the *Margins* panel (click on its tab), if necessary.
- Enter the new margin settings in the appropriate margin text boxes.
- Click on *OK* (or press *Enter*).

Let's practice changing margins from the Page Setup dialog box:

1. Move to the top of the document, if necessary.

2. Choose **File**, **Page Setup** to open the Page Setup dialog box, and click on the **Margins** tab, if necessary (see Figure 6.6).

Figure 6.6
The Margins tab in the Page Setup dialog box

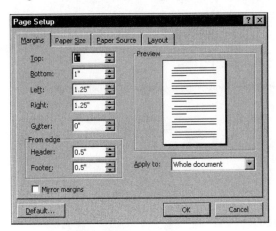

3. Verify that the Top text box is selected and type **1.5** to change the top margin to one and one-half inches. Note that you do not have to type the inch symbol (").

4. Press **Tab** to select the Bottom text box and type **1.5** to change the bottom margin to one and one-half inches.

5. Triple-click in the **Left** text box to select the current left margin setting (**1.25"**). Type **1** to change the left margin to one inch.

6. Press **Tab** to select the current right margin setting (**1.25"**). Type **1** to change the right margin to one inch.

7. Press **Enter** (or click on **OK**) to accept your margin changes. Due to the extra half-inch of text width that you gained (by decreasing the left and right margins by one quarter-inch each), your text lines now run off the right end of the screen (see Figure 6.7). Note that the screen representation of the left margin has not changed. When you are working in Normal view (as opposed to Print Preview or Page Layout view), Word always displays your left margin in the same place (approximately one-quarter inch to the right of the document window edge), no matter how large or small the margin actually is.

8. Save the file.

Figure 6.7
Overwide text lines

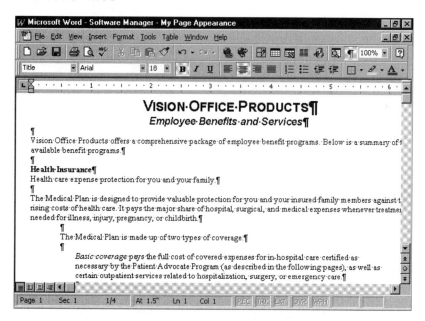

Let's use the Zoom Control feature (covered in Chapter 2) to shrink the display, so that the text lines no longer run off the screen:

1. Observe the status bar. The current magnification level is *100%*.

2. Click on the Zoom Control **down arrow** button to open the Zoom Control list box, and select **Page Width**. Observe the text and the Standard tool-

bar (see Figure 6.8). The magnification level automatically adjusts to fit the entire width (but not the length) of the page on the screen. In the Zoom Control box, you can see that the program has automatically adjusted the magnification level to *92%*.

Figure 6.8
Using the Zoom Control Page Width option

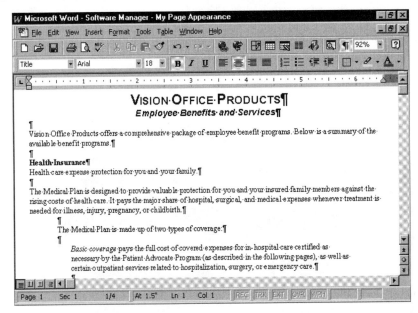

USING PAGE BREAKS TO PAGINATE A DOCUMENT

Pagination is the process of separating a document's text into pages. The separations between pages are called *page breaks*.

There are two types of page breaks in Word:

- *Automatic* page breaks, which Word automatically inserts into a document. An automatic page break appears as a loosely spaced dotted line across the text area.

- *Manual* page breaks, which you insert into the document. A manual page break appears as a tightly spaced dotted line with the words *Page Break* in the center of the line.

To insert a manual page break:

- Place the insertion point immediately to the left of the first character that you want on the new page.

- Choose *Insert, Break*, verify that *Page Break* is selected, and then click on *OK*; or, simply press *Ctrl+Enter*.

To delete a manual page break:

- Move the mouse pointer into the selection bar.

- Select the page break.

- Press *Del*.

You cannot delete automatic page breaks. However, if you insert a manual page break above an automatic page break, Word will remove the automatic page break.

Let's use the above procedure to insert some manual page breaks in My Page Appearance.doc:

1. Move to the top of page 2, and scroll up one line. Observe the automatic page break in the *Plan Cost* section. It is displayed as a loosely spaced dotted line.

2. Place the insertion point to the left of the *P* in the heading *Plan*, near the bottom of page 1.

3. Choose **Insert, Break** to open the Break dialog box. Verify that **Page Break** is selected.

4. Point to (but *don't* click on) OK and, while observing the automatic page break between pages 1 and 2, click on **OK**. Word inserts a manual page break (with the words *Page Break*) at your insertion point and then, shortly afterward, deletes the automatic page break. Because you changed the beginning of page 2 to *Plan Cost*, Word no longer needed to break pages automatically in the middle of the Plan Cost section.

5. Move to the bottom of page 2. Notice that there is an automatic page break at the bottom of page 2 and a manual page break at the bottom of page 3. Page 3 is only four lines long.

6. Place the insertion point before the *T* in the text *Time For Yourself*.

7. Press **Ctrl+Enter** to insert a manual page break. As mentioned earlier in this section, pressing Ctrl+Enter is the keyboard shortcut for using the Insert, Break command.

8. Note that the automatic page break disappears, but that the manual page break before *Sick Days* remains (see Figure 6.9). Automatic page breaks are deleted or repositioned automatically, as necessitated by changes you make to the document (resetting margins, changing font size, inserting new page breaks, and so on). Undesired manual page breaks, however, must be deleted manually.

9. In the selection bar, point to the manual page break before *Sick Days*. Click the mouse button to select the page break.

10. Press **Del** to delete the manual page break.

Figure 6.9
Inserting a manual page break

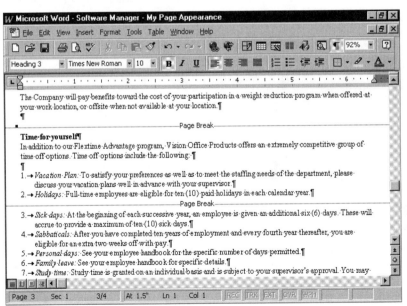

WORKING IN PAGE LAYOUT VIEW

Word's Page Layout view allows you to view all page areas, including headers, footers, and margins. Page Layout view is like a cross between Normal view (where you can edit and format body text, but cannot view headers and footers) and Print Preview (where you can see headers and footers but cannot edit text).

Note: Page Layout view can be useful for applying the finishing touches to your documents. However, you might find that this view significantly slows the operating speed of Word and makes it awkward to move around in the document. For this reason, we recommend that you do most of your work in Normal view.

To enter Page Layout view:

*   Choose *View, Page Layout*; or click on the *Page Layout View* button (to the left of the horizontal scroll bar; see Figure 6.10).

Figure 6.10
The Normal and Page Layout View buttons

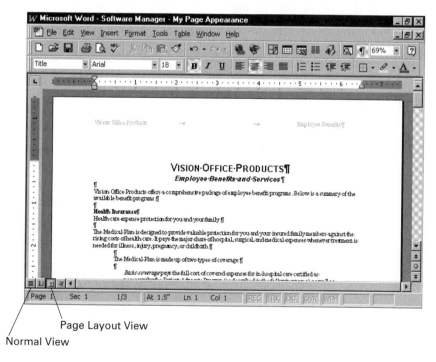

Page Layout View

Normal View

To return to Normal view:

- Choose *View*, *Normal*; or click on the *Normal View* button.

To edit a header or footer in Page Layout view:

- Double-click on the (dimmed) header or footer.

- Edit the header or footer text, as desired.

- Click on *Close*.

Let's edit your header and footer in Page Layout view. But first we'll open the Print Preview window to observe a page-positioning problem with the header and footer:

1. Move to the top of the document.

2. Open the Print Preview window (choose **File**, **Print Preview** or click on the Print Preview button). Notice that the header and footer text no longer aligns with the right margin. Why? Because you changed the document's margins in a previous activity, but did not adjust the position of the right-aligned tab stop in the header and footer. This tab stop does not reach the new right margin. (We'll fix the problem in a moment.)

3. Close the Print Preview window (click on **Close**).

4. Choose **View, Page Layout** to switch to Page Layout view. Notice that the Zoom Control is set to *100%*, which doesn't allow you to view the right margin.

5. Open the Zoom Control list box, and select **Page Width** to automatically adjust the magnification. In Page Layout view, you can both view and edit headers and footers, even though they are currently dimmed and cannot, therefore, be selected.

6. Double-click on the dimmed header. Eureka! The Header area is displayed in Page Layout view.

7. Place the insertion point in the header after the *s* in *Employee Benefits*. Type **and Services**.

8. Observe the ruler. The right-aligned tab stop at 6" did not automatically adjust when you changed the margins earlier.

9. Drag the right-aligned tab stop at 6" to **6.5"** to set it even with the right margin.

10. Click on the **Switch Between Header and Footer** button (in the Header and Footer toolbar) to view the footer.

11. Drag the right-aligned tab stop at 6" to **6.5"**. Then close the Footer area (click on **Close**).

12. Open the Print Preview window. Scroll through the document to verify that the headers and footers now align with the right margin on every page. Then close the Print Preview window.

13. Choose **View, Normal** to return to Normal view.

14. Open the Zoom Control drop-down list box, and select **100%** to return to 100% magnification.

15. Update the disk file (use **File, Save**).

HYPHENATING TEXT

Up to now, we have worked exclusively with unhyphenated text: Each of our documents' lines has ended with a whole word, rather than a *hyphenated* word—a word broken into two parts by a hyphen. You may, at times, wish to hyphenate a document to reduce the raggedness of its right margin (with left-aligned text) or to tighten things up by minimizing the blank space between words (with justified text). Word provides two methods for doing this: *manual hyphenation*, in which you can use either the keyboard or the Tools, Language, Hyphenation command; and *automatic hyphenation*, in which you use the Tools, Language, Hyphenation command.

MANUAL HYPHENATION

To hyphenate text manually:

- Place the insertion point between the desired letters of the word you wish to hyphenate.

- Insert your desired hyphen, choosing from the three types shown in the following table:

Type of Hyphen	How and When to Use
Regular	Press the *Hyphen* key (-); use when you always want the hyphen to appear, such as in compound words ("left-aligned," "right-aligned," and so on).

Type of Hyphen	How and When to Use
Optional	Press *Ctrl+Hyphen*; use when you only want the hyphen to appear if the word is broken at the end of a line (such as "auto-matic").
Hard	Press *Ctrl+Shift+Hyphen*; use when you always want the hyphen to appear, but you never want the word to be broken at the end of a line, such as with names ("Ann-Marie," for instance).

AUTOMATIC HYPHENATION

To hyphenate a document automatically:

- Move the insertion point to the top of the document.

- Choose *Tools, Language, Hyphenation* to open the Hyphenation dialog box.

- Check the Automatically Hyphenate Document option.

- Click on *OK* (or press *Enter*) to hyphenate the document.

PRACTICE YOUR SKILLS

1. Use the **Tools, Hyphenation** command to automatically hyphenate your entire document.

2. Scroll through the document to examine the results.

CONTROLLING THE PRINTING OF YOUR DOCUMENTS

Several times in this book, you've used the File, Print command to print your active document. Let's revisit this very powerful command and learn how to use some of its more advanced features. In addition to printing a single copy of your entire document, File, Print allows you to print the current page, multiple pages, multiple copies, selected text, or nondocument items such as Document Properties.

To use the Print dialog box to control how your documents print:

- If you wish to print selected text, select that text.
- Choose *File, Print* to open the Print dialog box.
- Choose the desired Print options (see Table 6.1).
- Click on *OK* (or press *Enter*).

PRINT DIALOG BOX OPTIONS

The Print dialog box provides the options shown in Table 6.1:

Table 6.1
Print Dialog Box Options

Option	Description
Print What	In this drop-down list box, you choose what you wish to print. The default choice is the current document, but you can also print, for example, comments, document properties (covered later in this section), styles, and AutoText (printing AutoText will be discussed in Chapter 9).
Copies	In this text box, you enter the number of copies that you wish to print. The default is 1 copy.
Page Range	In this area of the dialog box, you specify the portion of the document that you wish to print. Choose All to print the entire document. Choose *Current Page* to print the page where the insertion point is located. If you selected text in your document before issuing the File, Print command, the Selection button becomes active; choose it to print the selected text. Choose *Pages* and enter page numbers in the Pages text box to print a range of pages; separate page numbers with commas (for nonsequential pages) or dashes (for sequential pages)—for example, enter 3, 6, 10-12 to print pages 3, 6, 10, 11, and 12.
Print	From this drop-down list, you can specify the printing of all the pages in a specified range, only the odd-numbered pages, or only the even-numbered pages.

Let's practice using the print options in the Print dialog box. (If you do not have a printer, please skip this activity.)

1. Move to the top of the document.

2. Choose **File, Print** to open the Print dialog box (see Figure 6.11).

Figure 6.11
The Print dialog box

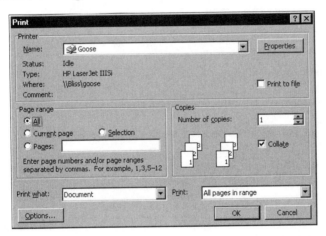

3. In the Page Range area of the box, choose the **Current Page** option (click on the radio button to the left of the option). Click on **OK** to print only the current page (the page on which the insertion point is located), which in this case is page 1. After the page has been sent to the printer, the Print dialog box is automatically closed.

4. Choose **File, Print** to reopen the Print dialog box. Note that Page Range has been reset to its default (*All*). Each time you open the Print dialog box, all of its settings are reset to their default values.

5. In the Page Range area of the box, select the **Pages** option. Type **1-2** in the Pages text box; this informs Word to print only from page 1 through page 2 of the document. Click on **OK** to print these pages.

6. Choose **File, Print** to reopen the Print dialog box. In the Page Range area of the box, notice that the Selection option is currently dimmed, because no text is selected in the document.

7. Select the **Current Page** option. Double-click in the Copies text box to select the current value (**1**); type **2** to tell Word to print two copies of the current page. Click on **OK** to print these copies.

8. Select all text from the heading *Vision Office Products* up to and including the empty paragraph above *Plan Cost*.

9. Choose **File, Print** to reopen the Print dialog box. Note that the Copies and Page Range options have been reset to their default values of *1* and *All*, respectively. Note also that the Selection option is now available.

10. Choose the **Selection** option and then click on **OK** to print only your selected text.

11. Press **Ctrl+Home** to deselect and move to the top of the document. Choose **File, Print** to reopen the Print dialog box. Note that the Selection option is once again dimmed (because there is no text selected in the document).

12. Click on the **down arrow** to the right of the Print What list box to display the Print options. Select **Document Properties** to tell Word to print the Document Properties for the current document. Click on **OK** to print this sheet.

USING THE PRINT BUTTON TO PRINT A DOCUMENT

In addition to the File, Print command, Word provides a Print button that you can use to print a single copy of an entire document. To do this, click on the Print button (the fourth from the left in the toolbar; it shows a printer).

Let's end this chapter's activities by using the Print button to print your entire document. (If you do not have a printer, please skip this activity.)

1. Click on ⬚ (the **Print** button). Word prints a single copy of your entire document.

2. Save the disk file and close the document.

QUICK REFERENCE

In this chapter, you learned the basics of page formatting. You now know how to create, edit, and view headers and footers; how to use Print Preview to preview a printed document; how to set margins; how to use page breaks to paginate a document; how to work in Page Layout view, how to hyphenate text; and how to control the printing of your documents.

Congratulations on completing your foundation of Word formatting techniques! You now know how to format your documents at the character, paragraph, and page levels. These skills will allow you to create highly professional-looking documents.

Here's a quick reference guide to the Word features introduced in this chapter:

Desired Result	How to Do It
Create a header or footer	Choose *View, Header and Footer.* Type header text, or click on *Switch Between Header and Footer* and type footer text. Click on *Close.*
Delete a header or footer	Follow previous procedure to open Header or Footer area. Choose *Edit, Select All* to select entire contents of area. Press *Del* to delete contents. Click on *Close* to close Header or Footer area.
Use Print Preview to preview a printed document	Choose *File, Print Preview.*
Set margins in Print Preview	In vertical or horizontal ruler, drag margin boundary to new margin position. Repeat previous step until all margin boundary lines are set as desired.
Set margins by using the Page Setup dialog box	Choose *File, Page Setup.* Enter new margin settings in appropriate margin text boxes. Click on *OK* (or press *Enter*).
Insert a manual page break	Place insertion point immediately to left of first character you want on new page. Choose *Insert, Break.* Verify that *Page Break* is selected. Click on *OK.* Or, place insertion point and press *Ctrl+Enter.*
Delete a manual page break	Move mouse pointer into selection bar. Select the page break. Press *Del.*
Enter Page Layout view	Choose *View, Page Layout.*

Desired Result	How to Do It
Return to Normal view	Choose *View, Normal.*
Hyphenate text manually	Place insertion point in word where you wish to hyphenate. Insert regular, optional, or hard hyphen.
Hyphenate a document automatically	Press *Ctrl + Home.* Choose *Tools, Hyphenation.* Check *Automatically Hyphenate Document.* Click on *OK.*
Use the Print dialog box to control document printing	If necessary, select text. Choose *File, Print.* Choose Print options. Click on *OK* (or press *Enter*).
Use the Print button to print a single copy of an entire document	Click on toolbar *Print* button.

In the next chapter, we'll explore ways in which Word can help you improve your writing. You'll learn how to check your documents' spelling, how to use the thesaurus to find alternative words, and how to check the grammar, style, and readability of your documents.

Checking the Spelling Of Your Documents

Using the Thesaurus to Find Alternative Words

Checking the Grammar and Style Of Your Documents

Using the AutoCorrect Feature

Quick Reference

Chapter 7
Proofing Your Documents

Misspellings and grammatical mistakes can severely undermine the credibility of your documents. In this chapter, we'll introduce you to tools that allow you to *proof* (check) your documents for potential spelling, grammar, and style errors. Wording is also a critical factor in determining the effectiveness of a document; using inappropriate words may alienate or confuse your readers. We'll explore Word's electronic thesaurus and see how easy it is to find vocabulary alternatives for your documents.

When you're done working through this chapter, you will know

- How to check the spelling of your documents

- How to use the thesaurus to find alternative words

- How to use the Word Count command to check your documents' statistical information

- How to check the grammar and style of your documents

- How to use the AutoCorrect feature

CHECKING THE SPELLING OF YOUR DOCUMENTS

Word provides a spell-check feature that you can use to proof the spelling of your documents. The *spell-check* feature checks each word in a document against the words in its own internal dictionary and highlights the words it does not recognize. The spell checker also checks for such common typing mistakes as repeated words (such as *the the*) and irregular capitalization (such as *tHe*).

Here are Word's options for spell checking documents:

- To spell check an entire document, press *Ctrl+Home* to move the insertion point to the top of the document; to spell check a portion of a document, select the text that you wish to check; to check a single word, select that word.

- Choose *Tools, Spelling and Grammar* or click on the *Spelling and Grammar* button to open the Spelling and Grammar dialog box and begin the spell check. Figure 7.1 illustrates the Spelling and Grammar dialog box.

Figure 7.1
The Spelling and Grammar dialog box

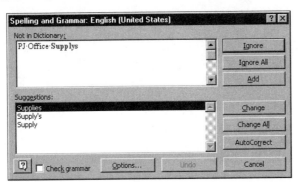

- Follow the dialog box prompts to spell check the document or selected text.

When spell checker finds a potential spelling error (a word not included in the internal dictionary), this word appears in the Not in Dictionary text box (see Figure 7.1), and a list of suggested spelling corrections appears in the Suggestions list box. The first of these suggested spellings is selected (highlighted). At this point, you can choose from the following options:

Option	Action Required
Leave the word unchanged	If you want to leave the word as it is and continue the spelling check, click on *Ignore*.
	To ignore all further occurrences of the word, click on *Ignore All*.
Correct the spelling	If the correction that you want is selected in the Suggestion text box, click on *Change*.
	If the correction that you want is in the Suggestions text box but not selected, click on that correction and then click on *Change*. (Or, as a shortcut, simply double-click on the desired correction.)
	If the correction that you want is not suggested, edit the correction in the Not in Dictionary text box and then click on *Change*.
	To change all the occurrences of the word throughout the document, click on *Change All*.
Add the word to a dictionary	Word allows you to build a custom dictionary that contains words not found in the spell checker's dictionary. This is particularly useful for proper names (such as *Peyton*), abbreviations (such as *ACCTDEPT*), and acronyms (such as *UNICEF*) that you use frequently in your documents. If you want to add the word to a custom dictionary, click on *Add*.
Delete the word	If you want to delete the highlighted word from the document, delete the word in the Not in Dictionary text box and then click on the *Change* button.
Undo the last correction	If you want to undo the last correction, click on *Undo Last*. Word allows you to undo your most recent corrections, one by one.

Option	Action Required
Stop the spelling check	If you want to cancel the spelling check procedure at any point, click on *Cancel* (or *Close*). All changes made up to that point will be preserved. If you used the Change All option, instances of these words that appear after the point where you canceled will not be changed or deleted.

If the error is repeated words (such as *the the*), you can

- Click on *Delete* to delete the second instance of the word.

- Click on *Ignore* to ignore the repeated words and continue the spelling check.

If you are not running Word, please start it now. Let's begin by opening a document and using the spell check feature on a selected portion of it:

1. Open **Proofing Tools** from your WordWork folder.

2. Select the address at the beginning of the document (the first four lines).

3. Choose **Tools, Spelling and Grammar** to open the Spelling and Grammar dialog box (see Figure 7.1). Note the dialog box title, *Spelling: English (United States)*. By default, United States English is the language against which the words in your document are checked. Word allows you to specify a different language (for example, UK English, French, German, Italian, and so on) by using the *Tools, Language, Set Language* command.

4. Observe the dialog box. In the Not in Dictionary text box, Word displays the first word it found that was not in its internal dictionary (*Supplys*, which appears in the second line of the address). In the Suggestions list box, Word displays a list of suggested spelling corrections (*Supplies, Supply's,* and *Supply*). The first of these suggestions (*Supplies*) is selected.

5. Click on **Change** to change *Supplys* to *Supplies* and to search for the next potential spelling error in your text selection. Word prompts: *Word finished checking the selection. Do you want to continue checking the remainder of the document?*

6. Click on **No** to end the spelling check and return to the document. Note that *Supplys* has been corrected to *Supplies* (see Figure 7.2).

Figure 7.2
A corrected spelling error

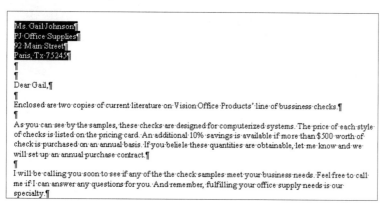

Ms. Gail Johnson¶
PJ Office Supplies¶
92 Main Street¶
Paris, Tx 75245¶
¶
¶
Dear Gail,¶
¶
Enclosed are two copies of current literature on Vision Office Products' line of bussiness checks.¶
¶
As you can see by the samples, these checks are designed for computerized systems. The price of each style of checks is listed on the pricing card. An additional 10% savings is available if more than $500 worth of check is purchased on an annual basis. If you beliele these quantities are obtainable, let me know and we will set up an annual purchase contract.¶
¶
I will be calling you soon to see if any of the the check samples meet your business needs. Feel free to call me if I can answer any questions for you. And remember, fulfilling your office supply needs is our specialty.¶

Now let's check the spelling of the entire document:

1. Press **Ctrl+Home** to deselect and move the insertion point to the top of the document.

2. Click on  (the **Spelling and Grammar** button).

3. The Spelling and Grammar dialog box opens and begins the spell check. Word displays the first word it finds that is not in its dictionary (*bussiness*). At the bottom of the dialog box, uncheck *Check Grammar* (if necessary).

4. Click on **Change** to replace *bussiness* with *business* (the entry that is selected in the Suggestions text box) and to search for the next potential spelling error. Word displays *samlpe*. Note that *samples* is listed in the Suggestions text box.

5. Select (click on) **samples**. Click on **Change** to change *samlpe* to *samples* and to search for the next potential spelling error. Word displays *the* in the uppermost text box, which is now titled *Repeated Word*, instead of *Not in Dictionary* (see Figure 7.3). Although *the* is not misspelled, it appears twice in a row (*the the*) in your document.

6. Click on **Delete** to delete the second *the* and to search for the next potential spelling error. Word displays *O'Malley*.

7. Click on **Ignore** to leave *O'Malley* unchanged and to continue the search. Word prompts: *The spelling check is complete.*

Figure 7.3
Correcting a repeated word

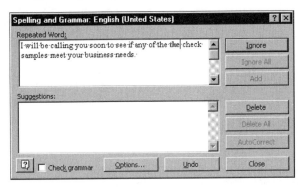

8. Click on **OK** (or press **Enter**) to close the message box.

9. Save the disk file as **My Proofing Tools**.

Now, let's try using the automatic spell check feature. This option is currently turned off. First, we have to turn it on:

1. Choose **Tools, Options**, and display the Spelling and Grammar panel.

2. Check the **Check Spelling As You Type** option to turn it on.

3. Click on **OK**.

Now, we'll have to purposely misspell a word in our newly corrected document:

1. Near the end of the document, select the word *Representative* and type in **Maneger** (to purposely misspell the word). Then press **Enter**. Notice that *Maneger* is underlined with a wavy red line.

2. Click the **right mouse button** on **Maneger** to open the automatic spell check menu (see Figure 7.4). The top portion of this menu lists suggested spellings of the word. The bottom portion of the menu offers three commands: Ignore All, Add (which adds the current spelling to the custom dictionary), AutoCorrect (which adds the current spelling as an AutoCorrect entry), and Spelling (which opens the Spelling dialog box).

3. Choose **Manager** from the menu to correct the word's spelling.

Figure 7.4
Using the automatic spell-check menu

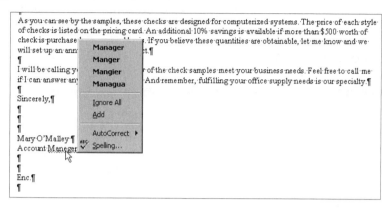

Clearly, the automatic spell-check feature can be handy, because any spellings unfamiliar to the spell-checker are immediately brought to your attention without having to run it manually. However, words such as proper names with odd spellings—for example O'Malley—would also be identified as potential misspellings. Documents with many such words or names would be littered with distracting wavy, red lines.

Let's turn off the automatic spell-check feature, so that we won't be distracted by wavy red lines for the remainder of this book:

1. Choose **Tools, Options**, and display the Spelling and Grammar panel.

2. Click on the **Check Spelling As You Type** option to uncheck it (turn it off).

3. Click on **OK**.

USING THE THESAURUS TO FIND ALTERNATIVE WORDS

You can use Word's internal thesaurus to look up vocabulary alternatives in your documents. The thesaurus provides a comprehensive source of *synonyms* (words with similar meanings) to assist you in finding just the right word for your documents. Having a powerful and lightning-fast electronic thesaurus at your fingertips can greatly enhance the quality of your writing.

To use the thesaurus to find alternative words:

• Select the desired word in your document, or simply place the insertion point anywhere within the word.

- Choose *Tools, Language, Thesaurus* (or press *Shift+F7*) to open the Thesaurus dialog box; a list of synonyms appears.

- To replace the selected word, select the desired synonym and click on *Replace.*

Let's practice using the thesaurus:

1. Place the insertion point in the word **specialty** (the last word in the paragraph that begins with *I will be calling*).

2. Choose **Tools, Language, Thesaurus** to open the Thesaurus dialog box and display a list of synonyms for *specialty* (see Figure 7.5). Note the dialog box title, *Thesaurus: English (United States)*. As with the spell checker, you can use the Tools, Language, Set Language command to change your thesaurus language.

Figure 7.5
The Thesaurus dialog box

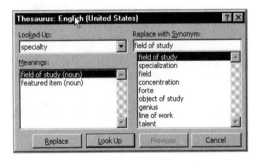

3. Under Replace with Synonym, select **forte** from the list of synonyms. The word *forte* now appears in the Replace with Synonym text box.

4. Click on **Replace** to replace *specialty* with *forte* and close the dialog box.

5. Place the insertion point anywhere in the word *designed* (located in the paragraph beginning with *As you can see*).

6. Press **Shift+F7** to use the shortcut keyboard method for opening the Thesaurus dialog box.

7. In the Replace with Synonym list box, **intended** is selected from a list of synonyms for *designed.*

8. Click on **Replace** to replace *designed* with *intended* and to close the dialog box.

WORD COUNT

The Word Count command enables you to view statistical information concerning your document, such as the number of pages, words, characters, paragraphs, and lines. To display this information:

- Open a document.

- Choose *Tools, Word Count.*

- View the dialog box, and click on *Close.*

Let's use the Word Count command to view statistical information concerning My Proofing Tools:

1. Choose **Tools, Word Count** to open the Word Count dialog box.

2. Observe the Word Count dialog box (see Figure 7.6).

Figure 7.6
141 words in the Word Count dialog box

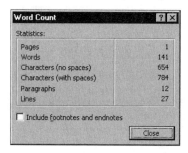

3. Click on the **Close** button to close the Word Count dialog box.

4. Save and close the document.

CHECKING THE GRAMMAR AND STYLE OF YOUR DOCUMENTS

You can use Word's grammar checker to identify and correct sentences in your document that contain grammatical errors and weak writing style.

Here's the general procedure for checking the grammar and style of a document:

- To check an entire document, press *Ctrl+Home* to move the insertion point to the top of the document; to check a portion of a document, select the text that you wish to check.

- Choose *Tools, Spelling and Grammar* to open the Spelling and Grammar dialog box and begin the grammar check.

When a potential grammar or style error is found, the dialog box displays the questionable sentence in the top text box, with words that are related to the potential error displayed in green letters. The dialog box might also provide one or more suggested corrections in the Suggestions list box. At this point, you can choose from the following options:

Option	Action Required
Accept a suggested correction	Select the desired correction in the Suggestions list box and click on *Change*. Or, as a shortcut, simply double-click on the desired suggestion.
Leave the sentence as it is and continue the grammar check	Click on *Next Sentence*.
Leave the sentence as it is and ignore similar potential grammar or style errors	Click on *Ignore*.
Undo the last correction	Click on *Undo*.
Get more information about the potential error or get help on using the grammar checker	Click on the *Help* button in the bottom-left corner of the dialog box. Or, click on the Office Assistant.
Stop the grammar check	Click on *Cancel* (or *Close*); all corrections made up to that point will be preserved.

CUSTOMIZING THE GRAMMAR CHECKER

You may disagree with certain rules that the grammar checker uses in assessing the correctness of a sentence. For example, you may find it perfectly acceptable to use the passive voice—a practice that the grammar checker considers to be a potential error. In recognition of the varying grammatical and style preferences of its users, Word allows you to customize the grammar checker to fit your needs. To do this:

- Click on *Options* in the Spelling and Grammar dialog box to open the Options dialog box with the Spelling and Grammar tab selected (or, choose Tools, Options and click on the Spelling & Grammar tab).

- Click on the *Settings* button.

- Set (check or uncheck) your desired grammar and style options.

- Click on *OK* (or press *Enter*) to return to the Options dialog box, then click on *OK* (or press *Enter*) to accept your customized settings and return to the Spelling and Grammar dialog box.

The changes you made to Word's grammar and style options will apply to all your grammar checks from this point on.

SPELL CHECKING WITH THE GRAMMAR CHECKER

By default, Word checks your document for spelling and grammar as you type, but for the purposes of this book, those options are turned off (in addition to the Check Grammar With Spelling option). In order to check your document for grammar you must first select the Check Grammar option in the Spelling and Grammar dialog box.

Once the Check Grammar option is selected, the dialog box will perform both a spell and grammar check in a document at the same time.

USING THE AUTOCORRECT FEATURE

You can use the AutoCorrect feature to correct text automatically as you type. For example, if you type "teh," AutoCorrect will replace it with "the" as soon as you press the Spacebar. Word supplies a number of default AutoCorrect entries. The AutoCorrect command also has other options available, such as correcting two initial caps and capitalizing days of the week. Choose Tools, AutoCorrect to activate or deactivate the various AutoCorrect options, to view the default AutoCorrect entries, or to add an AutoCorrect entry.

To turn off the AutoCorrect features:

- Choose *Tools, AutoCorrect* to open the AutoCorrect dialog box.

- Uncheck the options you want to turn off.

- Click on *OK*.

AUTOCOMPLETE

As you type some common words, dates or names, Word will suggest the complete word or phrase when you type the first four letters of certain items. This feature is called *AutoComplete.* When the suggestion appears, you can press Enter or F3 to accept the suggestion, or just keep typing to reject it.

Let's use AutoCorrect:

1. Click on the *New* button to open a new document.

2. Type *teh*. You are intentionally misspelling the word.

3. Press the *Spacebar.* AutoCorrect automatically corrects the mistyped word. The letter "T" was also capitalized because it was at the beginning of the sentence.

4. Press *Enter* twice.

5. Type *monday.* (Ignore the AutoComplete suggestion and continue to type.) Press *Enter*. AutoCorrect automatically capitalized the "M" in Monday.

PRACTICE YOUR SKILLS

Use the AutoCorrect feature to finish listing the days of the week.

Let's create our own AutoCorrect entry:

1. Select all the text (press *Ctrl+A*) and press *Del* to clear the document.

2. Choose *Tools, AutoCorrect* to open the AutoCorrect dialog box. Notice the options available in the dialog box: correct two initial caps; capitalize the names of the days; and correct accidental usage of the Caps Lock key.

3. In the *Replace text* box, type your initials. You are creating a shortcut that will replace your initials with your name. (Use a different abbreviation if your initials spell a word. Case does not matter.)

4. Press *Tab* to move to the With text box and type your full name.

5. Click on *Add* and click on *OK* to add your initials as an entry in Auto-Correct and return to the document.

6. In the document, type your initials. Press the Spacebar. Your initials are replaced with your complete name.

7. Close the document without saving.

QUICK REFERENCE

In this chapter, you learned how to proof your documents and improve their quality. Now you know how to check the spelling of your documents; how to use the thesaurus to find alternative words; how to use the Word Count command to count the number of words, lines and paragraphs; and how to check the grammar and style of your documents.

Here's a quick reference guide to the Word features introduced in this chapter:

Desired Result	How to Do It
Spell check a document	Press *Ctrl+Home* to move the insertion point to the top (to spell check an entire document), or select the desired text (to spell check part of a document).
	Choose *Tools, Spelling and Grammar* or click on the *Standard toolbar Spelling and Grammar* button.
	Follow the Spelling and Grammar dialog box prompts.
Use the thesaurus to find alternative words	Select the desired word or place the insertion point anywhere within the word.
	Choose *Tools, Language, Thesaurus*, or press *Shift+F7*.
	Follow the Thesaurus dialog box prompts.
Use Word Count command	Choose *Tools, Word Count*.
	Click on *Close* after you have reviewed the information.

Desired Result	How to Do It
Check the grammar and style of a document	Press *Ctrl+Home* to move the insertion point to the top (to check an entire document), or select the desired text (to check part of a document).
	Choose *Tools, Spelling and Grammar*.
	Follow the Spelling and Grammar dialog box prompts.
Customize the grammar checker	Click on *Options* in the Spelling and Grammar dialog box.
	Click on *Settings* in the Spelling and Grammar tab of the Options dialog box.
	Set (check or uncheck) your desired grammar and style options.
	Click on *OK* (or press *Enter*) to return to the Options dialog box.
	Click on *OK* (or press *Enter*) to accept your customized rule settings and return to the Spelling and Grammar dialog box.
Adding an AutoCorrect entry	Choose *Tools, AutoCorrect*.
	In the Replace text box, type the shortcut.
	In the With text box, type the commonly used text that corresponds to the shortcut.
	Click on *Add*.
	Click on *OK*.
	Type the shortcut in the document.
	Press the *Spacebar*.

In the next chapter, you will build on the basic formatting and editing skills that you have already acquired. You'll learn advanced techniques for moving and copying text, and we'll show you how to copy font formats using the mouse. You'll also learn how to add numbers and bullets to selected text and how to replace and revise font formats.

IF YOU'RE STOPPING HERE

If you need to break off here, please exit Word. If you want to proceed directly to the next chapter, please do so now.

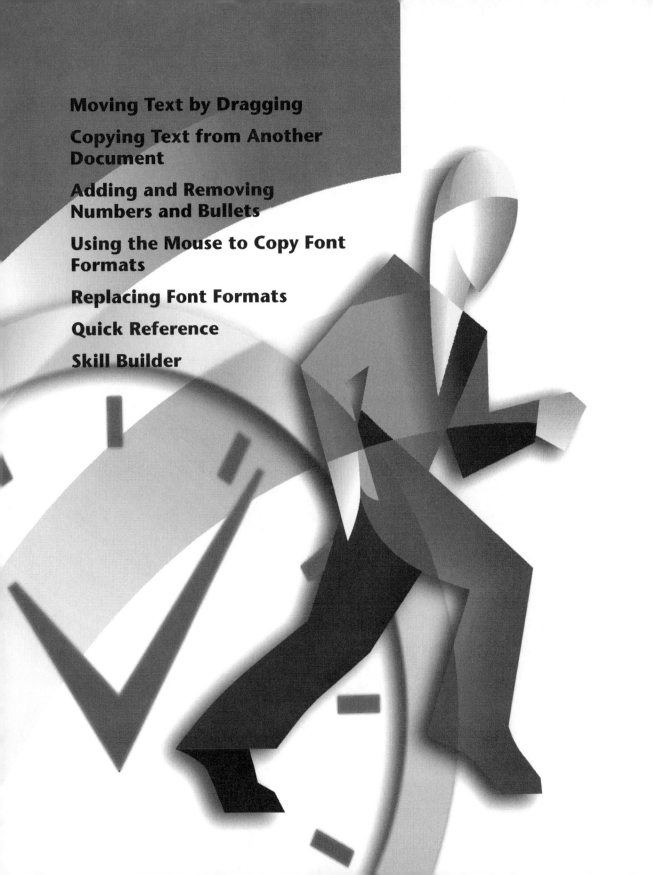

Chapter 8

Advanced Formatting and Editing Techniques

In Chapters 3 and 4, you learned basic techniques for editing and changing font formats of text. In this chapter, you will build on this information by learning more advanced methods of editing and formatting text. For example, you will learn how to copy text from one document to another and how to enhance the readability and visual appeal of your documents by turning selected text into a numbered or bulleted list.

When you're done working through this chapter, you will know

- How to move text using the mouse

- How to copy text from one document to another

- How to add bullets and numbers to selected paragraphs

- How to copy font formats

- How to replace font formats using the Edit, Replace command

MOVING TEXT BY DRAGGING

In Chapter 3, you learned how to copy and move text by using the Cut, Copy, and Paste buttons on the Standard toolbar. In addition to using the toolbar to move text, you can also use the mouse.

To move text (within the same document) using the mouse:

- Select the text you wish to move.

- Point to the selected text.

- Press and hold the mouse button (a small dotted box and dotted insertion point appear attached to the mouse pointer).

- Drag the dotted insertion point to where you want to place the text.

- Release the mouse button.

Let's begin by copying some text. Then we'll use the mouse to move text:

1. Open **VOP Draft**.

2. Select the two lines of the *Vision Office Products* heading and the blank line below them.

3. Click on the **Copy** button. A copy of the selected text is now placed on the Clipboard.

4. Go to the top of page 2.

5. Click on the **Paste** button. The contents of the Clipboard are now placed at the insertion point.

6. Go to the top of page 3.

7. Click on the **Paste** button to paste the contents of the Clipboard at the insertion point. Remember, the contents of the Clipboard will remain there until another selection is cut or copied.

8. Move to the top of page 2 to view the *Dental Insurance* section.

9. Drag to select the entire section, from the *Dental Insurance* heading through the blank line above the *Disability Plans* heading (see Figure 8.1).

Figure 8.1
Selected text to be moved

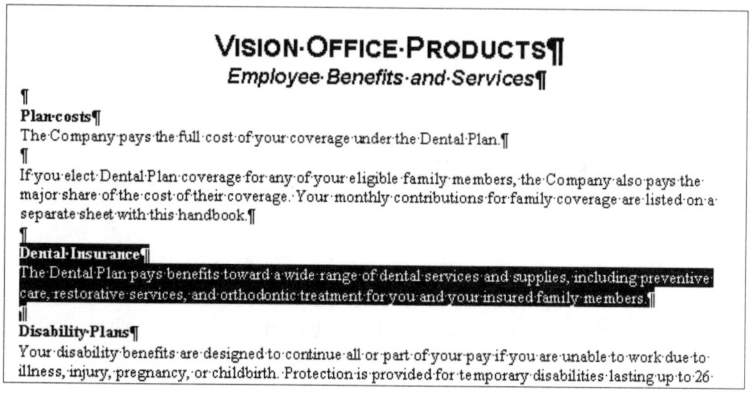

10. Point to the selected text. The mouse pointer becomes an arrow.

11. Press and hold the mouse button. A small, dotted box and a dotted insertion point appear.

12. Drag the dotted insertion point to the left of the *P* in *Plan costs* (toward the top of page 2) to place the *Dental Insurance* section above the *Plan costs* section.

13. Release the mouse button. The selected text is now displayed in its new location. Deselect the text.

14. Save the document as **My VOP Draft** and compare your screen to Figure 8.2.

Figure 8.2
The moved text

VISION·OFFICE·PRODUCTS¶
Employee·Benefits·and·Services¶

¶
Dental·Insurance¶
The·Dental·Plan·pays·benefits·toward·a·wide·range·of·dental·services·and·supplies,·including·preventive·
care,·restorative·services,·and·orthodontic·treatment·for·you·and·your·insured·family·members.¶

¶
Plan·costs¶
The·Company·pays·the·full·cost·of·your·coverage·under·the·Dental·Plan.¶

¶
If·you·elect·Dental·Plan·coverage·for·any·of·your·eligible·family·members,·the·Company·also·pays·the·
major·share·of·the·cost·of·their·coverage.·Your·monthly·contributions·for·family·coverage·are·listed·on·a·
separate·sheet·with·this·handbook.¶

¶
Disability·Plans¶
Your·disability·benefits·are·designed·to·continue·all·or·part·of·your·pay·if·you·are·unable·to·work·due·to·
illness,·injury,·pregnancy,·or·childbirth.·Protection·is·provided·for·temporary·disabilities·lasting·up·to·26·

COPYING TEXT FROM ANOTHER DOCUMENT

The first document you open appears in the document window. If you create or open a second document without closing the first one, Word opens the second document on top of the first document, so that both documents are open at the same time. The second document then becomes the active document. You can open several (how many depends on your computer's available memory) documents at one time, but only one document can be active.

The names of the documents appear in the title bars and under the Window menu. To make a document active, either click on the document window, if it is visible, or select the document name from the Window menu.

Once you have placed text on the Clipboard, you can move or copy the text from one document to another, in the same way that you would within a document.

Let's open a second document window, and then copy and paste between the two documents:

1. Place the insertion point to the left of the *P* in *Profit Sharing and Retirement*, near the middle of page 2.

2. Open **Flexible Spending Accounts**. The document consists of a two paragraphs, followed by a blank line.

3. Select the paragraphs and the blank line below them.

4. Click on the **Copy** button to place a copy of the selected text on the Clipboard.

5. Choose **Window, 2 My VOP Draft** to move to the My VOP Draft document window.

6. Click on the **Paste** button. The paragraph and blank line are now displayed above the *Profit Sharing and Retirement* heading.

7. Click on the **Save** button to update the document. This is the same as choosing File, Save from the menu.

8. Choose **Window, 1 Flexible Spending Accounts** to move to the *Flexible Spending Account* document window.

9. Choose **File, Close** to close *Flexible Spending Account*.

ADDING AND REMOVING NUMBERS AND BULLETS

The longer your document, the more important it is for you to clearly define its major sections and subsections. To achieve this, you can use headings, which you can format differently from the surrounding text. In fact, you've already seen several examples of headings in exercises throughout the course of this book. Furthermore, when your document contains lists of items that you would like to call attention to, such items can be numbered or bulleted. This section focuses on using numbers and bullets to improve your document's organization and appearance.

ADDING NUMBERS AND BULLETS

To add numbers to specific paragraphs, select the desired paragraphs and click on the Numbering button. To add bullets to specific paragraphs, select the desired paragraphs and click on the Bullets button. When you add bullets or numbers to paragraphs, Word automatically formats the paragraphs with hanging indents. (See "Setting Hanging Indents" in Chapter 5 for details on this feature.)

If you apply numbers to a series of paragraphs and then want to change them to bullets, or vice versa:

• Select the desired paragraphs.

• Click on the *Bullets* or *Numbering* button.

You can also create a numbered or bulleted list before you add the text to the list. To do so:

• Position the insertion point where you wish to place the list.

- Click on the *Numbering* or *Bullets* button.

- Create as many paragraphs as you like.

- Click on the *Numbering* or *Bullets* button again to turn off the feature.

Let's select a list of items, and then add numbers and bullets to the list:

1. Scroll to place the *Time for yourself* heading, on page 3, at the top of the screen.

2. Drag to select the paragraphs that begin *Vacation Plan...* through *Study time...*

3. Click on ⊞ (the **Numbering** button).

4. Numbers appear to the left of the selected paragraphs.

5. Deselect the text to view the numbers. Compare your screen to Figure 8.3.

Figure 8.3
The numbered list

> ¶
> ▪ **Time·for·yourself**¶
> In·addition·to·our·Flextime·Advantage·program,·Vision·Office·Products·offers·an·extremely·competitive·
> group·of·time·off·options.·Time·off·options·include·the·following:·¶
> ¶
> 1.→ *Vacation·Plan:*·To·satisfy·your·preferences·as·well·as·to·meet·the·staffing·needs·of·the·department,·
>   please·discuss·your·vacation·plans·well·in·advance·with·your·supervisor.¶
> 2.→ *Holidays:*·Full-time·employees·are·eligible·for·ten·(10)·paid·holidays·in·each·calendar·year·(in·addition·
>   to·the·Vacation·Plan).¶
> 3.→ *Sick·days:*·At·the·beginning·of·each·successive·year,·an·employee·is·given·an·additional·six·(6)·days.·
>   These·will·accrue·to·provide·a·maximum·of·ten·(10)·sick·days.¶
> 4.→ *Sabbaticals:*·After·you·have·completed·ten·years·of·employment·and·every·fourth·year·thereafter,·you·
>   are·eligible·for·an·extra·two·weeks·off·with·pay.¶
> 5.→ *Personal·days:*·See·your·employee·handbook·for·the·specific·number·of·days·permitted.¶
> 6.→ *Family·leave:*·See·your·employee·handbook·for·specific·details.¶
> 7.→ *Study·time:*·Study·time·is·granted·on·an·individual·basis·and·is·subject·to·your·supervisor's·or·
>   Mr.°Taylor's·approval.·You·may·be·eligible·if·you·↵
>   —·are·enrolled·in·a·company·approved·education·program·↵
>   —·have·been·with·the·company·for·at·least·one·year.¶
> ¶

6. Drag to select the numbered list. Be sure to select all the paragraph marks.

7. Click on ⊞ (the **Bullets** button).

8. Bullets now replace the numbers to the left of the selected paragraphs.

9. Deselect the text and compare your screen to Figure 8.4.

Figure 8.4
The bulleted list

> ▪ **Time·for·yourself¶**
> In·addition·to·our·Flextime·Advantage·program,·Vision·Office·Products·offers·an·extremely·competitive·
> group·of·time·off·options.·Time·off·options·include·the·following:·¶
> ¶
> ● → *Vacation·Plan:*·To·satisfy·your·preferences·as·well·as·to·meet·the·staffing·needs·of·the·department,·
>   please·discuss·your·vacation·plans·well·in·advance·with·your·supervisor.¶
> ● → *Holidays:*·Full-time·employees·are·eligible·for·ten·(10)·paid·holidays·in·each·calendar·year·(in·addition·
>   to·the·Vacation·Plan).¶
> ● → *Sick·days:*·At·the·beginning·of·each·successive·year,·an·employee·is·given·an·additional·six·(6)·days.·
>   These·will·accrue·to·provide·a·maximum·of·ten·(10)·sick·days.¶
> ● → *Sabbaticals:*·After·you·have·completed·ten·years·of·employment·and·every·fourth·year·thereafter,·you·
>   are·eligible·for·an·extra·two·weeks·off·with·pay.¶
> ● → *Personal·days:*·See·your·employee·handbook·for·the·specific·number·of·days·permitted.¶
> ● → *Family·leave:*·See·your·employee·handbook·for·specific·details.¶
> ● → *Study·time:*·Study·time·is·granted·on·an·individual·basis·and·is·subject·to·your·supervisor's·or·
>   Mr.°Taylor's·approval.·You·may·be·eligible·if·you·↵
>   — are·enrolled·in·a·company·approved·education·program·↵
>   — have·been·with·the·company·for·at·least·one·year.¶
> ¶

REMOVING NUMBERS AND BULLETS

You can remove bullets or numbers from a series of paragraphs. To do so:

● Select the numbered or bulleted list.

● Click on the *Numbering* or *Bullets* button.

Note: You can also use the Undo command to remove bullets or numbers.

Let's remove the bullets from our list:

1. Drag to select the bulleted list. Be sure to select all the paragraphs.

2. Click on the *Bullets* button to remove the bullets from the selected text.

CUSTOM BULLETS

You can customize bullets by selecting from additional symbols. To do so:

● Select the bulleted list.

● Choose Format, Bullets and Numbering.

● Click on the *Customize* button to open the Customize Bullet List dialog box.

● Click on the *Bullet* button to open the Symbol dialog box. The font *Wingdings* is selected by default, or you can select another font.

● Click on the bullet style that you want to apply.

● Click *OK* twice.

In the Bullets and Numbering dialog box, you can also set other options for the type of bullet or number character you want to use, such as varying its size (accessible through the customize option), and removing the hanging indent. There is also a tab for creating multilevel lists.

Let's customize a bulleted list:

1. Drag to select the paragraphs *Vacation Plan...* through *Study time....* Be sure to select all the paragraphs.

2. Choose **Format, Bullets and Numbering** to open the Bullets and Numbering dialog box (See Figure 8.5).

Figure 8.5
The Bullets and Numbering dialog box

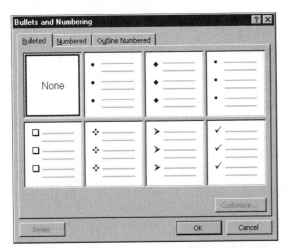

3. Select one of the seven bullets that are available and click on **OK**. The text has the bullet you selected applied to it.

4. With the text still selected, choose **Format, Bullets and Numbering**. Click on the **Customize** button to open Customize Bullet List dialog box, and then click on the **Bullet** button to open the Symbol dialog box. Notice that the font *Wingdings* is selected.

5. Click on the bullet style of your choice, and then click on **OK** twice to return to My VOP Draft.

6. Observe the bulleted list. The text now has the customized bullet that you chose applied to it.

USING THE MOUSE TO COPY FONT FORMATS

In Chapter 4, you learned how to apply multiple character, or font, styles using the Format menu. You learned that you could use the F4 (Repeat) key or choose Edit, Repeat Formatting to repeat the formatting on other text. Remember, however, that when you use either of these methods, only the *last* format applied will be repeated. For example, if you select text and apply first the bold and then the italic formats from the Formatting toolbar, then select different text and press F4, only the italic formatting will be applied.

You also began to use the Format Painter to copy formatting from one block of text and paste it onto another. Now, we'll use it again to make the task of formatting easier.

Note: Once the Format Painter button is active, you can only use the normal scroll bar, Go To dialog box, and keyboard techniques to navigate the document. If you use the Next Page or Previous Page double-arrows, the Format Painter will be deactivated.

Let's apply and copy some font formats:

1. Move to the top of the document. Select the **Health Insurance** heading, near the top of the document.

2. Open the **Font** drop-down list box (in the Formatting toolbar) and select **Arial**.

3. Click on the **Italic** and **Underline** buttons to apply those font styles to the selected text.

4. Select the **Plan costs** heading, below the *Health Insurance* section.

5. Open the Edit menu. Notice the second menu choice, *Repeat Underline*. If you were to choose this option (or press F4), only the underlining would be applied to the selected text.

6. Close the Edit menu. *Plan costs* is still selected.

7. Place the insertion point anywhere within the *Health Insurance* heading (this text contains the font formats that you will copy).

8. Click on 🖌 (the **Format Painter** button).

9. Move the mouse pointer down into the text area.

10. Scroll down and select the **Plan costs** heading (use the scroll bar). Notice that as you select the heading, the formatting from the *Health Insurance*

heading is copied or "painted" onto it. The Format Painter button is no longer depressed, and the mouse pointer returns to normal.

11. With the *Plan costs* heading still selected, click on the **Format Painter** button and then select **The Patient Advocate Program** heading to copy the formatting from the *Plan costs* heading.

PRACTICE YOUR SKILLS

1. Repeat the formatting (the font Arial and bold, italic, and underline styles) to the *Dental Insurance* and *Plan costs* headings.

2. Deselect the text.

3. Save the document and compare your screen to Figure 8.6.

Figure 8.6
Copied font formats

VISION·OFFICE·PRODUCTS¶
Employee·Benefits·and·Services¶

¶
<u>*Dental·Insurance*</u>¶
The·Dental·Plan·pays·benefits·toward·a·wide·range·of·dental·services·and·supplies,·including·preventive·
care,·restorative·services,·and·orthodontic·treatment·for·you·and·your·insured·family·members.¶
¶
<u>*Plan·costs*</u>¶
The·Company·pays·the·full·cost·of·your·coverage·under·the·Dental·Plan.¶
¶
If·you·elect·Dental·Plan·coverage·for·any·of·your·eligible·family·members,·the·Company·also·pays·the·
major·share·of·the·cost·of·their·coverage.·Your·monthly·contributions·for·family·coverage·are·listed·on·a·
separate·sheet·with·this·handbook.¶
¶
Disability·Plans¶
Your·disability·benefits·are·designed·to·continue·all·or·part·of·your·pay·if·you·are·unable·to·work·due·to·
illness,·injury,·pregnancy,·or·childbirth.·Protection·is·provided·for·temporary·disabilities·lasting·up·to·26·

Now let's apply and copy some more font formats:

1. Select the **Plan costs** heading, under the *Dental Insurance* section on page 2.

2. Double-click the **Format Painter** button and move the mouse pointer down into the text area. Notice that it becomes an I-beam with a paintbrush attached.

3. Select the **Disability Plans** heading (under the *Plan cost* heading—scroll down if necessary). Notice that the Format Painter button is still depressed. By double-clicking on the *Format Painter* button, you can use the "copied" formats until you turn off the Format Painter feature.

4. Format the remaining headings on pages 2 and 3 with the Format Painter (which is still active).

5. Click on the **Format Painter** button to deselect it. Move the mouse pointer onto the text area. Notice that it is returned to its normal shape.

6. Save and close My VOP Draft.

REPLACING FONT FORMATS

You can use the Replace dialog box to search for and replace font formats in a manner that is similar to the way you find and replace text.

To replace font formats:

- Choose *Edit, Replace*.

- Click on *More* and then click on *Format*.

- Choose *Font* from the Format pop-up list.

- In the Find Font dialog box, click on the *Font* tab, if necessary, and then select the font formats you want to find.

- Click on *OK* to return to the Find and Replace dialog box.

- Press *Tab* to move to the Replace With text box.

- Click on *Format*.

- Choose *Font* to open the Replace Font dialog box, and click on the *Font* tab, if necessary.

- Select the font formats that you want to change to.

- Click on *OK* and then click on *Less*.

- Click on *Find Next*.

- Click on *Replace* to replace the font formatting, or click on *Find Next* to leave the existing formatting intact.

- Click on *Cancel* to close the Find and Replace dialog box when you are finished.

In the Find Font dialog box, grayed or unchecked formats under Effects will not change. Clicking in the check box selects the format; clicking twice clears the check box, indicating that you want to remove the format.

QUICK REFERENCE

In this chapter, you learned a number of advanced formatting and editing techniques that make use of the Standard toolbar and mouse, including copying and moving text within a single document and between documents. You learned how to create numbered lists and bulleted lists by adding numbers or bullets to a continuous string of paragraphs. You also learned how to change a numbered list to a bulleted list, and vice versa. Finally, you learned how to copy and replace font formats.

Here is a quick reference guide to the Word features introduced in this chapter:

Desired Result	**How to Do It**
Copying text using the Standard toolbar	Select the desired text.
	Click on the *Copy* button.
	Place the insertion point in the desired destination.
	Click on the *Paste* button.
Moving text using the mouse pointer	Select the desired text.
	Point to the selected text.
	Drag the selection to the desired destination.
	Release the mouse button.
Copying text from one document to another	Open the second document.
	Select the desired text.
	Click on the *Copy* button.
	Choose *Window* and choose the file name of the destination document.
	Place the insertion point where you wish to place the copied text.
	Click on the *Paste* button.

Desired Result	How to Do It
Close an inactive document window	Choose *Window* and the name of the document you wish to close.
	Choose *File, Close.*
Adding numbers or bullets to existing text	Select the desired paragraphs.
	Click on the *Numbering* button or the *Bullets* button.
Changing numbers to bullets or vice versa	Select the numbered or bulleted list.
	Click on the *Bullets* or *Numbering* button, whichever you desire.
Removing numbers or bullets	Select the desired text.
	Click on the *Numbering* or *Bullets* button.
Copying font formats (pasting only once)	Place the insertion point anywhere within the text that has the formatting that you wish to copy.
	Click on the *Format Painter* button in the Standard toolbar.
	Select the text to which you wish to copy the formats.
Copying font formats (continuous pasting)	Place the insertion point anywhere within the text that has the formatting that you wish to copy.
	Double-click on the *Format Painter* button in the Standard toolbar.
	Select the text to which you wish to copy the formats.
	Click on the *Format Painter* button to turn off the feature.

Desired Result	How to Do It
Replacing font formats	Place the insertion point at the top of the document.
	Choose *Edit, Replace*.
	Click on *Format*, and choose *Font*.
	Select the settings you want to find.
	Click on *OK*. Press *Tab*.
	Click on *Format*, and choose *Font*.
	Select the replacement settings.
	Click on *OK*. Click on *Find Next*.
	Click on *Replace*.
	Continue clicking on *Find Next*, then *Replace*, until you have finished replacing the formats.

In the next chapter, you will learn how to create and use the AutoText feature to store frequently used text and graphics.

IF YOU'RE STOPPING HERE

If you need to break off here, please exit Word. If you want to proceed directly to the next chapter, please do so now.

SKILL BUILDER

The following instructions lead you through the steps necessary to edit the document Practice 8A to produce the document shown in Figure 8.7.

Follow these steps at your computer:

1. Open **Practice 8A**.

2. Use the mouse to select the *Northeastern Region* section, which is under the *3. Regional Updates* heading. Be sure to select the entire section and the blank line following it.

3. Drag the selected text to place it directly *above* the *Midwestern Region* section.

4. Use the Standard toolbar to copy the three-line heading and the blank line below it at the top of page 1, to the top of page 2.

5. Open **Practice 8B**.

6. Use the Standard toolbar to copy all of Practice 8B to the Clipboard.

7. Move to the Practice 8A window.

8. Paste the contents of the Clipboard below the *Northeastern Region* section. (**Hint:** Place the insertion point to the left of the *M* in *Midwestern* before you paste the contents of the Clipboard.)

9. Under the *5. Conclusion* heading, select the paragraphs *A. Marketing and sales* through *C. Development of the new.*

10. Add bullets to the selected paragraphs.

11. Change the font formatting of the *1. Introduction* heading to include **Arial**, **Bold**, and **Underline**.

12. Use the mouse to apply the font formats from the 1. *Introduction* heading to the *2. Computer Study* heading.

13. Apply the font formats from the *2. Computer Study* heading to the following headings:

    3. Regional Updates

    4. Quarterly Meeting

    5. Conclusion

Figure 8.7
The completed My Practice 8A document

Macco Plastics Inc.

Quarterly Sales Report

First Quarter

1. Introduction

Congratulations to all of you! An initial review of the sales figures for the nation reveals a surge in sales in all of Macco's sales regions. Major new clients have been added and many new products are on the way.

As we expected when we entered the field, computer-related products, such as keyboard housings and protective carrying cases, are accounting for a major portion of this upswing.

2. Computer Study

A companywide study will begin in March, under the direction of Cathy Donaldson and Bill Schuster in data processing, to determine how to most effectively implement automation in our firm. We will be making a large commitment to productivity gains via computerization sometime late this year.

3. Regional Updates

Northeastern Region

John Martinson and his group are doing a great job in Nashua. They have secured major contracts for a wide range of new and existing products. Much of this business is coming from Computer Equipment Corporation, a major client of Macco's.

Midwestern Region

After several years of falling sales due to the slump in the auto industry, Blair Williams and his folks have something to celebrate. The recent boom in auto manufacturing has led to renewed demand of Macco Products in Detroit.

Southern Region

Mark Daley and his group have done a fine job of maintaining relations with Becker's Product Development Division in Boca Raton. They have been working closely with Becker to decrease manufacturing costs.

Figure 8.7
The completed My Practice 8A document (Continued)

Macco Plastics Inc.
Quarterly Sales Report
First Quarter

4. Quarterly Meeting

The quarterly meeting will take place in Memphis this time. You will find the agenda attached to this report.

5. Conclusion

The following items will be discussed at the next managers' meeting:

- Marketing and sales strategies for the introduction of the new System 400 and System 500 product lines.

- Current available positions resulting from the early retirement program and normal attrition of personnel.

- Development of the new expense form to facilitate the prompt payment of
  - travel reimbursements
  - other out-of-pocket expenses and
  - commissions.

If the recovery continues at the current pace, this year should be a banner year for all of us at Macco. We want to thank all of you for the outstanding jobs you have done and, most important, for standing by Macco in hard times. Keep up the good work!

John Smith
Regional Coordinator
Macco Plastics Inc.

14. Save the document as **My Practice 8A**.

15. Print the document and compare your printout to Figure 8.7.

16. Close both documents.

Creating AutoText Entries
Inserting AutoText Entries
Modifying AutoText Entries
Printing AutoText Entries
Quick Reference

Chapter 9

Storing Frequently Used Text with the AutoText Feature

Suppose you needed to send out a large number of letters with the same letterhead and closing. It would certainly save you a great deal of time to enter the letterhead and closing only once, and then simply paste them into each document, as needed. You could copy the information to the Clipboard and paste it into each letter. However, you already know that the Clipboard is only a temporary storage area; as soon as you cut or copied other text or exited Windows, the information would be lost.

Word enables you to save such information as an AutoText entry. Word's *AutoText* feature is a kind of shorthand that allows you to save text (or graphics), and then retrieve it whenever you need it. You can insert Auto-Text entries anywhere in your documents.

When you're done working through this chapter, you will know

- How to create AutoText entries

- How to modify and delete AutoText entries

- How to print AutoText entries

CREATING AUTOTEXT ENTRIES

AutoText entries enable you to store frequently used text and graphics so that you can insert them into your documents quickly and easily.

To create an AutoText entry using the AutoCorrect dialog box with the Auto-Text tab selected:

- Select the text or graphics you want in the AutoText entry.

- Choose *Insert, AutoText, AutoText* to open the AutoCorrect dialog box with the AutoText tab selected.

- In the Enter AutoText Entries Here text box, type a name for the AutoText entry (or accept the default one). The AutoText entry can be seen in the Preview box.

- Click on *Add*.

To create an AutoText entry using the Create AutoText dialog box:

- Select the text or graphics you want in the AutoText entry.

- Choose *Insert, AutoText, New* to open the Create AutoText dialog box.

- In the text box, type a name for the AutoText entry (or accept the default one).

- Click on *OK*.

AutoText entries can contain any type of formatting. Entry names can have up to 32 characters and can contain spaces. For ease of use, you might want to keep your AutoText entry names brief.

Let's create an AutoText entry for letterhead text:

1. Click on the **New** button (the first Standard toolbar button on the left) to open a new document window.

2. Type **Vision Office Products** and press **Enter**.

3. Type **2345 Industrial Parkway** and press **Enter**.

4. Type **Chicago, Illinois 60603** and press **Enter** three times.

5. Select all of the text. Do *not* select the blank lines below the text.

6. Change the font to **Arial** (use the **Font** drop-down list box) and apply the **Bold** character style.

7. Center the selected text.

8. Deselect the text and compare your screen to Figure 9.1.

Figure 9.1
The completed letterhead

Vision·Office·Products¶
2345·Industrial·Parkway¶
Chicago,·Illinois·60603¶

9. This time, select all of the text *and* the three blank lines. The heading and blank lines will be included in the AutoText entry.

10. Choose **Insert, AutoText, AutoText** (see Figure 9.2) to open the Auto-Correct dialog box with the AutoText tab selected.

11. Observe the Preview box at the bottom of the dialog box. It allows you to verify the desired selection. Notice that a default name is provided in the Enter AutoText Entries Here text box (the default name is the first line of the selected text); however, let's change the name.

12. In the text box, verify that the name is selected and type **letterhead** to name the AutoText entry. Compare your screen to Figure 9.3.

13. Click on **Add** to add the AutoText entry to the list.

14. Close the document without saving it; saving is not necessary because the document's text has already been saved as an AutoText entry.

Let's create an AutoText entry for closing text using the Create AutoText dialog box:

1. Click on the **New** button (the first Standard toolbar button on the left) to open a new document window.

Figure 9.2
Choosing Insert, AutoText, AutoText

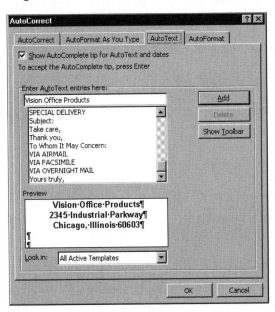

Figure 9.3
Naming the letterhead AutoText entry

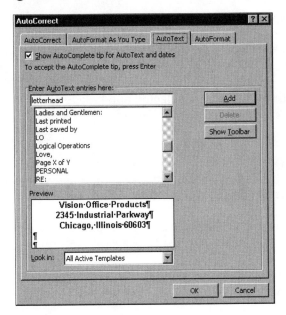

2. Type **Cordially,** (press Enter to accept the AutoComplete tip for *Cordially,*) and press **Enter** four times.

3. Type *your name* and press **Enter**.

4. Type **Corporate Sales Coordinator** and press **Enter** twice.

5. Type **CC:** and press **Tab** to move to the first tab stop.

6. Type **R. Allen** and press **Enter**.

7. Press **Tab**, type **G. Berg** and compare your screen to Figure 9.4.

Figure 9.4
Completed letter closing

Cordially,¶
¶
¶
¶
(your name)¶
Corporate Sales Coordinator¶
¶
cc: → R. Allen¶
  → G. Berg¶

8. Select all of the text and paragraph marks. The selected text will be included in the AutoText entry.

9. Choose **Insert, AutoText, New** to open the Create AutoText dialog box.

10. In the Name text box, type **cordially** (type *cordially to* replace *Cordially,*)to name the AutoText entry. Compare your screen to Figure 9.5.

Figure 9.5
Naming the letter-closing AutoText entry

11. Click on **OK** to add the AutoText entry.

12. Choose **Insert, AutoText, AutoText**. Scroll through and observe the Auto-Text entries. Notice that the *letterhead* and *cordially* entries, which you created earlier, are listed in the Name list box.

13. Click on **Cancel** to close the dialog box.

14. Close the document without saving it.

INSERTING AUTOTEXT ENTRIES

Word includes various AutoText entries that are stored in the Insert, AutoText drop-down menu under different category names. To insert an AutoText entry in a document:

- Place the insertion point where you want to insert the AutoText entry.

- Choose *Insert, AutoText* and then choose a category drop-down menu that corresponds to the AutoText entry.

- Click on the name of the AutoText entry you want to insert.

To insert an AutoText entry in a document using the AutoText toolbar:

- Place the insertion point where you want to insert the AutoText entry.

- Choose *View, Toolbars, AutoText;* or choose *Insert, AutoText, AutoText* and click on the *Show Toolbar* button.

- On the AutoText toolbar, click on the All Entries button to display the category drop-down lists; choose one of the drop-down lists; and click on an AutoText entry.

If you want to insert an AutoText entry quickly, type the name of the entry in the document to display the AutoComplete tip and then press Enter to enter the AutoText. For example, as you type *letterhead* an AutoComplete tip will be displayed. Press Enter and the AutoText will be inserted.

Note: If you type the AutoText entry name in front of text, be sure to type a space after the AutoText name, and if you type an entry after text, make sure there is a space before the name. Otherwise, Word will not insert the AutoText. Also remember that the AutoText name must be typed exactly the way you typed it when you named it.

Let's insert the AutoText entries in a document:

1. Open **VOP Letter**. This letter contains no letterhead or closing.

2. Verify that the insertion point is at the top of the document.

3. Choose **Insert, AutoText, Normal** and select **letterhead**. Compare your screen to Figure 9.6.

Figure 9.6
The inserted letterhead AutoText entry

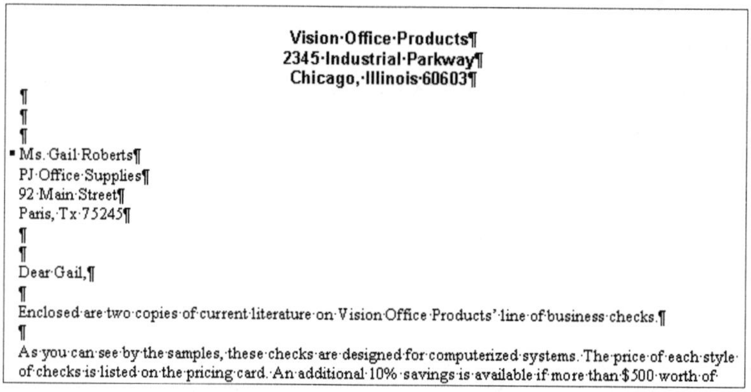

```
                              Vision·Office·Products¶
                             2345·Industrial·Parkway¶
                             Chicago,·Illinois·60603¶
     ¶
     ¶
     ¶
   ▪ Ms.·Gail·Roberts¶
     PJ·Office·Supplies¶
     92·Main·Street¶
     Paris,·Tx·75245¶
     ¶
     ¶
     Dear·Gail,¶
     ¶
     Enclosed·are·two·copies·of·current·literature·on·Vision·Office·Products'·line·of·business·checks.¶
     ¶
     As·you·can·see·by·the·samples,·these·checks·are·designed·for·computerized·systems.·The·price·of·each·style·
     of·checks·is·listed·on·the·pricing·card.·An·additional·10%·savings·is·available·if·more·than·$500·worth·of·
```

4. Move the insertion point to the end of the document.

5. Choose **Insert, AutoText, Normal** and select **cordially** to insert the Auto-Text entry. Compare your screen to Figure 9.7.

Figure 9.7
Inserted closing AutoText entry

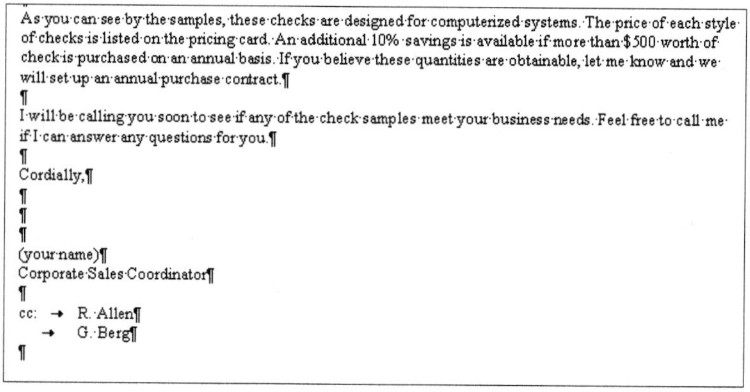

```
     As·you·can·see·by·the·samples,·these·checks·are·designed·for·computerized·systems.·The·price·of·each·style·
     of·checks·is·listed·on·the·pricing·card.·An·additional·10%·savings·is·available·if·more·than·$500·worth·of·
     check·is·purchased·on·an·annual·basis.·If·you·believe·these·quantities·are·obtainable,·let·me·know·and·we·
     will·set·up·an·annual·purchase·contract.¶
     ¶
     I·will·be·calling·you·soon·to·see·if·any·of·the·check·samples·meet·your·business·needs.·Feel·free·to·call·me·
     if·I·can·answer·any·questions·for·you.¶
     ¶
     Cordially,¶
     ¶
     ¶
     ¶
     (your·name)¶
     Corporate·Sales·Coordinator¶
     ¶
     cc:  →  R.·Allen¶
          →  G.·Berg¶
     ¶
```

6. Save the document as **My VOP Letter**.

Note: The "extra" paragraph mark (¶) after the closing in Figure 9.7 was produced by inserting the AutoText entry before an existing paragraph mark.

MODIFYING AUTOTEXT ENTRIES

After you have created an AutoText entry, you can go back and edit the text of the entry, in much the same way as you would a normal document.

EDITING AUTOTEXT ENTRIES

To edit an AutoText entry:

- Insert the AutoText entry that you want to edit into your document.

- Make the desired changes.

- Select the text and/or graphics you want in the AutoText entry.

- Choose *Insert, AutoText, New*.

- If necessary, type the original name of the AutoText entry. (If you wish to keep the original entry intact, type a new name for the entry.)

- Click on *OK*; a message box displays, asking if you want to redefine the AutoText entry. (If you used a new name for the revised entry, no message box will be displayed.)

- Click on *Yes*.

Let's edit one of our AutoText entries:

1. Verify that the insertion point is at the end of the document.

2. Press **Tab**, then type **K. Donnelly**, and press **Enter** (to add more names to the list).

3. Press **Tab**, then type **J. Hutton**, and press **Enter**.

4. Select the entire closing, from *Cordially* through *J. Hutton*. Do *not* select the last paragraph mark.

5. Choose **Insert, AutoText, New**.

6. In the Name list box, type **cordially** (if necessary).

7. Click on **OK**. A message box displays, asking if you wish to redefine the AutoText entry (see Figure 9.8). If the Office Assistant is open, the prompt will come from there.

8. Click on **Yes** to redefine the *cordially* AutoText entry under the same name.

Figure 9.8
Editing an AutoText entry

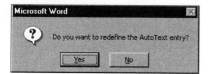

PRACTICE YOUR SKILLS

1. Delete the selected text. Do *not* move the insertion point.

2. Insert the new *cordially* AutoText entry.

DELETING AUTOTEXT ENTRIES

To remove an AutoText entry:

* Choose *Insert, AutoText, AutoText*.

* In the Name list box (under the *Enter AutoText Entries* text box), select the name of the AutoText entry that you want to delete.

* Click on *Delete*.

* Click on *OK*.

Let's edit the AutoText entry, give it a new name, and then delete the old entry:

1. Select **Cordially,** and type **Sincerely,**

2. Select the entire closing, from *Sincerely* through *J. Hutton*. Do not select the last paragraph mark.

3. Choose **Insert, AutoText, New**.

4. In the Name text box, type **sincerely** to name the AutoText entry.

5. Click on **OK** to add the AutoText entry to the list.

6. Delete the selected text. Do *not* move the insertion point.

7. Type **sincerely** and press **Enter** to insert the AutoText entry using the AutoComplete tip. Notice that the AutoText entry replaced the word *sincerely*.

8. Save the document and compare your screen to Figure 9.9.

Figure 9.9
The new *sincerely* AutoText entry

check·is·purchased·on·an·annual·basis.·If·you·believe·these·quantities·are·obtainable,·let·me·know·and·we·will·set·up·an·annual·purchase·contract.¶

¶

I·will·be·calling·you·soon·to·see·if·any·of·the·check·samples·meet·your·business·needs.·Feel·free·to·call·me·if·I·can·answer·any·questions·for·you.¶

¶

Sincerely,¶

¶

¶

¶

(your·name)¶

Corporate·Sales·Coordinator¶

¶

cc: → R.·Allen¶

    → G.·Berg¶

    → K.·Donnelly¶

    → J.·Hutton¶

¶

9. Open the AutoText dialog box (choose **Insert, AutoText, AutoText**).

10. Select **cordially** (if necessary), not *Cordially,*.

11. Click on **Delete** to delete the selected AutoText entry.

12. Scroll through the AutoText entries to verify that the *cordially* entry is gone.

13. Click on **OK** to close the AutoText dialog box.

PRACTICE YOUR SKILLS

Delete the *letterhead* AutoText entry.

PRINTING AUTOTEXT ENTRIES

You can print your AutoText entries so that you can see the contents of each entry. To print AutoText entries:

- Choose File, Print.

- In the Print What drop-down list box, select *AutoText Entries*.

- Click on *OK*.

All AutoText entries available to the active document are printed in alphabetical order. The formatting appears as it would if it were inserted in a document.

Let's print our AutoText entries:

1. Choose **File, Print**.

2. In the Print What drop-down list box, select **AutoText Entries** to print only AutoText entries (see Figure 9.10). Notice that under Page Range, all options are dimmed.

Figure 9.10
Printing AutoText entries

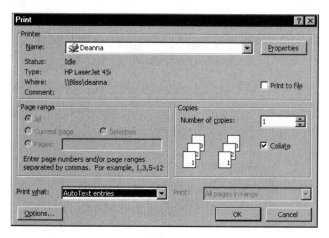

3. Click on **OK** to print the AutoText entries. Observe the printout to view all of the available AutoText entries.

4. Save and close the document.

QUICK REFERENCE

In this chapter, you learned how to create AutoText entries and insert them in your documents. You also learned how to edit, delete, save, and print your AutoText entries.

Here is a quick reference guide to the Word features introduced in this chapter:

Desired Result	How to Do It
Create an AutoText entry	Select the desired text and/or graphics to be placed in the entry.
	Choose *Insert, AutoText, AutoText* (or *Insert, AutoText, New*).
	Name the entry in the Enter AutoText Entries Here text box.
	Click on *Add*.
Insert an AutoText entry in a document using the mouse	Place the insertion point at the desired destination for the AutoText entry.
	Choose *Insert, AutoText* and the corresponding category drop-down list.
	Select the name of the desired entry.
Insert an AutoText entry using the AutoText toolbar	Place the insertion point at the desired destination for the AutoText entry.
	Choose *View, Toolbars, AutoText* (or *Insert, AutoText, AutoText* and click on the *Show Toolbar* button).
	Click on the All Entries button
	Choose one of the category drop-down lists and select the name of the desired entry.
Insert an AutoText entry using the keyboard	Place the insertion point at the desired destination for the AutoText entry.
	Type the name of the entry.
	Press *Enter*.

Desired Result	**How to Do It**
Edit an AutoText entry	Insert the AutoText entry to be edited in the document.
	Make the desired changes.
	Select the desired contents of the entry.
	Choose *Insert, AutoText, New* (or click on the *New* button on the AutoText toolbar).
	Type the original name of the entry, if necessary.
	Click on *OK*.
	Click on *Yes*.
Delete an AutoText entry	Choose *Insert, AutoText, AutoText*.
	Select the name of the AutoText entry to be deleted.
	Click on *Delete*.
	Click on *OK*.
Print all AutoText entries	Choose *File, Print*.
	In the Print What box, *select AutoText Entries*.
	Click on *OK*.

In the next chapter, you will learn how to create, modify, and enhance tables.

IF YOU'RE STOPPING HERE

If you need to break off here, please exit Word. If you want to proceed directly to the next chapter, please do so now.

Chapter 10
Working with Tables

If you want to arrange information in a table, you can do so by setting tabs. However, creating tabbed tables is a slow and tricky process; you must figure out exactly how the table should look, measure the width of each column, and then set tabs that correspond to each measurement. (You've already seen an example of a tabbed table in Chapter 5.) You can also run into problems if your text does not fit between your tabs.

Word's Table feature allows you to create rows and columns of information without having to set tabs. You can even convert tabbed text to a table. A table can be useful for enhancing the presentation of data in your document, for creating side-by-side paragraphs, and for organizing information used in form letters.

When you're done working through this chapter, you will know:

- How to create a table

- How to modify a table

- How to enhance a table

- How to convert tabbed text to a table

CREATING TABLES

To insert a table into your document:

- Place the insertion point where you want to insert the table.

- Choose *Table, Insert Table*, or click on the *Insert Table* button in the Standard toolbar.

When you create tables by using the menu command, you specify the number of columns and rows in the Insert Table dialog box. You can also specify the width of the columns. When you use the Insert Table button to create tables, you select the number of columns and rows on the Insert Table button grid (the grid is displayed when you click on the Insert Tables button). This is similar to the technique you used to print-preview multiple pages in Chapter 6. (You'll use the Insert Table button grid later in this section.)

Word creates a table that fills the area inside the margins. The width of the columns adjusts automatically according to the amount of space available between the left and right margins.

A table consists of vertical *columns* and horizontal *rows* (see Figure 10.1). The intersection of a column and a row is called a *cell*. By default, Word applies a border to tables when you create them (displayed between the cells), but under the border are dotted lines called *gridlines*. You can hide the gridlines by choosing Table, Gridlines. The dotted lines called *column boundaries* are displayed between the columns (under the border). The gridlines and column boundaries are for visual reference only; they do not appear when you print the document.

If you display nonprinting characters, *end-of-cell* marks appear in each cell and *end-of-row* marks appear at the end of each row. You can use these marks to select and edit the table. Squares are displayed in the ruler above the column boundaries; these are called *column markers*. You can use these column markers to adjust the width of the columns by dragging them left or right. When you place the insertion point in a column, indent markers for that column are displayed on the ruler, enabling you to indent selected text as you desire.

Note: When you Print Preview the table, the gridlines, end-of-cell marks, and end-of-row marks are not displayed.

Figure 10.1
Table components

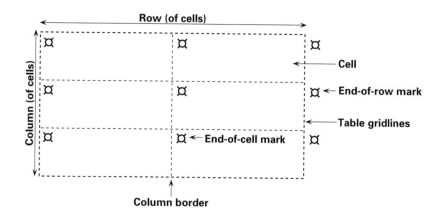

Let's create and examine a table:

1. Open **Car Rental Memo**.

2. Scroll down to place the paragraph that begins *A full list of surcharge cities* near the top of the document window. Place the insertion point two blank lines above the paragraph that begins *All rates include.*

3. Choose **Table, Insert Table** to open the Insert Table dialog box, shown in Figure 10.2.

Figure 10.2
The Insert Table dialog box

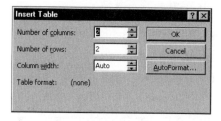

4. Observe the *Number of Columns* text box. You can change the number of columns by typing a number in the text box or by clicking on the increment indicators (see Figure 10.2).

5. Observe the *Number of Rows* text box. You can change the number of rows by typing a number in the text box or by clicking on the increment indicators.

6. Click on **Cancel** (or press **Esc**) to close the dialog box without inserting the table.

7. Click on [icon] (the **Insert Table** button).

8. The Insert Table button grid is displayed.

9. Using Figure 10.3 as a guide, point to the cell in column three, row four on the grid to select it. The bottom of the grid displays *4x3 Table*.

Figure 10.3
Specifying table size in the Insert Table button grid

4 x 3 Table

10. Click the mouse button to display the table at the insertion point.

11. Observe the following features:

   • The *columns* are displayed vertically on the page.

   • The *rows* are displayed horizontally on the page.

   • The *cells* are the intersections of columns and rows.

   • The *end-of-cell marks* are the small circles inside the cells.

   • The *end-of-row marks* are at the end of each row.

   • The *column markers* in the ruler are the square buttons placed above the column boundaries.

   • The border is a thin black line that outlines the columns, rows and cells of the table.

Note: Underneath the border (which is on by default) are the gridlines, the dotted lines between the cells. The column boundaries are the vertical dotted lines between the columns (also under the border).

MOVING IN A TABLE

You can use the mouse to move to from one table cell to another, or you can use the keyboard. To move to a specific cell using the mouse, simply place the I-beam on (or to the right of) the end-of-cell mark in the desired cell, and click. Table 10.1 lists the keystrokes used for moving within a table.

Table 10.1
Moving in a Table Using the Keyboard

Desired Result	How to Do It
Move one cell to the right	Press *Tab*.
Move one cell to the left	Press *Shift+Tab*.
Move up one row	Press *Up Arrow*.
Move down one row	Press *Down Arrow*.

Note: If you use the arrow keys on the numeric keypad, Num Lock must be turned off.

Let's practice moving in the table we've created:

1. Press **Tab** to move the insertion point one cell to the right (the second column of the first row).

2. Press **Tab** twice to move the insertion point to the next row.

3. Press **Shift+Tab** to move back one cell to the third cell in the first row.

4. Press **Down Arrow** to move down one row.

5. Press **Up Arrow** to move up one row.

6. Place the I-beam in the last cell of the table on (or to the right of) the end-of-cell mark, and click the mouse button to place the insertion point in the last cell.

PRACTICE YOUR SKILLS

Place the insertion point in the first cell of the table.

SELECTING TABLE COMPONENTS

You can select a cell, a row, a column, or the entire table. Table 10.2 lists the methods used for making these selections.

Table 10.2
Selecting in a Table

Desired Selection	How to Do It
Cell	Place the insertion point in the cell to the left of the text; press and hold the mouse button; drag to select the cell; and release the mouse button. Place the insertion point in the cell and triple-click.
Row	Place the insertion point anywhere within the desired row and choose *Table, Select Row*. Click in the selection bar to the left of the row.
Column	Place the I-beam on the top border of the desired column until it becomes a downward-pointing arrow, and click the mouse button. Or, place the insertion point anywhere in the column, and choose *Table, Select Column*.
Entire table	Place the insertion point anywhere within the table and choose *Table, Select Table*.

Let's try various selection techniques within our table:

1. Point to the left of the end-of-cell mark in the first cell. (Make sure that the mouse pointer is still located within the cell.)

2. Triple-click (or drag to the end of the cell) to select the cell. Compare your screen to Figure 10.4.

Figure 10.4
The selected cell

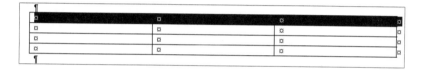

3. In the selection bar, point to the left of the first row. Click the mouse button to select the entire row (see Figure 10.5).

Figure 10.5
The selected row

4. Point to the top border of the second column, until the mouse pointer becomes a downward-pointing arrow. Then click to select the entire column (see Figure 10.6).

Figure 10.6
The selected column

5. Choose **Table, Select Table** to select the entire table. Compare your screen to Figure 10.7.

Figure 10.7
The selected table

6. Deselect the table (click above or below the table).

7. Choose **Table**. Notice that when the insertion point is not in the table, only five Table menu commands are available. Close the Table menu (click on **Table**).

ENTERING TEXT IN A TABLE

To enter text in a table, either select a cell or place the insertion point in the cell; then begin typing.

Let's enter text in our table:

1. Place the I-beam on the end-of-cell mark in the first cell and click.

2. Type **City**.

3. Press **Tab** to move to the next cell.

4. Type **Surcharge** and press **Tab**.

PRACTICE YOUR SKILLS

1. Complete the table as shown in Figure 10.8.

Figure 10.8
The completed table

City¤	Surcharge¤	Additional·Costs¤	¤
Boston¤	9.9%¤	$25.50¤	¤
New·York¤	10.9%¤	$29.95¤	¤
Washington¤	8.9%¤	$24.00¤	¤

2. Print Preview the table to see how the table will print and compare it to Figure 10.8. (We'll add formatting to improve its appearance as the chapter progresses.)

3. Save the document as **My Car Rental Memo**.

MODIFYING TABLES

After you have created your table—even after you have entered all the desired data—you can still change its structure. You can insert rows and columns within the table, add rows to the bottom or columns to the right side of the table, change the width of the columns, and delete rows and columns.

INSERTING ROWS AND COLUMNS

To insert a row at the end of a table, place the insertion point in the last cell of the table and press the Tab key. To insert a row *within* a table, select the row where you want to insert the new row (the new row will be inserted above the selected row) and choose *Table, Insert Rows*, or click on the *Insert Rows* button (the erstwhile *Insert Table* button). To insert more than one row in a table, select as many rows as you want to insert (the new rows will be inserted above the selected rows) and choose *Table, Insert Rows*, or click on the *Insert Rows* button. The number of rows that you select is the number of rows that will be inserted.

To insert a column at the end of a table, select all of the end-of-row marks (by placing the I-beam directly above the marks until it becomes a downward-pointing arrow and clicking once); then choose *Table, Insert Columns* or click on the *Insert Columns* button (you guessed it—the same button as Insert Table and Insert Rows). To insert a column within a table, select the column where you want to insert a new column (the new column will be inserted to the left of the selected column) and choose *Table, Insert Columns* or click on the *Insert Columns* button. To insert more than one column within a table, select as many columns as you want to insert (the new columns will be inserted to the left of the selected columns) and choose *Table, Insert Columns* or click on the *Insert Columns* button. The number of columns that you select is the number of columns that will be inserted.

Let's insert rows and columns in our table:

1. Verify that the insertion point is in the last cell of the table.

2. Press the **Tab** key. Voilà! A new row is inserted at the end of the table.

3. Type **Baltimore** and press **Tab**.

4. Type **7.9%**. Press **Tab** and type **$19.95**.

5. In the selection bar, point to the left of the second row. Press and hold the mouse button, and drag to select the second and third rows (to tell Word to insert two rows); then release the mouse button.

6. Place the mouse pointer (but do *not* click) on ▣ (the *Insert Rows* button).

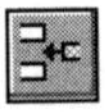

   Notice that the button has changed from the *Insert Tables* button, because you selected a row. Let's use the menu to insert our rows.

7. Choose **Table, Insert Rows** to insert two rows above the selected rows. Compare your screen to Figure 10.9.

Figure 10.9
The inserted rows

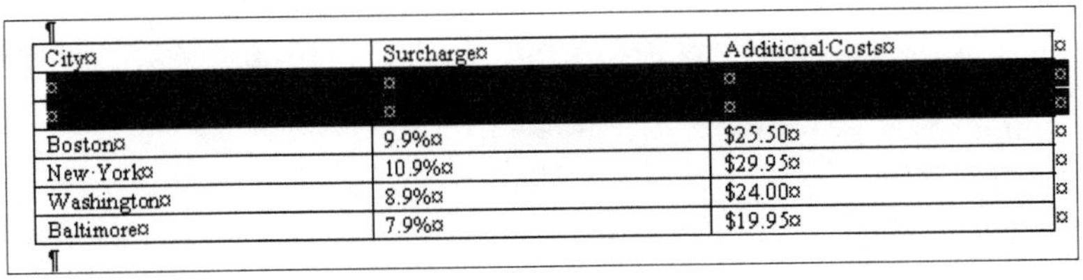

City¤	Surcharge¤	Additional·Costs¤	¤
¤	¤	¤	¤
¤	¤	¤	¤
Boston¤	9.9%¤	$25.50¤	¤
New·York¤	10.9%¤	$29.95¤	¤
Washington¤	8.9%¤	$24.00¤	¤
Baltimore¤	7.9%¤	$19.95¤	¤

8. Select the entire second column (click on the top border of the second column).

9. Open the Table menu. Notice (but do *not* choose) the second menu option: *Insert Columns.* This time, let's use the Standard toolbar. Click on **Table** to close the menu.

10. Place the mouse pointer on ▣ (the *Insert Columns* button).

11. Notice that the button has changed from the *Insert Rows* button, because you selected a column.

12. Click on the **Insert Columns** button, and then compare your screen to Figure 10.10.

Figure 10.10
The inserted column

City¤	¤		Surcharge¤	A
¤	¤		¤	¤
¤	¤		¤	¤
Boston¤	¤		9.9%¤	$
New·York¤	¤		10.9%¤	$
Washington¤	¤		8.9%¤	$
Baltimore¤	¤		7.9%¤	$

13. Scroll right to view the rest of the table. The table extends beyond the right margin.

PRACTICE YOUR SKILLS

1. In the first row of the second column, enter the heading **Mileage Included**.

2. Complete the second column as shown in Figure 10.11.

Figure 10.11
The data entered in the second column

City¤	Mileage·Included¤	Surcharge¤	A
¤	¤	¤	¤
¤	Yes¤	¤	¤
Boston¤	No¤	9.9%¤	$
New·York¤	No¤	10.9%¤	$
Washington¤	Yes¤	8.9%¤	$
Baltimore¤	Yes¤	7.9%¤	$

3. In the third row of the first column, type **Buffalo**.

4. Press **Tab** twice and type **5.9%**. Press **Tab** and type **$14.95**. Scroll back to the left.

5. Save the document.

DELETING ROWS, COLUMNS, AND ENTIRE TABLES

To delete one or more contiguous rows in a table, select the row or rows that you want to delete; then choose *Table, Delete Rows*.

To delete one or more contiguous columns, select the column or columns that you want to delete; then choose *Table, Delete Columns*.

To delete an entire table, select the table; then choose *Table, Delete Rows*.

Let's delete a row in our table:

1. Select the second row (click in the selection bar, to the left of the second row).

2. Choose **Table, Delete Rows** to delete the selected row (see Figure 10.12).

Figure 10.12
The table after deleting a row

City¤	Mileage·Included¤	Surcharge¤	A
Buffalo¤	Yes¤	5.9%¤	$
Boston¤	No¤	9.9%¤	$
New·York¤	No¤	10.9%¤	$
Washington¤	Yes¤	8.9%¤	$
Baltimore¤	Yes¤	7.9%¤	$

CHANGING COLUMN WIDTH

To change column width by dragging column boundaries:

- Point to the column boundary that you want to move; the mouse pointer will become a horizontal, double-headed arrow.

- Press and hold the mouse button.

- Drag the column boundary to the desired location.

- Release the mouse button.

To change column width by using the ruler:

- On the ruler, point to the column marker that you want to move (the mouse pointer will become a horizontal, double-headed arrow).

- Press and hold the mouse button.

- Drag the column marker to the desired location.

- Release the mouse button.

To change column width by using the menu:

- Select the desired column (or the entire table).

- Choose *Table, Cell Height and Width*.

- Click on the *Column* tab.

- Type the desired width in the Width of Column text box.

- Click on *OK*.

When you change the column width using the first two of these techniques (dragging column boundaries and column markers), the column to the right of the column boundary you are moving is resized, and the width of the entire table does not change. If you change column width using the third technique (the Cell Height and Width menu command), the width of the table changes to accommodate the adjusted width of its columns and the entire table is resized.

Note: Before you print a document that contains a table, use Print Preview to make sure that the entire table fits on the page.

To automatically adjust column width so that the table fits on the page:

- Choose Table, Cell Height and Width.
- Click on the *Column* tab.
- Click on *AutoFit*.

Let's try using all three manual methods to change the width of columns in our table:

1. Point to the column boundary between the *City* and *Mileage Included* headings. The mouse becomes a double-headed arrow.

2. Press and hold the mouse button, and drag the column border to the left until it is just to the right of the end-of-cell mark in the *Washington* cell. This decreases the width of the first column. Release the mouse button. The second column is now considerably wider.

3. In the ruler, point to the column marker near the 4" mark. Hold down the Alt key as you drag the column marker to decrease the width of the second column to 1.01" on the ruler (holding down the Alt key displays the exact column width as you drag the column marker).

4. Select the entire table (choose **Table, Select Table**).

5. Choose **Table, Cell Height and Width** to open the Cell Height and Width dialog box, and click on the **Column** tab (if necessary).

6. In the Width of Columns 1-4 text box, click to place the insertion point, and type **1.25** to set the width of all columns in the table to 1.25" (see Figure 10.13).

7. Click on **OK** to close the dialog box, and deselect the table. Notice that all four columns are now equal in width and fit in-between the margins. Compare your screen to Figure 10.14.

Figure 10.13
Setting column width

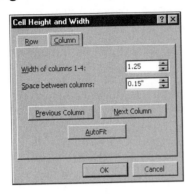

Figure 10.14
The table with columns of equal width

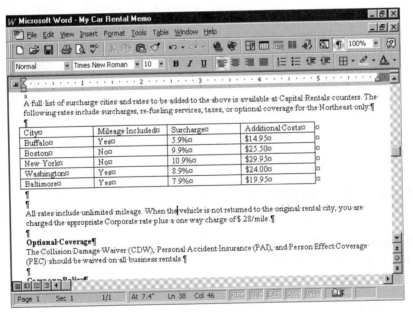

ENHANCING TABLES

You already know how to enhance text in your document; doing so can improve its appearance and often its readability. Accentuating important text helps the eye to locate these reference points. The same text enhancements that are available in standard document text are also available when working in tables, including, for example, bold and italic font styles, changes in font and font size, and text alignment within a cell. In addition, you can alter the alignment of the entire table relative to the margins you're using. You can apply any font formats to text within a table. You can also enhance a table by adding a border or gridlines that will appear when the document is printed.

ALIGNING A TABLE

To align a table between the left and right margins:

- Select the entire table.

- Click on the Center alignment button.

- Or, choose Table, Cell Height and Width; click on the *Row* tab (if necessary); under Alignment, select the desired alignment; and click on *OK*.

Let's format and align text in our table, and then center the table between the left and right margins:

1. Select the first row, which contains the column headings.

2. Make all of the text in the first row bold and centered.

3. Select the **Yes** cell (under the *Mileage Included* heading), hold the mouse button, and drag down to select the rest of the second column. The second column is selected except for the column heading.

4. Center-align the selected text. All of the text in the selected columns is now centered.

5. Select the third column except for the *Surcharge* heading.

6. Click on the Alignment Tab button to select the Decimal tab. Set a **Decimal** tab stop at the **3"** mark on the ruler to center the selected numbers by the decimal point.

7. Select the fourth column except for the *Additional Costs* heading. Center the selected numbers by placing a **Decimal** tab stop at the **4.25"** mark on the ruler.

8. Click on the **Show/Hide** button to hide the end-of-cell marks. Now you can view the table without all the extraneous marks.

9. Click on the **Show/Hide** button to display the end-of-cell marks.

10. Select the entire table. Then click on the **Center Alignment** button to center the table between the left and right margins (see Figure 10.15).

Figure 10.15
Centering the table

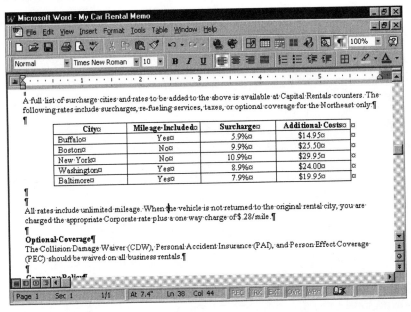

11. Print Preview the document. The table is centered between the left and right margins.

12. Close Print Preview.

13. Save the document.

ADDING OR REMOVING BORDERS

Borders are decorative lines added around text, objects or tables to place emphasis on them. To add or remove a border to a table:

- Select the table, column, row, or cell around which you want to add or remove a border.

- On the Formatting toolbar, click on the downward-pointing arrow next to the Border button.

- Click on the desired border type to apply.

In addition to the Border button on the toolbar, you click on the Tables and Borders button to open the Tables and Borders toolbar. You can use the Tables and Borders toolbar to perform many tasks associated with tables, such as: draw tables, add borders, customize line size and color, add shading, merge cells, split cells, distribute rows and columns, AutoFormat, Sort, and AutoSum.

To add or remove a border to a table using the Table and Borders toolbar:

- Click on the *Table and Borders* button to display the Tables and Borders toolbar.

- Select the table, column, row, or cell around which you want to add or remove a border.

- On the Tables and Borders toolbar, click on the downward-pointing arrow next to the Border button.

- Click on the desired border type to apply.

Shading is a degree of gray or other color that can be added to text, object or table to also place emphasis. To add or remove shading to a table using the Table and Borders toolbar:

- Select the table, column, row, or cell around which you want to add or remove shading.

- On the Tables and Borders toolbar, click on the downward-pointing arrow next to the Shading Color button.

- Click on the desired color or shade to apply.

Note: When you are finished using the Tables and Borders toolbar, it is a good idea to close it. The fewer obstructions that you have on your screen the better.

Let's remove and add borders to our table:

1. Select the entire table.

2. Click on the downward pointing arrow next to the Border button to view the border selections.

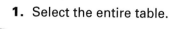

3. Use ToolTips to find the **No Border** option and click on it to remove the borders from the table.

4. Deselect the table and view the gridlines (see Figure 10.1)

5. Select the table and open the Border drop-down list box. Click on the **Inside Vertical Border** (use ToolTips to locate the option).

6. Select the first row and open the Borders drop-down list. Click on the **Bottom Border**.

7. Deselect the table. Notice the change in the table. You can see some of the dotted gridlines (see Figure 10.16).

Figure 10.16
The completed table with border and gridlines

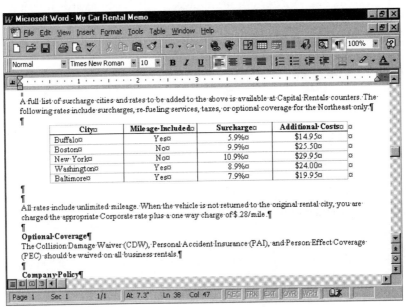

MODIFYING TABLE STRUCTURE

Word enables you to *merge cells* in a table; for example: to create one long row from several adjacent cells. Once the cells have been merged into one long row, you could type in the table's title or create a custom table.

Merging cells in a table ensures that your information will be included as part of the table, and can be formatted independently.

To merge cells:

- Select the cells you want to merge (they can be across a row or column).

- Choose *Table, Merge Cells* to merge the selected cells into one cell.

In addition to merging cells and adding borders and shading to your table, you might want to consider changing the direction of the text to *vertical*.

A vertical format means that while the majority of the table text flows horizontally, the vertical text is placed up and down in the column or row. The text direction can be changed in rows or columns, and is used to customize your table. For example, you may want to apply the vertical format to the column headings in a table in order to limit the amount of space each column contains.

To change the direction of text in a table:

- Select the text, cell, column or row you want to format.

- Choose *Format, Text Direction* to open the Text Direction dialog box.

- Select one of the vertical directions.

- Click on *OK*.

CONVERTING TABBED TEXT TO A TABLE

Word enables you to convert a tabbed table created by inserting tabs between columns of text into an actual table consisting of cells, rows, and columns. To convert tabbed text to a table:

- Select the text that you want to convert to a table.

- Choose Table, Convert Text to Table.

- In the Number of Columns text box, enter the desired number of columns.

- Click on *OK*.

Note: In addition to converting text separated by tabs, you can convert text that is separated by paragraph marks, commas, and other characters. To indicate the type of character you want to use to separate the text, select the character under *Separate Text At* in the *Convert Text to Table* dialog box.

You can also convert table text into ordinary text.

Let's convert tabbed text to a table:

1. Scroll to view the tabbed text near the middle of the page.

2. Select all of the lines in the tabbed table, from *Car Class* to *$63.00*, that will be placed in the table. Notice that our tabbed table consists of two columns of information in seven rows. We'll retain this structure.

3. Choose **Table, Convert Text to Table**. The Convert Text to Table dialog box is displayed. Word knows how many rows we want in our table (determined by the paragraph marks), and how many columns (determined by the tabs separating the text).

4. Under Separate Text At, verify that **Tabs** is selected to tell Word that tab marks currently indicate column boundaries (if necessary). Compare your screen to Figure 10.17.

Figure 10.17
Converting tabbed text to a table

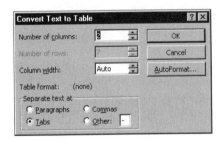

5. Click on **OK**. The selected text appears in a table. Notice that the column widths need some adjustment.

6. Verify that the entire table is selected. Then choose **Table, Cell Height and Width** to open the Cell Height and Width dialog box. Display the Column tab (if necessary).

7. In the Width of Columns 1-2 text box, type **1.5** to set the width of all of the columns to 1.5", and click on **OK**. The table now consists of two equally spaced columns.

PRACTICE YOUR SKILLS

1. Remove the grid border around the table and between all the cells.

2. Place an **Inside Vertical Border** to the entire table and a **Bottom Border** to the first row.

3. Center all the information in the table.

4. Center the table between the left and right margins.

5. Deselect the table.

6. Save the document and compare your screen to Figure 10.18.

**Figure 10.18
The converted table**

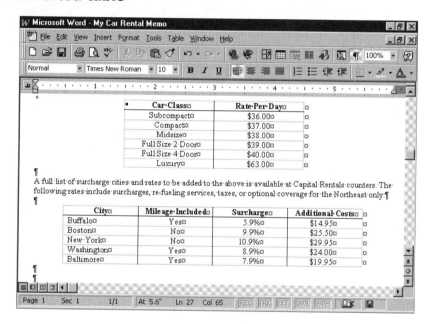

7. Close the document.

QUICK REFERENCE

In this chapter, you learned how to create tables using the Insert Table button in the Standard toolbar or the Table, Insert Table command from the menu. You learned how to move within a table; how to select cells, rows, columns, and the entire table; and how to enter data in a table. You also learned how to insert and delete rows and columns, how to change column width, how to change the alignment of a table between the left and right margins, and how to enhance the appearance of a table by creating various types of borders. Finally, you learned how to convert tabbed text to a table.

Here is a quick reference guide to the Word features introduced in this chapter:

Desired Result	How to Do It
Create a table using the menu	Choose *Table, Insert Table*. Type the desired number of columns in the Number of Columns text box. Type the number of rows in the Number of Rows text box. Click on *OK*.
Create a table using the Standard toolbar	Click on the *Insert Table* button.
Move within the table using the mouse	Place the I-beam on (or to the right of) the end-of-cell mark of the desired cell. Click the mouse button.
Move within the table using the keyboard:	
Move one cell to the right	Press *Tab*.
Move one cell to the left	Press *Shift+Tab*.
Move up one row	Press *Up Arrow*.
Move down one row	Press *Down Arrow*.
Select a cell	Move the mouse pointer into the cell. Triple-click the mouse button.
Select a row	Click the mouse button in the selection bar, to the left of the row. Or, place the insertion point anywhere within the desired row, and choose *Table, Select Row*.
Select a column	Click on the top border of the desired column. Or, place the insertion point in any cell within the desired column, and choose *Table, Select Column*.
Select an entire table	Place the insertion point anywhere within the table. Choose *Table, Select Table*.
Add a row at the end of a table	Place the insertion point in the last cell of the table. Press *Tab*.

Desired Result	How to Do It
Insert a row within a table	Select the row before which you want to insert the new row. Choose *Table, Insert Rows,* or click on the *Insert Rows* button.
Insert more than one row in a table	Select as many rows as you want to insert. Choose *Table, Insert Rows,* or click on the *Insert Rows* button.
Add a column to the right side of a table	Select all the end-of-row marks. Choose *Table, Insert Columns* or click on the *Insert Columns* button.
Insert a column within a table	Select the column to the left of where you want to insert the new column. Choose *Table, Insert Columns* or click on the *Insert Columns* button.
Insert more than one column within a table	Select as many columns as you want to insert. Choose *Table, Insert Columns* or click on the *Insert Columns* button.
Delete one or more rows	Select the row or rows that you want to delete. Choose *Table, Delete Rows.*
Delete one or more columns	Select the column or columns that you want to delete. Choose *Table, Delete Columns.*
Delete an entire table	Select the table. Choose *Table, Delete Rows.*
Change column width by dragging column boundaries	Point to the column boundary that you want to move until the mouse pointer becomes a horizontal, double-headed arrow. Drag the column boundary to the desired location. Release the mouse button.
Change column width by using the ruler	On the ruler, point to the column marker that you want to move. Drag the column marker to the desired location. Release the mouse button.

Desired Result	**How to Do It**
Change column width by using the menu	Select the desired column (or the entire table). Choose *Table, Cell Height and Width*. Click on the *Column* tab (if necessary). Type the desired width in the Width of Column text box. Click on *OK*.
Align a table between the left and right margins	Select the entire table. Click the *Center* alignment button. Or, choose *Table, Cell Height and Width*; click on the *Row* tab (if necessary); under Alignment, select the desired alignment; and click on *OK*.
Add or remove a table border	Select the table, column, row, or cell around which you want to add a border. Click on the downward-pointing arrow next to the Borders button. Place the mouse pointer over the border option of your choice. Click the mouse button.
Convert tabbed text to a table	Select the tabbed text that you want to convert to a table. Choose *Table, Convert Text to Table*. Enter the desired number of columns (if necessary). Under Separate Text At, select the desired separation character (if necessary). Click on *OK*.

In the next chapter, you will learn how to create newspaper-style columns and add graphics to your documents.

IF YOU'RE STOPPING HERE

If you need to break off here, please exit Word. If you want to proceed directly to the next chapter, please do so now.

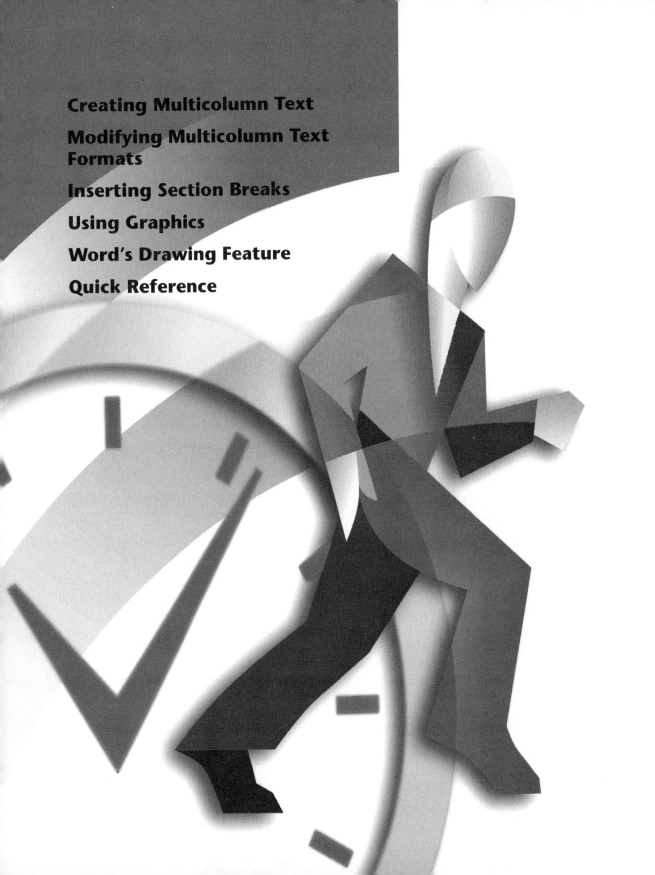

Creating Multicolumn Text

Modifying Multicolumn Text Formats

Inserting Section Breaks

Using Graphics

Word's Drawing Feature

Quick Reference

Chapter 11

Newspaper-Style Columns and Graphics

This chapter introduces ways to format text into *newspaper-style columns* (two or more columns running side-by-side down the page). Newspaper-style columns are useful in creating documents such as newsletters, brochures, and reports. In newspaper columns, the document text "snakes," or flows, down the length of one column, then continues at the top of the next column, and so on. If all of the columns on the page become filled, any additional text continues onto the first column of the next page.

Word also provides you with powerful tools for incorporating graphic images, or *graphics,* into your documents and for creating drawings.

When you're done working through this chapter, you will know:

- How to format text into newspaper-style columns

- How to insert a section break

- How to insert a graphic into your document

- How to size and move a graphic

- How to create a border around a graphic

- How to draw in your document

CREATING MULTICOLUMN TEXT

You can define your columns before typing the text, or you can reformat existing text into newspaper-style columns.

To create newspaper-style columns using the Format, Columns command:

- Place the insertion point where you want the columns to begin.

- Choose *Format, Columns* to open the Columns dialog box.

- Specify the desired number of columns in the *Number of Columns* text box, or click on one of the predefined column formats under Presets.

- In the *Apply To* drop-down list box, select *This Point Forward, Whole Document*, or *This Section* (as explained below).

- Click on *OK.*

Note: There is a limit to the number of columns you can specify, based on your document's margins and the default tab stops. Each column must be at least as wide as the distance between the default tab stops (0.5").

When you select *This Point Forward* in the Apply To drop-down list box, Word applies your specified multicolumn format from the insertion point to the end of the document. Word then inserts a *section break* directly before the insertion point; the section break is displayed as a double dotted line marked *Section Break*. Compare this to a page break, which is displayed as a single dotted line marked *Page Break*. Dividing a document into sections—each of which consists of a small portion of text, one page, or multiple pages—allows you to apply different page-formatting options to each section. The status bar displays the section number in which the insertion point is placed.

When you select *Whole Document* in the Apply To drop-down list box, Word sets your specified multicolumn format for the entire document, regardless of where the insertion point is placed.

When you select *This Section* in the Apply To drop-down list box, Word sets your specified multicolumn format for the entire section in which the insertion point is placed. (This option will only be available if your document already contains section breaks.)

To create newspaper-style columns using the Columns button:

- Place the insertion point anywhere in the section of the document where you want to create your newspaper-style columns.

- Click on the *Columns* button in the Standard toolbar to open a miniature four-column window.

- Click on the first (leftmost) miniature column to specify a single-column format; click on the second column to specify two columns; click on the third column to specify three columns; or click on the fourth (rightmost) column to specify four columns.

Note: When you use the Columns button to create newspaper-style columns, Word automatically applies your specified number of columns (1, 2, 3, or 4) to the entire section in which the insertion point is placed and changes the view to Page Layout.

Columns will not appear in the document window in Normal view. To display the text in columns, you must either Print Preview the document or change to Page Layout view.

Let's open a new document and create a newspaper-style column format:

1. Open **Customer Focus**.

2. Click on the **Print Preview** button. Notice that all of the text is currently in one standard, single-column format.

3. Click on the **Close** button to return to Normal view.

4. Place the insertion point at the top of the document (if necessary).

5. Choose **Format, Columns** to open the Columns dialog box.

6. In the Presets option, click on **Two** to select a two-column format. Notice that the Number of Columns box has changed to the number *2*.

7. Verify that the *Apply To* drop-down list box is set to *Whole Document* to format the document as two columns. Observe the Preview box, as shown in Figure 11.1.

8. Click on **OK**.

Figure 11.1
Changing to two-column format

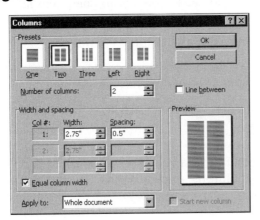

9. Observe the document. The view has changed to Page Layout (if Word prompts you, click OK to view the document in Page Layout view), and the text is formatted into two side-by-side columns.

10. Choose **View, Normal**. The side-by-side columns are not visible in Normal view.

11. Scroll to view the document.

12. Return to Page Layout view (choose View, Page Layout).

MODIFYING MULTICOLUMN TEXT FORMATS

When you create multiple (newspaper-style) columns, Word automatically apportions even amounts of space within each column and between columns, based on your document's margins. However, you can modify these values. For example, by default, Word places one-half inch of space between each column. Depending on the effect you desire, as well as how many columns appear on the page, you might want to increase or reduce this amount.

To change the space between columns:

• Place the insertion point in the section containing the columns.

• Choose *Format, Columns* to open the Columns dialog box.

• In the *Spacing* box, specify the desired width between columns.

• Click on *OK.*

You can also insert a vertical dividing line between adjacent columns, which can produce a visually pleasing effect and help the eye separate the columns. This is particularly true of columns that are by necessity spaced closely together.

To add a vertical line between columns:

- Place the insertion point in the section containing the columns.
- Choose *Format, Columns* to open the Columns dialog box.
- Check the *Line Between* option.
- Click on *OK.*

Let's change the space between our columns, and then add a vertical line to highlight their readability:

1. Observe the space between the columns. It is large enough to be reduced slightly to make more room within the columns for text.

2. Choose **Format, Columns** to open the Columns dialog box.

3. Click twice on the *Spacing* down increment indicator to decrease the amount of space between the columns of text to **0.3"**.

4. Click on **OK**. The text columns now appear closer together. Notice that the text that earlier wrapped to the second column has now moved to the bottom of the first column.

5. Choose **Format, Columns**.

6. Check the **Line Between** option. Compare your screen to Figure 11.2.

Figure 11.2
Inserting a vertical line between columns

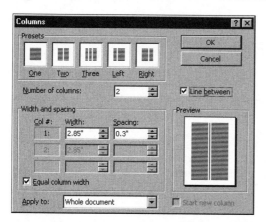

7. Click on **OK**.

8. Print Preview the document to see how it will look printed (see Figure 11.3).

Figure 11.3
Print Previewing the column modifications

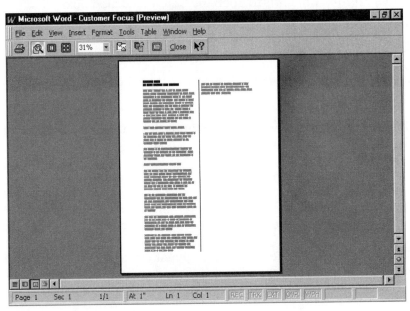

9. Close Print Preview.

10. Save the document as **My Customer Focus**.

INSERTING SECTION BREAKS

You can use sections to change formatting in one section of your document without affecting the rest of your document. For example, you could divide a five page report into two sections. The first section includes the first page (1.5" margins on all sides, and the report title in large bold letters centered in the middle of the page). The second section includes pages two through five (a 1" margin on all sides and a two-column format with left-aligned text).

When you create a new section, Word inserts a section break at the bottom of the section. Sometimes, Word will automatically insert section breaks for you, but you can also insert section breaks manually by using the Insert, Break command. The type of section break determines where the next section will begin.

The following chart determines how the four types of section breaks control where the next section will begin:

Table 11.1
Section Breaks

Type of Section Break	Where the Next Section Will Begin
Continuous	On the same page.
Next Page	On the next page.
Odd Page	On the next odd-numbered page.
Even Page	On the next even-numbered page.

To insert a section break in your document:

- Place the insertion point where you want the section break.
- Choose *Insert, Break* to open the Break dialog box.
- Under the Section Breaks option, select a type of section break.
- Click on *OK*.

Word uses section breaks to store formatting information, so you should be careful when you are deleting section breaks. To delete a section break, select the section break using the selection bar and press Delete. Section formatting is controlled by the break at the end of a section. Therefore, when you delete a section break, the section above the break's former location takes on the formatting of the section below that location.

VERTICAL ALIGNMENT

In the Layout section of the Page Setup dialog box, you have three choices for the vertical alignment of text on a page. These options control how Word aligns a partial page of text between the top and bottom margins. The options are:

Option	Effect
Top	The top of the paragraph is aligned to the top margin (this is the default setting).
Center	All paragraphs are aligned midway between the top and bottom margins.

Option	Effect
Justified	The paragraphs are arranged evenly between the top and bottom margins, with the top of the first paragraph aligned with the top margin and the bottom of the last paragraph aligned with the bottom margin.

After creating a section break, a common formatting applied to text is vertical alignment.

To apply vertical alignment to a section:

- Place the insertion point in the section you wish to format.

- Choose *File, Page Setup* to open the Page Setup dialog box.

- Select the *Layout* tab.

- In the Vertical Alignment drop-down list box, select the desired alignment (*Top* is the default setting).

- In the Apply To drop-down list box, select *This section*.

- Click on *OK*.

Let's divide the document, My Customer Focus, by inserting a section break and formatting the two sections differently:

1. Move the insertion point to the top of the document (the insertion point is next to the *C* in *Customer Focus*) if necessary.

2. Type **The Vision** (to enter text for the heading) and press **Enter**.

3. Verify that the insertion point is next to the C in Customer Focus. Choose **Insert, Break** to open the Break dialog box, and select **Continuous** under the Section breaks option (see Figure 11.4).

Figure 11.4
Inserting a continuous section break

4. Click on **OK** to insert the continuous section break. Notice the dotted line (with *Section Break (Continuous)* in the middle) is only one column wide.

5. Move the insertion point into the two-column text (if necessary). Observe the status bar; it reads *Sec 2*. This document now includes two sections.

6. Place the insertion point in *The Vision* heading (*Sec 1* on the status bar) and choose **Format, Columns** to open the Columns dialog box.

7. In the Presets option, select **One** (to select one column). Verify that the Apply To drop-down list box is set to *This Section*.

8. Click on **OK** to apply the new column formats. Notice that the section break now extends to the right margin.

9. Using the selection bar, select *The Vision* heading and apply the following formats: **Arial**, **24 pts**, and **centered**.

10. Click on the *Tables and Borders button* (on the Standard Toolbar) to open the Tables and Borders toolbar.

11. Change the *Line Weight* drop-down list box to **3 pt** (use ToolTips to locate the button on the Tables and Borders toolbar). Open the Borders button drop-down list box and select **Outside Border** to apply a 3 pt. border to the one-column heading text.

12. Click on the *Shading Color* button to open the drop-down list box, and select **Gray-25%** (use ToolTips to locate the color). Notice the fill is applied inside the border and the border is still black. Close the Tables and Borders dialog box.

13. Click on the **Print Preview** button to view the document. The document includes two sections; one is formatted with one column and the second is formatted with two columns. The left and right columns in the second section are uneven.

14. Return the document to Page Layout view (click on the Close button).

USING GRAPHICS

You can place graphics in any Word document, as well as in headers and footers. Graphics can be imported into a document from many draw or paint software programs or from *clip art* (sources of digitized images). Word also comes with a number of graphics files, which you can use in your documents and even edit.

To insert a graphic in your document:

- Switch to Page Layout view.

- Place the insertion point where you want to insert the graphic.

- Choose *Insert, Picture, Clip Art* to open the Microsoft Clip Gallery 3.0 dialog box.

- From the categories list, select the category of your choice.

- Click on the file name of the desired graphic.

- If you want to preview your selected graphic, click on the Preview button (if necessary) and observe the Preview box.

- Click on *Insert.*

Let's insert a graphic in our document:

1. Verify that you are still in Page Layout view.

2. Place the insertion point to the left of the *C* in the *Customer Focus* at the top of the first column.

3. Choose **Insert, Picture, Clip Art** to open the Microsoft Clip Gallery 3.0 dialog box.

4. From the Clip Art panel, select the graphic of your choice (see Figure 11.5).

5. Click on **Insert** to place the graphic in your document.

6. Observe the results. The graphic is inserted at the top of the first column in the second section. The graphic might be very large, depending upon what you selected. We'll have to resize it, so that it can fit in the document.

SIZING A GRAPHIC

The simplest way to size a graphic is by using the mouse to drag one of the selection handles. When you drag a handle on the side of the graphic, only the width of the graphic changes. When you drag a handle on the top or bottom of the graphic, only the height of the graphic changes. When you drag a corner handle, the width *and* height of the graphic change proportionately.

If you have sized the graphic and it appears distorted, you can restore it to its original size by: selecting the graphic; choosing Format, Picture; clicking on the Size tab; clicking on the Reset button; and then clicking on OK.

Figure 11.5
Selecting a graphic

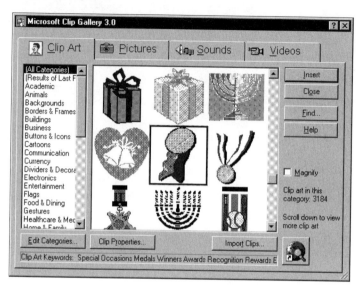

Once a graphic has been placed and modified, you might want to have text wrap around it. Word enables you to wrap text around an object or picture by using the Format, Picture command. To use this feature:

- Select the graphic.

- Choose *Format, Picture* to open the Format Picture dialog box.

- Click on the *Wrapping* tab to view the available options.

- Click on the *Wrapping Style* of your choice.

- Click on the *Wrap To* option of your choice.

- Click on *OK*.

Let's experiment with sizing our graphic:

1. Click once on the graphic to select it, if necessary. Place the mouse pointer on the selection handle in the middle of the right side of the graphic. The mouse pointer becomes a horizontal, two-headed arrow.

2. Press and hold the mouse button. Drag the handle leftward about 1" and release the mouse button. The width of the graphic is now disproportional to the height of the graphic.

3. Click on the **Undo** button to return the graphic to its original size.

4. Place the mouse pointer on the handle in the middle of the bottom of the graphic. The pointer becomes a vertical, two-headed arrow.

5. Drag the handle up about 1" and release the mouse button. The graphic is disproportional to the width.

6. Click on **Undo**.

7. Verify that the graphic is still selected.

8. Place the mouse pointer on the handle in the bottom-right corner of the graphic. The mouse pointer becomes a diagonal, two-headed arrow.

9. Drag the handle up or down until the graphic is about half the size of the column (the graphic will vary, depending on which graphic you choose).

10. Release the mouse button and compare your screen to Figure 11.6. The width and height of the graphic have changed proportionately.

Figure 11.6
Resizing the graphic proportionately

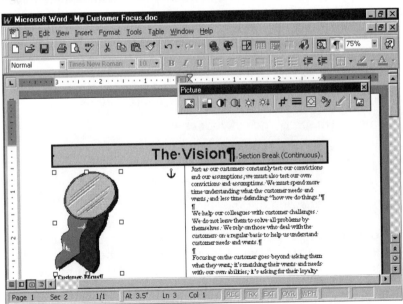

11. Verify that the graphic is selected. Choose **Format, Picture** and select the **Wrapping** tab. Currently, the text in column one is below the graphic, but it can wrap around, next to, or through the graphic to fill in the space.

12. Under the Wrapping Style option, select **Tight**, and Under the Wrap To option, select **Largest Side**. Click on **OK**.

13. Observe the document. The text in column one now wraps to the right of the graphic.

PRACTICE YOUR SKILLS

1. Place the mouse pointer in the title, *The Vision.*

2. Choose **Format, Paragraph** to open the Paragraph dialog box. Change the After text box (under the Spacing option) to **12 pt**.

MOVING A GRAPHIC

Suppose that you insert a graphic, and perhaps even size it, and then decide that you don't like its placement in your document. After you have inserted a graphic in your document, you do have the option of moving it.

To move a graphic:

- Select the graphic.
- Point to the graphic and press and hold the mouse button.
- Drag the dotted frame to the desired location.
- Release the mouse button.

Let's move our graphic to see if it would be more appropriate somewhere else in the document:

1. Use the Zoom Control box in the Standard toolbar to set the magnification to **50%**, and then scroll your window until you can see the graphic. When moving large graphics, you'll find it much easier to work at a lower magnification.

2. Verify that the graphic is selected.

3. Drag the graphic to the top of the right column next to the line in-between the columns. As you move the graphic it is displayed as a dotted frame.

4. Release the mouse button. The graphic is displayed in the right column (see Figure 11.7).

Figure 11.7
Moving the Graphic

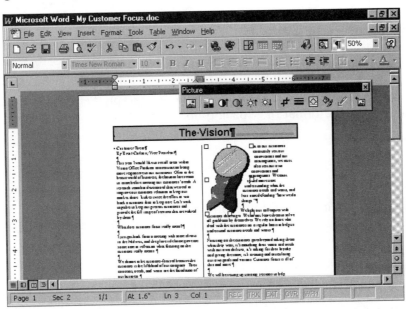

5. Move the graphic to the bottom of the left column. Notice how the text wraps around the graphic.

6. Move the graphic back to its original position, at the top of the left column next to the left margin.

ADDING A BORDER TO A GRAPHIC

To add a border around a graphic:

- Select the graphic.

- Choose *Format, Borders and Shading* to open the Format Picture dialog box.

- Click on the *Colors and Lines* tab, if necessary, to display the Borders settings.

- Under the Line option, open the Color drop-down list box and select your desired border color.

- Under the Line option, select your desired settings in the Style, Dashed, and Weight drop-down list boxes.

- Click on *OK.*

Let's add a border to our graphic:

1. Verify that the graphic is selected.

2. Choose **Format, Borders and Shading** to open the Format Picture dialog box.

3. Click on the **Colors and Lines** tab, if necessary, to display the Borders settings.

4. Under the Line option, open the Color drop-down list box and select **Black** (use ToolTips to locate the color).

5. Under the Line option, set the Weight box to **1 pt** and click on **OK**.

6. Deselect the graphic. A border now frames the graphic. Change the magnification back to **75%** to see this more clearly. Compare your screen to Figure 11.8.

MODIFYING A GRAPHIC BORDER

After you have applied a border to a graphic, you can change its thickness and style (or remove it altogether).

To modify the border:

- Select the graphic.

- Choose *Format, Borders and Shading* to open the Format Picture dialog box.

- Click on the *Colors and Line* tab, if necessary, to display the Borders settings.

- Under the Line option, select your desired options in the Color, Style, Dashed, and Weight drop-down list boxes.

- Click on *OK.*

**Figure 11.8
Adding a border**

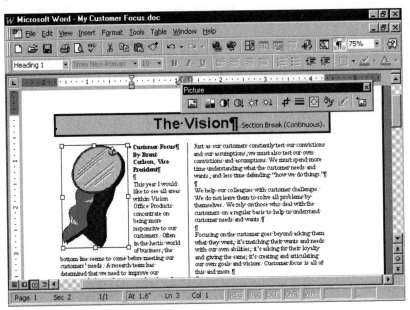

Let's remove our graphic's border:

1. Select the graphic.

2. Choose **Format, Borders and Shading** to open the Format Picture dialog box with the Colors and Lines tab selected.

3. Under the Line option, change the Color drop-down list to **No Line**. Click on **OK**.

4. Observe the graphic. It no longer has a 1 pt. black line border on all sides. The text wrapping is no longer set to tight, instead the text wraps in a square shape.

Now let's make a few final adjustments to our document, and then print it:

1. Place the insertion point at the blank line above the paragraph that begins with *Just as our customers* (near the bottom of column one).

2. Choose **Insert, Break** to open the Break dialog box.

3. Under the Insert option, click on **Column Break** to insert a column break at the insertion point.

4. Click on **OK**. The blank line and the paragraph that begins with *Just as our customers* is now at the top of the second column.

5. Print (or Print Preview) the completed document, shown in Figure 11.9.

Figure 11.9
The completed My Customer focus document

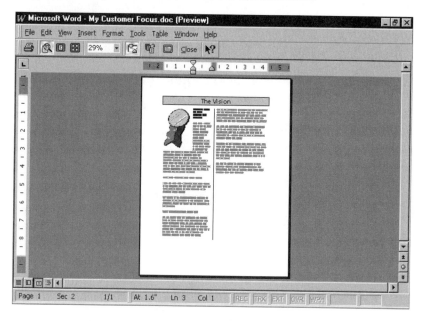

6. Close Print Preview, if necessary.

7. Save the document and then close it.

WORD'S DRAWING FEATURE

Word provides an easy-to-use drawing feature that allows you to create simple drawings in your documents. To do this:

- Open a document or create a new document.

- If the Drawing toolbar is not displayed, click on the *Drawing* button in the Standard toolbar to display it.

- Use the drawing tools to draw your picture within the document.

To edit a drawing in a document:

- Modify the drawing as desired.

- When you are finished, close the Drawing toolbar.

Let's use the Drawing toolbar to draw a simple map:

1. Open **Customer Focus Memo.**

2. View the end of the document. We are going to draw a map to go with the memo.

3. If the Drawing toolbar is not already displayed on your screen, click on ▨ (the **Drawing** button—on the Standard toolbar).

4. The Drawing toolbar appears at the bottom of the screen, and the view is changed to Page Layout view.

5. Click on ◹ (the **Line** button).
   The mouse pointer changes to a cross-hair because the Line button is activated.

6. Press and hold down the **Shift** key, and then drag (from left to right) at the bottom of the document within the document as shown in Figure 11.10. Holding down Shift while you drag allows you to draw straight lines easily. (**Note:** Don't release Shift until you're done drawing the line or it might not be straight.)

7. With the line still selected, click on ▤ (the **Line Style** button).

8. A list of line sizes and options is available. Select the **6 pt.** line.

9. Use the technique outlined in steps 5 and 6 to draw the other straight line shown in Figure 11.10. These are two of the roads.

10. Draw the diagonal line as shown in Figure 11.10 (you do not need to press Shift).

Lets add the road names and other text:

1. Click on ▣ (the **Text Box** button).
   The text box option is active and the Line button is deactivated.

2. Using Figure 11.10 as a guide, drag the text box for the text *Business Cooperative*. The Text Box toolbar is displayed.

Figure 11.10
The map

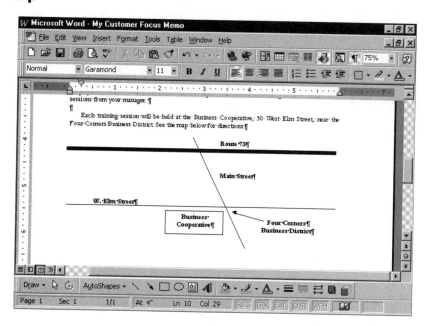

3. Type **Business Cooperative** in the text box (make sure the text is on two lines), **center** and **bold** the text. Resize the text box, if necessary.

4. Open ![Line Color button] (the **Line Color** drop-down list).

5. The available line colors are now visible. Select the color **Black** (if necessary).

6. Using Figure 11.10 as a guide, move the text box (with the border around it) into position.

7. Click on the **Text Box** button and drag a text box for a road name anywhere on the document (we'll move it into place later). Type **Route 73**. **Bold** the text. Resize the text box, if necessary.

8. Click on the **Line Color** to open the drop-down list box and select **No Line** (if necessary).

9. Click on ![Fill Color button] (the **Fill Color** button).

10. From the drop-down list box, select **No Fill** (if necessary).

11. Using Figure 11.10 as a guide, move the *Route 73* text box into place.

12. Repeat steps 6, 7, 8, and 9 to create and place the text boxes for **Main Street**, **W. Elm Street**, and **Four Corners Business District.**

13. Click on ↖ (the **Arrow** button) to activate the Arrow function.

14. Draw an arrow from the *Four Corners Business District* text to the intersection of *W. Elm Street* and *Main Street*.

15. View the finished document in Print Preview. Click on the Close button.

16. Save the document as **My Customer Focus Memo.**

In addition to the two-dimensional drawing tools, Word has enabled you to add another dimension and perspective to your drawings by using the *3-D* and *Shadow* buttons.

Let's add a third dimension to our map:

1. Click on the *Business Cooperative* text box to select it.

2. On the Drawing toolbar, click on 🔲 (the **3-D** button).

3. Select **3-D Style 7** (use ToolTips to locate it).

4. Deselect and observe the *Business Cooperative* text box. It has a 3-dimensional look with two shades of gray fill added. The text box looks like a building.

5. Select the arrow pointing to the intersection.

6. Click on 🔲 (the **Shadow** button).

7. Select **Shadow Style 14** to apply a light gray shadow under the arrow and to make it look 3-dimensional.

8. Deselect and observe the map and compare it to Figure 11.11.

9. Close all toolbars except for the Standard and Formatting toolbars (choose **View, Toolbars**).

10. Save and close the document.

Figure 11.11
The completed map

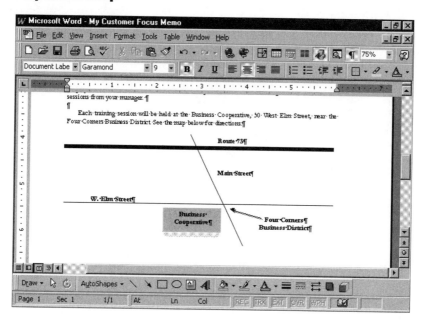

QUICK REFERENCE

In this chapter, you learned how to create newspaper-style columns of text, how to import a graphic image into your document, how to move and size the graphic, how to change the style of its border, how to create a drawing in a document, how to size and move the drawing, and how to superimpose text over it.

Here is a quick reference guide to the Word features introduced in this chapter:

Desired Result	How to Do It
Create newspaper-style columns	Place the insertion point where you want the columns to begin.
	Choose *Format, Columns*.
	In the Number of Columns text box, specify the desired number of columns or click on the desired column format under Presets.
	In the Apply To drop-down list box, select the portion of the document you wish to affect.
	Click on *OK*.
	Or, Click on the *Columns* button and select the number of columns.

Desired Result	How to Do It
Display multicolumn text	Choose *Print, Preview* or *View, Page Layout*.
Change the space between columns	Place the insertion point in the section containing the columns to be affected.
	Choose *Format, Columns*.
	In the Spacing box, type the desired value, or use the increment arrows.
	Click on *OK*.
Insert a line between columns	Place the insertion point in the desired section.
	Choose *Format, Columns*.
	Check *Line Between*.
	Click on *OK*.
Create a section	Place the insertion point where you want to insert the section break.
	Choose *Insert, Break*.
	Select a section break (Continuous, Next Page, Odd Page, or Even Page).
	Click on *OK*.
Insert a graphic	Place the insertion point where you want to insert the graphic.
	Choose *Insert, Picture, Clip Art*.
	From the categories list, select a category.
	Select the file name of the desired graphic.
	Click on *Insert*.
Size a graphic	Select the graphic.
	Drag the middle handle on the left or right edge of the graphic frame to affect the width.
	Drag the middle handle on the top or bottom edge to affect the height.
	Or drag one of the corner handles to increase or decrease the width and height proportionally.

Desired Result	How to Do It
Restore a graphic to its original size	Select the graphic. Choose *Format, Picture*. Click on the *Size* tab. Click on *Reset*. Click on *OK*.
Move a graphic	Select the graphic. Drag it to the desired location, using the dotted rectangle as a reference. Release the mouse button.
Add a graphic border	Select the graphic. Choose *Format, Borders and Shading*. Click on the *Colors and Lines* tab, if necessary. Under the Line option, select the desired settings in the Color, Style, Dashed, and Weight drop-down list boxes. Click on *OK*.
Modify a graphic border	Select the graphic. Choose *Format, Borders and Shading*. Click on the *Colors and Lines* tab, if necessary. Under the Line option, select the desired settings in the Color, Style, Dashed, and Weight drop-down list boxes. Click on *OK*.
Create a drawing in a document	Place the insertion point where you want your drawing to appear. If the Drawing toolbar is not displayed, click on the *Drawing* button. Use the drawing tools to draw your picture within the document. When you are finished, close the *Drawing* toolbar.

Desired Result	How to Do It
Edit a drawing in a document	Modify the drawing as desired.
	When you are finished, close the *Drawing* toolbar.

In the next chapter, you will learn how to create form letters.

IF YOU'RE STOPPING HERE

If you need to break off here, please exit Word. If you want to proceed directly to the next chapter, please do so now.

Chapter 12
Creating Form Letters

In word processing, *merging* or *mail-merge* is the process of transferring selected information from one document to another document. For example, you can write a form letter and instantly merge it with your mailing list to produce a customized letter for everyone on the mailing list. Other common mail-merge documents include mailing labels, interoffice memos, and reports.

Word's Tools, Mail Merge command enables you to take information from two documents—for example, a form letter and a list of names and addresses—and combine them into a single document. Of equal importance, perhaps, is the ability to sort the information in the mailing list, say, in alphabetical order by last name.

When you're done working through this chapter, you will know:

- How to create and attach the components of form letters

- How to generate form letters

- How to sort data

- How to create and print envelopes and labels

COMPONENTS OF A FORM LETTER

Before using Word's Mail Merge feature, you should be familiar with three important terms that correspond to the three main components of the merge process: the main document, the data file, and the merged document.

THE MAIN DOCUMENT

The *main document* contains normal text plus *field names,* which contain the instructions for carrying out the merge. The basic information in the main document remains the same. For example, suppose a form letter of invitation were to serve as the main document. The main document would contain the invitation text and various field names that would cause Word to retrieve names and addresses from a data file (discussed after the next section). Word would then insert the names and addresses in specific places in the merged document. Before you can instruct Word to merge documents, you must have inserted field names in your main document.

FIELD NAMES

In the main document, field names are used to indicate where variable information is to be inserted. In the data file (discussed next), field names indicate the category of information in each column. The field names inserted in the main document must match the field names in the data file. You can insert field names in your main document before the data file is attached; however, then you would have to enter field names twice. Thus, it is easier to insert the field names *after* the two files have been attached (you'll learn how to attach files later in this chapter).

THE DATA FILE

The *data file* stores information to be brought into the main document. You can think of the data file as a name-and-address list from which the program gets what you want to include in the main document. However, not only can you store names and addresses in the data file, you can also use it to store sentences and whole paragraphs, as well as any text or data you expect to use repeatedly. You can set up your data file as ordinary paragraphs or as a table. In this chapter, we use a table to compile data file information. In Chapter 10, you saw how compiling data in a table is an efficient way to keep the data organized. For this reason, when you create a data file using the Mail Merge Helper dialog box, Word automatically sets up the data as a table.

The *data-file table* contains a column for each category of information, or *data field*, in the data file. The *header row* is the first row of the table; it contains field names, which indicate the type of information in each column. Except for the header row, each additional row of the table contains a set of related information, known as a *data record*. Each record includes all of the information for one person in the name-and-address list. The various types of information in each record are known as *fields*, which are the equivalent of cells in a standard table.

There are several important guidelines for naming fields in data files:

- Each field name must be unique.

- It must begin with a letter.

- It can contain up to 40 characters.

- It can contain letters, numbers, and underscore characters; however, it cannot contain spaces.

Let's open a data file with missing records and then complete it:

1. Open **Data Source** and return to Normal view if necessary.

2. Observe the header row, the top row of the table.

3. Observe the data records, located in the rows below the header row.

4. Place the insertion point in the first field of the last row.

5. Type **Dudley** and press **Tab**.

6. Type **Long** and press **Tab**.

7. Type **Unique Rugs** and press **Tab**.

8. Type **125 North Road** and press **Enter**. Then type **Suite 3904**. Notice that you can press Enter to force information to a separate line in the record. The second line of information remains within the same record, and the insertion point remains in the same field.

PRACTICE YOUR SKILLS

1. Complete the table with the following information:

Yuma   AZ   85365   West

2. Save the disk file as **My Data Source** and compare your screen to Figure 12.1.

Figure 12.1
The completed My Data Source document

Header Row ———

Data records ——

Fields

First¤	Last¤	Company¤	Address¤	City¤	State¤	Zip¤	Sales· Region¤	¤
Kimberly¤	Reese¤	¤	1105·West·10th· Street¤	Omaha¤	NE¤	68127¤	West¤	¤
Andrew¤	Neel¤	Carl·Farms¤	119·Culver·Avenue¤	La·Jolla¤	CA¤	93108¤	West¤	¤
Carol¤	Hunter¤	¤	246·Eastman·Street¤	Chicago¤	IL¤	60604¤	Mid-west¤	¤
Dudley¤	Long¤	Unique·Rugs¤	125·North·Road¶ Suite·3904¤	Yuma¤	AZ¤	85365¤	West¤	¤

3. Close the document.

ATTACHING THE DATA FILE TO THE MAIN DOCUMENT

Attaching the data file to the main document identifies the data file as the one to be used for the variable information when the two documents are merged. Make sure that the main document is open when you attach the data file.

To attach a data file to a main document:

- Make the main document the active window.

- Choose *Tools, Mail Merge* to open the Mail Merge Helper dialog box.

- Click on *Create*, and choose the desired type of main document; for example, Form Letters.

- Click on *Active Window*.

- Click on the *Get Data* button.

- Click on *Open Data Source*.

- Specify the location and the name of the data file.

- Click on *OK*.
- Click on *Close* to close the Mail Merge Helper dialog box.

When you attach the data file, the *Mail Merge* toolbar is displayed above the ruler (see the following exercise). The Mail Merge toolbar enables you to quickly and accurately insert the field names and perform the merge.

To insert field names in the main document by using the Mail Merge toolbar:

- Place the insertion point where you want to add a field name.
- Click on the *Insert Merge Field* button.
- From the Insert Merge Field drop-down list, choose the desired field name.

Once the field name is inserted in the main document, it is enclosed by chevrons—for example, *<<First>>*, which represents the first-name field.

To enter a field name in the main document without using the Mail Merge toolbar, press Ctrl+F9 and type the field name between the braces ({ }) that appear. Be sure to use the identical field names used in the data file. If you are unsure of the field names, you can click on the Edit Data Source button in the Mail Merge toolbar to display the data file.

Let's view the main document, attach the data file, and then complete the main document:

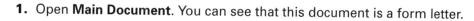

1. Open **Main Document**. You can see that this document is a form letter.

2. Observe the field names in the document (<<First>>, <<Last>>, and <<Company>>).

3. Choose **Tools, Mail Merge** to open the Mail Merge Helper dialog box. Notice that the dialog box conveniently places the three steps of the mail-merge process in a numbered list. As you can see, only the Create button is not dimmed. This tells us that we first need to create the main document. However, in this case, we want the current document to serve as our main document, so we must first instruct Word to use Main Document as the main document.

4. Click on **Create**. Notice the various choices for a main document available in the drop-down list box (see Figure 12.2).

5. Choose **Form Letters**. A message box is displayed telling you that you can use the Main Document file in the active window as the main document or select another one.

Figure 12.2
The Create options in the Mail Merge Helper dialog box

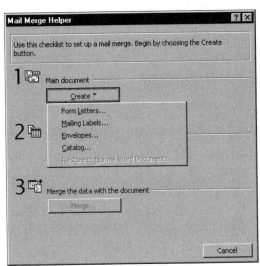

6. Click on the **Active Window** button to select Main Document as the main document and return to the Mail Merge Helper dialog box. Notice that under the Create button, the selected type of merge is displayed, as well as the name and location of the main document. Next to the Create button, an Edit button has appeared, allowing you to edit data in the main document.

7. Click on the **Get Data** button, and choose **Open Data Source** from the drop-down list (see Figure 12.3). The Open Data Source dialog box is displayed, along with the contents of the WordWork folder.

8. From the list of files, select **My Data Source**, the data file you saved earlier.

9. Click on **Open** to attach the data file to the main document and return to the Mail Merge Helper dialog box. The selected data file is now listed below the Get Data button, and next to it is displayed another Edit button, this one for editing data in the data file.

10. Click on **Close** to close the Mail Merge Helper dialog box. (Before we perform the merge, we'll insert some fields in our document.) The Mail Merge toolbar is now displayed above the ruler in the main document window (see Figure 12.4).

Figure 12.3
The Get Data drop-down list

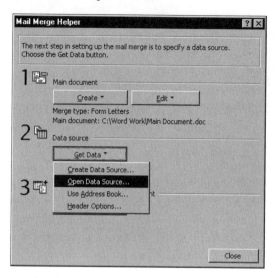

Figure 12.4
The Mail Merge toolbar

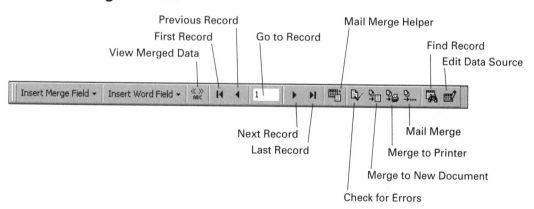

11. Place the insertion point on the first blank line below the *<<Company>>* field. Then click on the **Insert Merge Field** button. A drop-down list of fields is displayed (see Figure 12.5). These are the fields in the My Data Source Data file.

12. Choose **Address** from the list box to tell Word to place the information from the Address column of the data file in the completed form letter. The *<<Address>>* merge field is inserted in the document.

Figure 12.5
The Insert Merge Field drop-down list

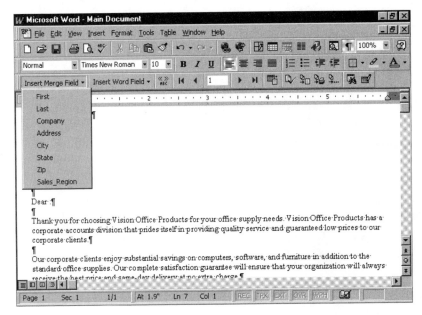

13. Press **Enter** so that three blank lines will remain between the address and the greeting.

14. Click on the **Insert Merge Field** button, and click on **City** to place the information from the City column of the data file in the completed form letter.

15. Type **,** and press the **spacebar** to place a comma and space after the city name.

PRACTICE YOUR SKILLS

1. Complete the form letter contained in the Main Document file, using Figure 12.6 as a guide. Also include the *Sales_Region* merge field in the last sentence of the letter (before the words S*ales Office*) and any spaces where necessary.

2. Save the disk file as **My Main Document**.

Figure 12.6
The form letter with inserted fields

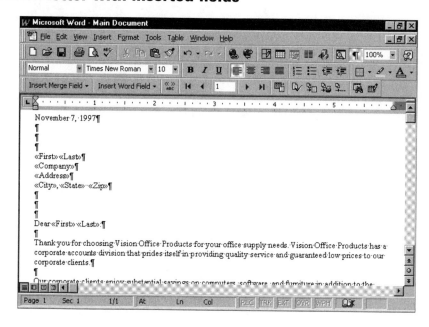

GENERATING YOUR FORM LETTERS

After you have completed and attached the data file and the main document, you can then merge the two documents. However, before you do so, you can preview your merged data in the main document window. This allows you to make any last-minute changes before committing the merge to a separate document or printing its results.

To preview the merge results, click on the View Merged Data button in the Mail Merge toolbar (see Figure 12.4). This switch is a toggle, which allows you to turn the feature on or off. With the View Merged Data feature turned on, you can:

- Select specific merged records for viewing by entering a record number in the Go to Record box on the Mail Merge toolbar

- Cycle through contiguous records by using the Previous Record and Next Record buttons

- View the first or last record by clicking on the First Record or Last Record button, respectively

There are three ways to merge the documents in Word using the Mail Merge toolbar:

- Click on the *Merge to New Document* button to save the merged files in a single, new file.

- Click on the *Merge to Printer* button to print the resulting merged documents.

- Click on the *Mail Merge* button to specify a range of data records to be merged or to choose other options in the Merge dialog box.

When you click on the Merge to New Document button to merge documents, a new document is created with the name Form Letters1 (if the type of merge you've selected is Form Letters). If you merge another document before you exit Word, the new document's name will be Form Letters2, and so on. A form letter is created for each record in the data file. You can print all the form letters by clicking on the Merge to Printer button, or you can print individual form letters by merging the documents first using the Merge to New Document or Mail Merge button, and then by displaying the desired merged form letter and choosing File, Print from the menu.

Note: By default, Word deletes any blank lines in the merged document that are created by empty fields in the data file. For this reason, records should not be left blank.

Let's merge the main document and the data file to create our form letters:

1. Observe the name of the current document, *My Main Document.*

2. Click on the **View Merged Data** button in the Mail Merge toolbar (see Figure 12.4). The merged data is displayed for the first record listed in the data file, that of Kimberly Reese (see Figure 12.7). Notice how the various fields have been "filled-in" with their corresponding information.

3. Click on the **Next Record** button in the Mail Merge toolbar to advance to the next record of information. Kimberly Reese's information is replaced with that of Andrew Neel.

4. This time, double-click in the **Go to Record** box to select the current record number (*2*); then type **3** and press **Enter** to advance to the third record of information contained in the data file. The data for Carol Hunter is displayed.

5. Click on the **Last Record** button in the Mail Merge toolbar to go to the last record, that of Dudley Long.

6. Click on the **First Record** button to return to Kimberly Reese's data.

Figure 12.7
Viewing the merged data

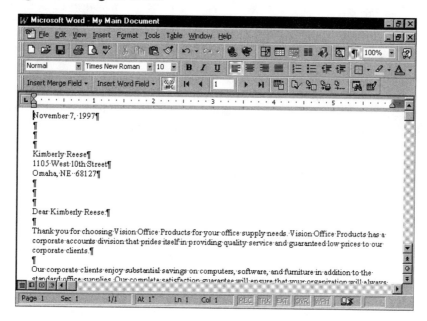

7. Click on the **View Merged Data** button to turn off the feature. Notice that the button is no longer depressed. The field codes are once again displayed in the document instead of actual merged data.

8. Click on the **Merge to New Document** button in the Mail Merge toolbar. My Data Source and My Main Document are now merged. Notice that the new document is named *Form Letters1*. Each letter is placed in a separate section within the document.

9. Scroll through the document to view the three remaining form letters. Notice the section breaks inserted between them. A letter has been created for every data record in the My Data Source file. Notice that the first and third letters do not have a company name, and the fourth letter has a two-line address.

10. Close all of the documents *without* saving them.

SORTING THE INFORMATION IN A DATA FILE

There will probably come a time when you will need to arrange a list of data, such as an address list, in alphabetical or numerical order. For example, you might want your data file records to appear in ascending alphabetical order by last name, or in descending numerical order by zip code.

You can use the Table, Sort command to sort columns of text in tables alphabetically, numerically, or by date. If you want to sort by a column other than the first one, you need to specify the column number. Columns are numbered from left to right. (For more information about tables, see Chapter 10.)

To sort data in a table:

- Select all of the text in the column that you want to sort; do not select headings or blank lines.

- Choose Table, Sort.

- Under Sort By, select the desired column number from the drop-down list box.

- In the Type drop-down list box, select the type of sort: *Text, Number,* or *Date*.

- Select a sort order: *Ascending* or *Descending*.

- Click on *OK*.

Note: You can select the header row of a table before performing a sort. However, if you do so, be sure to click on the Header Row option under *My List Has* in the Sort dialog box. If you do not select the Header Row before sorting, or if your table truly has no header row and you'd like the *entire* table sorted, the No Header Row option should be selected.

Let's experiment with sorting the records in a data file a couple of ways:

1. Open **Records**. Observe the second column, which contains last names. The last names are not arranged alphabetically.

2. Select all of the rows except the header row (see Figure 12.8).

Figure 12.8
Selected records to be sorted

First¤	Last¤	Company¤	Address¤	City¤	State¤	Zip¤	Sales· Region¤	¤
Kimberly¤	Reese¤	¤	1105·West·10th· Street¤	Omaha¤	NE¤	68127¤	West¤	¤
Andrew¤	Neel¤	Carl·Farms¤	119·Culver·Avenue¤	La·Jolla¤	CA¤	93108¤	West¤	¤
Carol¤	Hunter¤	¤	246·Eastman·Street¤	Chicago¤	IL¤	60604¤	Mid-west¤	¤
Dudley¤	Long¤	Unique·Rugs¤	125·North·Road¶ Suite·3904¤	Yuma¤	AZ¤	85365¤	West¤	¤

3. Choose **Table, Sort** to open the Sort dialog box.

4. Under Sort By, select **Column 2** from the column-number drop-down list box to instruct Word to sort by the second column of the table.

5. In the Type drop-down list box, verify that **Text** is selected.

6. Verify that **Ascending** order is selected, in order to sort the last names from A to Z. Compare your screen to Figure 12.9.

Figure 12.9
The specified sort criteria

7. Click on **OK** to perform the sort.

8. Deselect the records and observe that they have been sorted, and that the last names in column 2 are listed in ascending alphabetical order (see Figure 12.10). Observe that the zip-code data is not sorted in any particular order.

Figure 12.10
The records sorted by last name

First¤	Last¤	Company¤	Address¤	City¤	State¤	Zip¤	Sales-Region¤	¤
Carol¤	Hunter¤	¤	246·Eastman·Street¤	Chicago¤	IL¤	60604¤	Mid-west¤	¤
Dudley¤	Long¤	Unique·Rugs¤	125·North·Road¶ Suite·3904¤	Yuma¤	AZ¤	85365¤	West¤	¤
Andrew¤	Neel¤	Carl·Farms¤	119·Culver·Avenue¤	La·Jolla¤	CA¤	93108¤	West¤	¤
Kimberly¤	Reese¤	¤	1105·West·10th·Street¤	Omaha¤	NE¤	68127¤	West¤	¤

9. Select all of the rows of the table except for the header row, and choose **Table, Sort** to open the Sort dialog box.

10. Under Sort by, select **Column 7,** and select **Descending** order, to sort the zip codes from 9 to 0. Notice that *Number* is already selected in the Type box; because we selected Column 7 for sorting, Word has detected that we want to sort by number.

11. Click on **OK** to perform the sort.

12. Deselect the data and observe that the zip-code data is sorted in descending numeric order (see Figure 12.11).

Figure 12.11
The records sorted in descending order by zip code

First¤	Last¤	Company¤	Address¤	City¤	State¤	Zip¤	Sales·Region¤	¤
Andrew¤	Neel¤	Carl·Farms¤	119·Culver·Avenue¤	La·Jolla¤	CA¤	93108¤	West¤	¤
Dudley¤	Long¤	Unique·Rugs¤	125·North·Road¶ Suite·3904¤	Yuma¤	AZ¤	85365¤	West¤	¤
Kimberly¤	Reese¤	¤	1105·West·10th· Street¤	Omaha¤	NE¤	68127¤	West¤	¤
Carol¤	Hunter¤	¤	246·Eastman·Street¤	Chicago¤	IL¤	60604¤	Mid-west¤	¤

PRACTICE YOUR SKILLS

1. Sort the records by zip code in ascending order.

2. Save the disk file as **My Records**.

3. Close the document.

SORTING RECORDS IN THE MAIN DOCUMENT

In the previous section, you learned how to sort records in a data file. However, you can also sort the records from the main document window, even after you've already attached the data file to the main document.

To sort records in the main document:

• Activate the main document window.

• Choose Tools, Mail Merge.

• Under step 3—Merge the Data with the Document—click on the *Query Options* button to open the Query Options dialog box.

• Display the *Sort Records* tab.

- Under Sort By, select the field you wish to sort by from the drop-down list box.

- Select the desired sort order.

- Click on *OK*.

Let's sort the records in a main document:

1. Open **New Main Document**. This is a copy of My Main Document, which we created earlier in this chapter. Notice that the Mail Merge toolbar is automatically displayed, since Word knows this is a main document.

2. Open the Mail Merge Helper dialog box (choose **Tools, Mail Merge**, or click on the **Mail Merge Helper** button on the Mail Merge toolbar). Notice that **New Main Document** is listed as the main document. The data file remains *My Data Source*. Notice the Query Options button next to the Merge button under step 3.

3. Click on the **Query Options** button to open the Query Options dialog box, and click on the Sort Records tab.

4. Under Sort By, select **State** from the drop-down list, and retain the Ascending order. Compare your screen to Figure 12.12.

Figure 12.12
Specifying sort criteria in the Query Options dialog box

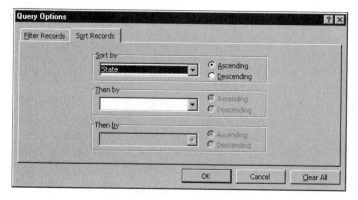

5. Click on **OK** to accept the sort criteria and return to the Mail Merge Helper dialog box. Under Options in Effect, near the bottom of the dialog box, notice the statement:

Query Options have been set

6. Close the Mail Merge Helper dialog box to return to the main document.

7. Preview the merge results (click on the **View Merged Data** button in the Mail Merge toolbar). Then view each record. Notice that the form letters are now displayed in ascending order by state. Dudley Long's data is displayed first, because his address is in Arizona (see Figure 12.13).

8. Close the file without saving your changes.

Figure 12.13
Previewing the results of the sort in the main document

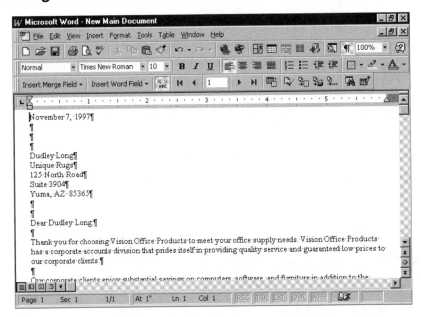

ENVELOPES AND LABELS

When creating envelopes or labels for a large mailing, the most effective method is to use the Tools, Mail Merge command. What if you only needed a few envelopes or labels? Word also includes the Tools, Envelopes and Labels command for such situations. For example, if you wanted to print one or two envelopes for a letter you wrote or if you wanted to print a few labels to place on some video tapes, you would use the Envelopes and Labels dialog box (choose Tools, Envelopes and Labels).

Note: Once the envelopes or labels are created, you'll need to print them. Because each printer is different, we suggest that you consult the owner's manual that came with your printer and follow the prompts in Word's Print dialog box.

To create an envelope for a document, such as a letter:

- Choose *Tools, Envelopes and Labels* to open the Envelopes and Labels dialog box.

- Click on the *Envelopes* tab, if necessary.

- Fill in the Return Address text box, if necessary. Word uses the inside address from the letter to fill in the Delivery Address text box (or fill in the address of your choice).

- Click on Add To Document or Print.

To create labels for a document or a short mailing:

- Choose *Tools, Envelopes and Labels* to open the Envelopes and Labels dialog box.

- Click on the *Labels* tab, if necessary.

- Fill in the Address text box, if necessary. If the document is a letter, Word uses the inside address from the letter to fill in the Address text box (or fill in the address of your choice).

- Click on the *Options* button to open the Label Option dialog box. In this dialog box, you can change the printer settings and the type of label you are going to use (such as selecting an Avery product number).

- Click on the *Print* button to print the labels, or click on the New Document button to create a document with the label layout (corresponding to the Avery product number you choose).

Note: If you have questions about how to use labels with your printer, consult the owner's manual for your printer or the label packaging. Each box of labels usually comes with directions on how to use the product.

QUICK REFERENCE

In this chapter, you learned how to create form letters by merging the main document and the data file. You learned how to insert merge fields in a main document, and then attach the corresponding data file. You also learned how to sort a data file in alphabetical and numerical order.

Here is a quick reference guide to the Word features introduced in this chapter:

Desired Result	How to Do It
Attach data file to main document	Activate the main document window.
	Choose *Tools, Mail Merge*.
	Click on *Create*.
	Click on *Active Window*.
	Click on *Get Data*.
	Click on *Open Data Source*.
	Select the desired data file.
	Click on *Open*.
Insert field names in main document	Place the insertion point in the desired location.
	Click on the *Insert Merge Field* button.
	Select the desired field name.
Merge documents	Attach the data file.
	Activate the main document window.
	Click on the *Merge to New Document* button.
Sort data in data file table	Select all data to be sorted.
	Choose *Table, Sort*.
	Under Sort By, select the desired sort criteria.
	Click on *OK*.
Sort records in main document	Activate the main document window.
	Choose *Tools, Mail Merge*.
	Click on *Query Options*, and display *Sort Records* tab.
	Under Sort By, select the desired sort criteria.
	Click on *OK*.

In Chapter 13, you will work with templates and styles.

SKILL BUILDER

This exercise gives you the opportunity to practice the skills you learned in the last four chapters. The following instructions lead you through the steps necessary to edit Practice 4A to produce the document in Figure 12.14.

Follow these steps at your computer:

1. Open **Practice 4A** (Chapter 2).

2. Type the following information into the table titled *Projected Quarterly Sales Table*:

   Row 3:   Trader Tom's   2300   1.49

   Row 4:   Aunt Emily's Market   4900   1.29

   Row 5:   Hamlet Farms   6500   1.29

3. Delete the second row that contains no information.

4. Right-align the second and third columns.

5. Change the column width for the *Boxes Sold* column to **1"**.

6. Change the column width for *Profit (per box)* to **1.25"**.

7. Center the table on the page.

8. Save the disk file as **My Practice 4A** (Chapter 1).

9. Print the document and compare it to Figure 12.14 (Chapter 1).

10. Close the document (Chapter 1).

If you have finished the activity, you might like to try a more challenging one requiring similar skills. In the next activity you will edit Practice 4B to create the document shown in Figure 12.15.

Follow these steps at your computer:

1. Open **Practice 4B** (Chapter 2).

2. Below the *Projected Quarterly Sales Table* heading, create a table that contains three columns and four rows.

3. Enter the data as shown in Figure 12.15.

Figure 12.14
The completed My Practice 4A document

The Garden Patch
Product Line Announcement

Introduction

The Garden Patch is pleased to announce the unveiling of a new food line in the Garden Patch series: the Fruit Patch. The Fruit Patch product line was developed after two years of intense work through the cooperation and dedication of Dr. Faye Shad and her staff. The FDA recently approved the food and it will be released for public sale in three weeks.

The Fruit Patch includes a variety of organically grown fruit: berries (cherries, strawberries, raspberries, blackberries, and blueberries), apricots, peaches, grapes, and plums.

Projected Quarterly Sales

Our finance department has been hard at work, determining sales projections for the next quarter. The results are shown in the following table.

Projected Quarterly Sales Table

Vendors	Boxes Sold	Profit (per box)
Trader Tom's	2300	1.49
Aunt Emily's Market	4900	1.29
Hamlet Farms	6500	1.29
B and J's	10000	.79
Hout and Wallace Inc.	11500	.79

Figure 12.15
The completed My Practice 4B document

The Garden Patch
Product Line Announcement

Introduction

The Garden Patch is pleased to announce the unveiling of a new food line in the Garden Patch series: the Fruit Patch. The Fruit Patch product line was developed after two years of intense work through the cooperation and dedication of Dr. Faye Shad and her staff. The FDA recently approved the food and it will be released for public sale in three weeks.

The Fruit Patch includes a variety of organically grown fruit: berries (cherries, strawberries, raspberries, blackberries, and blueberries), apricots, peaches, grapes, and plums.

Projected Quarterly Sales

Our finance department has been hard at work, determining sales projections for the next quarter. The results are shown in the following table.

Projected Quarterly Sales Table

Vendors	Boxes Sold	Total Profit
Trader Tom's	2,300	3,427.37
Aunt Emily's Market	4,900	6,321.25
Hamlet Farms	6,500	7,085.98

4. Make the column headings in the first row bold.

5. Right-align the second and third columns.

6. Decrease the column width for the second and third columns to **1.5"**.

7. Center the table on the page.

8. Place a grid border on the table.

9. Save the disk file as **My Practice 4B** (Chapter 2).

10. Print the document and compare it to Figure 12.15 (Chapter 1).

11. Close the document (Chapter 1).

The following instructions lead you through the steps necessary to complete and attach the components of a form letter.

Follow these steps at your computer:

1. Open **Practice 4C Data** (Chapter 2).

2. Enter the data shown in Figure 12.16 (Chapter 10, this chapter).

Figure 12.16
The completed data file

First¤	Last¤	Company¤	Address¤	City¤	State¤	Zip¤	¤
Joy¤	Stevens¤	Design·One,·Inc.¤	49·March·Street¤	Chicago¤	IL¤	60606¤	¤
Andrew¤	Neel¤	Fantasy·Sport·Cards¤	2730·South·Carl·Street¤	Yuma¤	AZ¤	85365¤	¤
Patty¤	Morse¤	PLM·Advertising¤	558·Charleston·Avenue¤	New·York¤	NY¤	10051¤	¤
Joe¤	Glenn¤	Glenn·Construction¤	3948·East·Avenue¤	Pittsburg¤	PA¤	15222¤	¤
Pat¤	Fisk¤	Frisky·Pet·Supplies¤	213·Driscoll·Road¤	Torrence¤	CA¤	90504¤	¤

3. Save the disk file as My **Practice 4C Data** (Chapter 2).

4. Open the disk file **Practice 4C Main** (Chapter 2).

5. Create the form letter and attach the data file **My Practice 4C Data**. (**Hint:** When the message box is displayed, click on the **Edit Main Document** button as suggested. Word displays this message only if you haven't yet inserted field names into your main document.)

6. Enter the field names shown in Figure 12.17. (**Hint:** Use the **Insert Merge Field** button on the Mail Merge toolbar.)

Figure 12.17
The entered fields

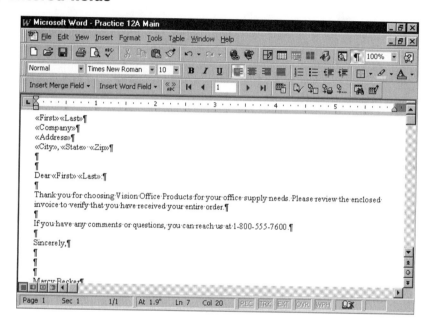

7. Save the disk file as **My Practice 4C Main** (Chapter 2).

8. Merge the files to create a new document.

9. Print the merged form letters and compare them to Figure 12.18.

10. Close all of the documents (Chapter 2) without saving them as disk files.

If you have finished the activity, you might like to try a more challenging one requiring similar skills. In this activity, you will create a data file, complete a main document, and merge the files to create form letters.

Follow these steps at your computer:

1. Open a new document (Chapter 2).

2. Create a table with six columns and four rows (Chapter 10).

3. Enter the data shown in Figure 12.19.

Figure 12.18
The merged form letters

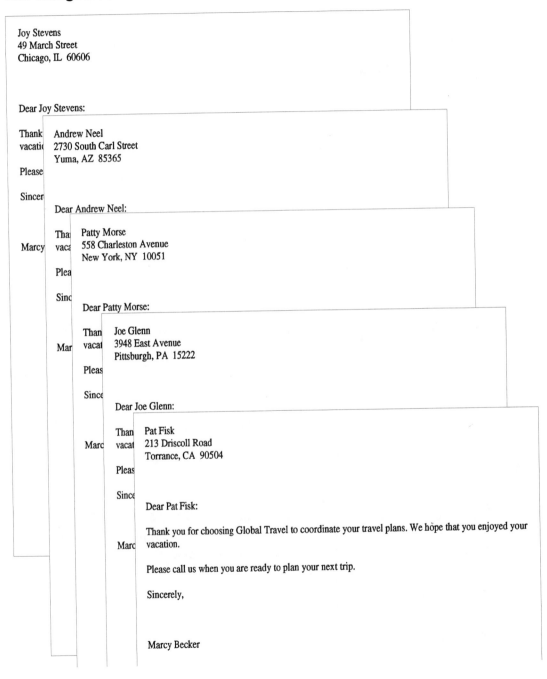

Joy Stevens
49 March Street
Chicago, IL 60606

Dear Joy Stevens:

Thank
vacati

Please

Sincer

Marcy

Andrew Neel
2730 South Carl Street
Yuma, AZ 85365

Dear Andrew Neel:

Tha
vaca

Plea

Sin

Patty Morse
558 Charleston Avenue
New York, NY 10051

Dear Patty Morse:

Than
vaca

Pleas

Since

Joe Glenn
3948 East Avenue
Pittsburgh, PA 15222

Dear Joe Glenn:

Than
vaca

Pleas

Since

Pat Fisk
213 Driscoll Road
Torrance, CA 90504

Dear Pat Fisk:

Thank you for choosing Global Travel to coordinate your travel plans. We hope that you enjoyed your vacation.

Please call us when you are ready to plan your next trip.

Sincerely,

Marcy Becker

Figure 12.19
The completed data file

First¤	Last¤	Company¤	Address¤	City¤	State¤	Zip¤	¤
Kimberly¤	Zona¤	KZ·Catering¤	96·Haven·Drive¤	Lee's·Summit¤	MO¤	64063¤	¤
Ashley¤	Benson¤	Smith,·Campbell·&·Young·Inc.¤	318·Acapulco·Trail¤	Thousand·Palms¤	CA¤	92276¤	¤
Andy¤	Fagan¤	Southside·Garage¤	2350·Southern·Way¤	Mesa¤	AZ¤	85210¤	¤

4. Save the disk file as **My Practice 4D Data** (Chapter 2).

5. Open the document **Practice 4D Main** (Chapter 2).

6. Attach the data file **My Practice 4D Data**.

7. In line 6, enter the following field names: <<First>> <<Last>>

8. In line 8, enter the following fields: <<Company>>, <<State>>

9. Save the disk file as **My Practice 4D Main** (Chapter 2).

10. Merge the files to create a new document.

11. Print the merged form letters and observe the results.

12. Close all of the documents without saving them as disk files (Chapter 2).

Chapter 13

Using Templates and Styles to Automate Your Work

Each time you instruct Word to create a document, the program does so according to a template. A *template* is a stored file that contains boilerplate text and/or special formatting information. It serves as a kind of skeleton or blueprint, providing your documents with an underlying structure. Templates also include styles, which contain special character and paragraph formats. (You were introduced to character and paragraph formats in Chapters 4 and 5, respectively.) Each style is stored under a specific name—for example, *Heading 1.*

Word comes with a number of useful templates, each designed for a specific kind of document. For example, the Normal template is used to create a standard document, while the Professional Letter template can be used to create a business letter. Word also comes with several *wizards*, which are specialized templates that walk you through the steps required to create a specific type of document. For example, the Fax Wizard leads you through the process of creating a business fax.

The primary benefit of using a template or a wizard is that all, or at least some, of the document's characteristics have been defined in advance. This enables you to create documents that have similar character and paragraph formats, as well as similar page setups, without having to specify each parameter for each document.

When you're done working through this chapter, you will know:

- How to create a document using the Normal template
- How to create a document using the Fax Wizard
- How to use styles
- How to create and modify styles
- How to create and modify an outline based on styles

USING THE NORMAL TEMPLATE

Every document that you create in Word uses a template. By default, Word uses the Normal template for each new document. You can select a different template for a new document by choosing File, New to open the New dialog box and selecting a template in one of the available tabs.

To attach a different template to a document:

- Choose *Tools, Templates and Add-Ins* to open the Templates and Add-ins dialog box.
- Click on *Attach* to open the Attach Template dialog box.
- Select the desired template.
- Click on *Open* to apply the template and close the Attach Template dialog box.
- Click on *OK* to close the Templates and Ad-ins dialog box.

Let's create a fax using the Normal template:

1. Choose **File, New** to open the New dialog box, shown in Figure 13.1. The Blank Document template (which refers to the Normal template) is selected by default.

2. Click on **OK**.

3. Type **FAX** and press **Enter** twice.

Figure 13.1
The New dialog box

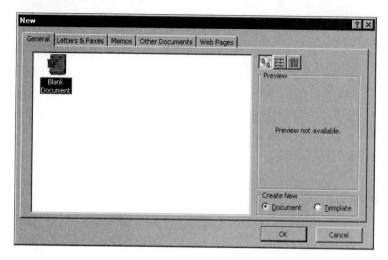

4. Type **To:** and press **Tab**.

5. Type **Ruth Allen** and press **Enter**.

6. Type **From:** and press **Tab**.

7. Type **Nancy Wright** and press **Enter**.

8. Press **Tab**, type **Vision Office Products** and press **Enter**.

9. Type **Date:** and press **Tab**. We'll insert the date in the next exercise.

INSERTING THE CURRENT DATE

Rather than typing the current date in every document that you create, you can have Word enter your computer's current system date.

To insert the current date:

- Place the insertion point where you want to add the date.

- Choose Insert, Date and Time.

- In the Available Formats list box, select the desired format.

- Click on *OK*.

Let's insert your computer's current system date:

1. Choose **Insert, Date and Time** to open the Date and Time dialog box.

2. In the Available Formats list box, select the third option (see Figure 13.2), which gives the full month, followed by the day, followed by the full year. (The date displayed is the current date.)

Figure 13.2
Selecting a date format

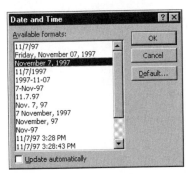

3. Click on **OK**. The system date is displayed in the document.

4. Press **Enter**.

5. Type **Fax #:** and press **Tab**.

6. Type **716-555-4343** and press **Enter**.

7. Type **Subject:** and press **Tab**.

8. Type **Change in Additional Services** and press **Enter** four times.

9. Type **Please review the text below and comment. Thank you.** Press **Enter** twice.

INSERTING A FILE

In Chapter 8 you learned how to use the Edit, Copy and the Edit, Paste commands to copy and move selected text from one document to another document. However, the easiest way to insert the entire contents of one document in another document is to use the Insert, File command.

To insert an entire file:

- Place the insertion point where you want the document to appear.
- Choose Insert, File.
- Select the desired folder in the Look In list box, if necessary.
- Select the desired disk file.
- Click on *OK*.

Note: If you have more than one window open, remember to activate the window of the document receiving the inserted disk file before you choose Insert, File. The inserted file is always placed in the active window.

Let's insert the contents of the Fax Text A disk file in our fax:

1. Choose **Insert, File** to open the Insert File dialog box.

2. Double-click on **Fax Text A** in the WORD WORK directory to place the contents of the file in the current document.

3. Save the disk file as **My Fax A**.

4. At the top of the document, select *Fax,* apply the **bold** font style, change the point size to **24**, and **center** alignment.

5. Select the six paragraphs beginning with *To:* and ending with *Subject:.* Then set a left-aligned tab at the 1" mark.

6. Deselect the text.

7. Select *To:* (do *not* select the entire line) and apply the **bold** font style.

8. Apply **bold** to *From:*, *Date:*, *Fax #:* and *Subject:.*

9. Select *Additional Services* (two lines below the paragraph that begins *Please review*) and apply **bold**. Change the point size to **14**.

10. Select the *Newsletter* heading, and apply **bold**. Then select *Consultations* and repeat the character formatting. Deselect the text, and compare your screen to Figure 13.3.

Figure 13.3
Formatting the fax

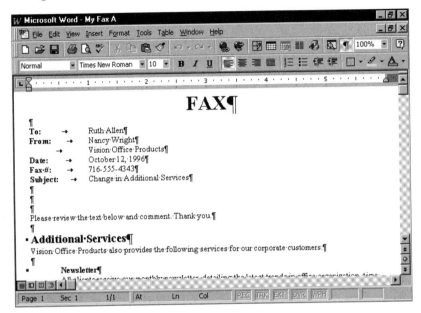

PRACTICE YOUR SKILLS

1. Apply the bold font style to the *Fax* heading.

2. Print Preview the document.

3. Save the disk file and close the document.

CREATING A FAX WITH FAX WIZARD

Word's *wizards* provide you with a fast way to create letters, memos, newsletters, resumes, calendars, faxes, and other common types of documents. For example, earlier you learned how to create a fax using the Normal template. However, you can also create a business-style fax by using Word's Fax Wizard.

To create a document using a wizard:

● Choose *File, New* to open the New dialog box.

● Select the desired tab; for example, Letters & Faxes.

- Select the desired wizard; for example, Fax Wizard.
- Click on *OK*.
- In the wizard dialog box, follow the steps provided.
- Click on *Next* to move to the next step, and fill-in the necessary options.
- Repeat this procedure until the *Next* button is dimmed (meaning that you have completed the last step).
- To change a setting, click on *Back* until that step is displayed; then change the setting.
- Click on *Finish*.

Note: If you do not wish to change any settings in the Fax Wizard dialog box, simply click on Finish when the first prompt (or any thereafter) is displayed.

Let's create a fax using the Fax Wizard:

1. Choose **File, New,** and click on the **Letters & Faxes** tab. (Remember, clicking on the New button in the Standard toolbar does *not* open the New dialog box.)

2. Select **Fax Wizard** (see Figure 13.4; the files in your list box may differ from those shown). A typical fax is displayed in the Preview box.

Figure 13.4
Choosing the Fax Wizard

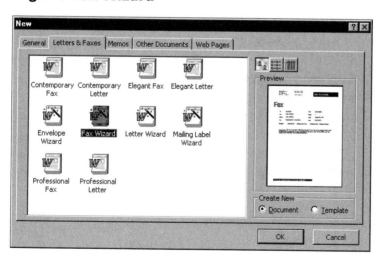

3. Click on **OK**. After some furious hard-disk activity, the Fax Wizard dialog box is displayed (see Figure 13.5). Notice that the left side of the box contains an outline of the steps necessary to create a fax.

Figure 13.5
The Fax Wizard dialog box

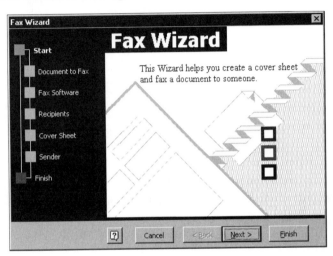

4. Click on **Next** to move to the first step, *Document to Fax*. Verify that *Just a cover sheet with a note* is selected (see Figure 13.6). If a document had been open, we could include that document in the fax.

Figure 13.6
Step 1—Document to Fax

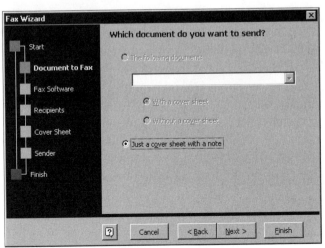

5. Click on **Next** to move to the second step, *Fax Software.* Select **I want to print my document so I can send it from a separate fax machine** (see Figure 13.7). You can send the fax directly from your computer (if your computer has a modem installed) or print the fax to send it from a separate fax machine.

Figure 13.7
Step 2—Fax Software

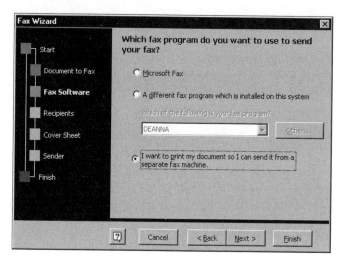

6. Click on **Next** to move to the third step, *Recipients.* The insertion point is in the first text box under *Name.* Type **Ruth Allen**, press **Tab**, and type **716-555-4343** (see Figure 13.8). You can choose from a list of predefined names and fax numbers or type one in, as we have just done.

7. Click on **Next** to move to the fourth step, *Cover Sheet.* You have three cover sheets to choose from. Verify that *Professional* is selected (see Figure 13.9).

8. Click on **Next** to move to the fifth step, *Sender.* In the *Name* text box, type **Nancy Wright**. Use Figure 13.10 as guide to fill in the remaining text boxes.

9. Click on **Next** to move to the last step, *Finish.* The Fax Wizard has now been completed (see Figure 13.11).

10. Click on **Finish** to close the Fax Wizard dialog box and to view the document, which is named *Document4* (the number to the right of *Document* may be different on your screen) and in Page Layout view. If necessary, close the Office Assistant.

Figure 13.8
Step 3—Recipients

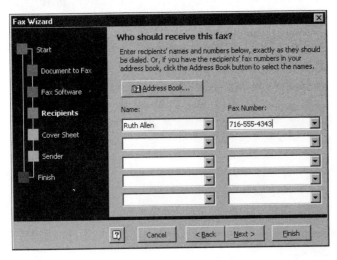

Figure 13.9
Step 4—Cover Sheet

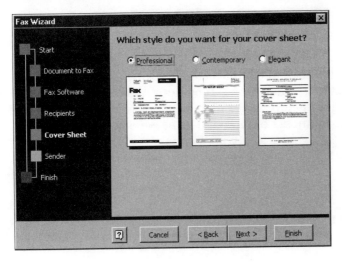

Figure 13.10
Step 5—Sender

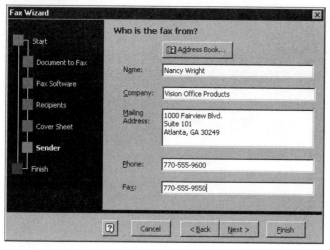

Figure 13.11
Last Step—Finish

11. If necessary, change *Zoom Control* to **75%** to view the fax. Observe the document and compare it to Figure 13.12.

Figure 13.12
A fax created with the Fax Wizard

12. Click on the placeholder text to the right of *Re:* to select it. Type **Change in Additional Services**. Use Figure 13.13 as guide, to fill in the rest of the fax. (Double-click on the boxes to place a check mark next to *Urgent* and *Please Reply.)*

13. Click on the placeholder text to the right of *Comments:*. Type **Please review the text below and comment. Thank you.** Press **Enter** twice.

14. Choose **Insert, File** and double-click on **Fax Text A** to insert the entire document.

15. Select **Additional Services** and apply the following formats: **Bold** and **14 pt**.

16. Bold the **Newsletter, Consultants**, and **Fax** subheads under *Additional Services.*

17. Save the document as **My Fax B**.

Figure 13.13
The fax with completed fields

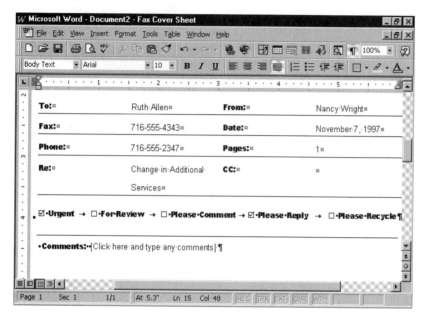

18. Observe the document and compare it to Figure 13.14.

19. Close all open documents.

USING STYLES

Templates contain styles, which are named sets of formatting instructions. Styles enable you to quickly and easily format the paragraphs in a document. You can use the styles included in the templates, or you can create your own.

Note: These styles differ from the ones you learned about in Chapter 4 in that here each style might contain a set of instructions, as opposed to a single instruction. For example, in Chapter 4 you saw how a word can have the bold font style applied to it. As it is used here, a style might refer to bold, 10 point, Times Roman, and underline. Furthermore, these styles are applied to whole paragraphs. All of the paragraphs using the same style will contain the same formatting.

The Style drop-down list box, at the left end of the Formatting toolbar, displays all of the styles included in the template of the current document.

Figure 13.14
The completed document, My Fax B

1000 Fairview Blvd.
Suite 101
Atlanta, GA 30249
Phone: 716-555-9600
Fax: 716-555-9550

**Vision Office
Products**

Fax

To:	Ruth Allen	**From:**	Nancy Wright
Fax:	716-555-4343	**Date:**	November 7, 1997
Phone:	716-555-4300	**Pages:**	1
Re:	Change in Additional Services	**CC:**	

☑ Urgent   ☐ For Review   ☐ Please Comment   ☑ Please Reply   ☐ Please Recycle

•**Comments:** Please review the text below and comment. Thank you.

Additional Services

Vision Office Products also provides the following services for our corporate customers:

Newsletter
All clients receive our monthly newsletter, detailing the latest trends in office organization, time management, and tips for a more efficient work place.

Consultations
Our corporate clients are invited to discuss their organizational and office needs with an agent from Vision Office Products' Professional Division. Our Professional Division is trained in the latest time management and managerial theory.

Fax
Office supply orders may be faxed to our office. If the order is faxed before 11:30 a.m., same-day delivery is guaranteed.

To apply a style to one or more paragraphs:

- Select (or place the insertion point in) the appropriate paragraph, or, for more than one paragraph, select the paragraphs.

- Open the Style drop-down list box.

- Select the desired style.

Let's examine styles that have already been applied, and then apply some of our own:

1. Open Style A.

2. Verify that the insertion point is at the top of the document, and take a look at the text in the first line, *Vision Office Products*. Observe the Style list box (in the Formatting toolbar). The style applied to the header is named (appropriately enough) *VOP Title*.

3. Observe the font, font size, bold font style, and alignment. The *VOP Title* style applies the following formats to the text: Arial, 18 pt., bold, and centered.

4. Place the insertion point anywhere in the text *Employee Benefits and Services* (under *Vision Office Products*). Notice that the current style name applied is *Subhead*.

5. Observe the font style, size and alignment. The *Subhead* style applies the following formats: Arial, 11 pt., bold, italic, and centered.

6. Place the insertion point in the paragraph that begins with *Vision Office Products offers* (two lines below *Employee Benefits and Services*). Notice that the current style applied is *Normal*.

7. Observe the font style and size. The Normal style applies the following formats: Times New Roman, 10 pt., and left-aligned. Had we applied, say, the *Heading 2* style, the body text would have been Arial, 12 pt., bold, and italic with additional paragraph formatting (line spacing).

8. Place the insertion point in the *Health Insurance* heading (below the paragraph that begins with *Vision Office Products offers*).

9. Open the Style drop-down list box and select the **Heading 1** style. The *Heading 1* style applies the following formats: Times New Roman, 14 pt., and bold.

10. Place the insertion point in the paragraph that begins with *Basic Coverage* (under the *Health Insurance* heading). Open the Style drop-down list box, and select the **Indent** style. This style applies a left indent at *0.75"* and a right indent at *5.5"*.

11. Place the insertion point in the paragraph that begins with *Major Medical coverage* (under the *Health Insurance* heading) and apply the *Indent* style to it (press **F4**). Do *not* use the Format Painter button; doing so will copy only the font formatting and not the heading style. Compare your screen to Figure 13.15.

Figure 13.15
The applied Heading 1 and Indent styles

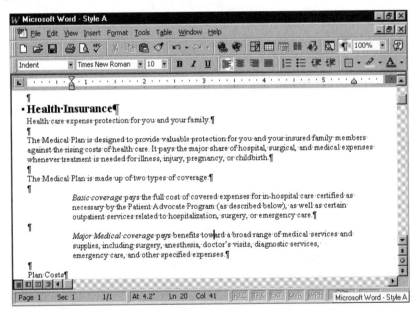

PRACTICE YOUR SKILLS

1. Apply the *Heading 1* style to the *Plan Costs, The Patient Advocate Program, Dental Insurance,* and *Plan Costs* headings.

2. Print Preview the document.

3. Save the disk file as **My Style A**

4. Close the document.

CREATING STYLES

You now know how to select an existing style from the Style list box. You can also create customized styles. The first step is to apply the desired formatting to text, or place the insertion point in text that already has the desired formatting applied to it. Then, either choose Format, Style from the menu or use the Style list box in the Formatting toolbar. We recommend using the Style list box, as it is simpler and faster.

To create a style based on a formatted paragraph:

- Select the formatted paragraph.
- Select the style name in the Style list box (or press *Ctrl+Shift+S*).
- Type the new style name.
- Press *Enter*.

Style names can contain up to 253 characters, though we recommend keeping them as short as possible. They can include any combination of characters and spaces, except the backslash (\), braces ({}), and semicolon (;). Of course, style names should be as descriptive as possible, and they must be unique; you can't have two styles with the same name. However, as you saw in the previous section, styles with names such as "Heading 1," "Heading 2," and so on, are perfectly acceptable.

When you create a new style for a document, it is saved whenever you save the disk file. The styles created in a document can be used only in that document. If you create a style in a template, it can be used in any new documents that are based on that template.

Let's examine the styles in the Normal template and then create our own style:

1. Open Style B.

2. Verify that the insertion point is in the text *Vision Office Products* (at the top of the document).

3. Observe the Formatting toolbar. The *Normal* style applies the following formats: Times New Roman, 10 pt., and left aligned.

4. Apply the **Heading 1** style (or any heading style that your printer can support). The *Heading 1* style applies the following formats: Arial, 14 pt., and bold (in addition to paragraph spacing).

5. Apply the **Heading 2** style. This style applies: Arial, 12 pt., bold, and italic (in addition to paragraph spacing).

6. Apply the **Heading 3** style. This style applies: Times New Roman, 12 pt., and bold (in addition to paragraph spacing).

7. Apply the **Normal** style.

8. Select the text *Vision Office Products.*

9. Use the Font dialog box to apply the following formats: **Arial**, **18 pt.**, **bold**, and **Small Caps**. Use the Formatting toolbar to change the alignment to **Centered**. These formats will be used in our new style.

10. Drag across the style name *Normal* in the Style box (or double-click on **Normal**) to select it.

11. Type **VOP Title** to name the new style (see Figure 13.16).

12. Press **Enter**.

Figure 13.16
Naming a style

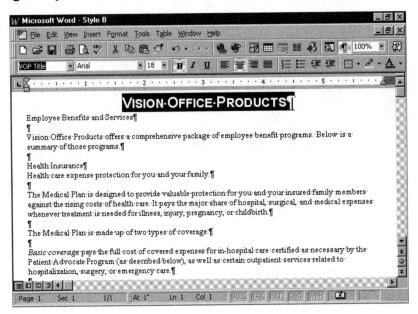

13. Open the Style list box and observe the list of styles. The *VOP Title* style is included near the bottom of the list. Normal was not replaced, but a new style was created.

14. Close the Style list box.

15. Select the text *Employee Benefits and Services* (under *Vision Office Products*) and apply the following formats: **Arial, 11 pt., bold, italic,** and **centered** alignment.

16. Select the style name *Normal* in the Style box and type **Subhead.**

17. Press **Enter.** Observe the list of styles. The *Subhead* style is included.

18. Place the insertion point in the paragraph that begins with *Basic Coverage* (under the *Health Insurance* heading).

19. Use the mouse to move the **Left-Indent** marker (use ToolTips to locate the marker if necessary) to the **0.75"** mark on the ruler. Then, move the Right-Indent marker to the **5.5"** mark on the ruler.

20. Select the style name *Normal* in the Style box, type **Indent,** and press **Enter** to create the *Indent* style.

21. Move the insertion point down one paragraph into the paragraph that begins with *Major Medical coverage.* Apply the **Indent** style.

PRACTICE YOUR SKILLS

Apply the *Heading 1* style to the following headings:

Health Insurance

Plan Costs

The Patient Advocate Program

Dental Insurance

Plan Costs

MODIFYING STYLES

Using styles to format a document is an easy way to make formatting changes. For example, if you format the Heading 1 style to include italics, and then want to remove the bold font style and add underlining, all you have to do is redefine, or modify, the style. When you modify the style, all of the paragraphs that have the Heading 1 style applied to them will be updated with the new formatting.

To modify a style:

- Select or place the insertion point in the paragraph containing the desired style.
- Choose Format, Style.
- Click on *Modify*.
- To modify the style's font, click on *Format*, and choose *Font*.
- Make the desired modifications in the Font dialog box.
- Click on *OK*.
- To modify the style's line spacing, click on *Format*, and choose *Paragraph*.
- Make the desired modifications in the Paragraph dialog box.
- Click on *OK*.
- Click on *OK*.
- Click on *Apply*.

Let's modify our Heading 1 style:

1. Place the insertion point in the *Health Insurance* heading.

2. Choose **Format, Style** to open the Style dialog box (see Figure 13.17). In the *Styles* list box, notice that the *Heading 1* style is currently selected (because of where the insertion point is located). The Paragraph Preview box displays a sample of the text. The Description box describes the characteristics of the style. Notice that the *Heading 1* style is defined as based on the Normal style, which we indeed used to create it.

3. Click on **Modify** to open the Modify Style dialog box, and click on **Format** to open the Format drop-down menu (see Figure 13.18).

Figure 13.17
The Style dialog box

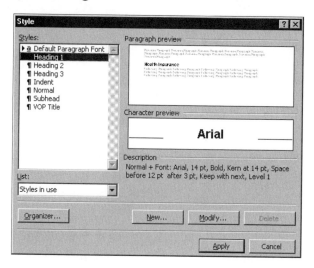

Figure 13.18
The Format drop-down menu in the Modify Style dialog box

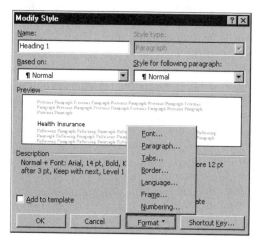

4. In the Format drop-down menu, choose **Font** to open the Font dialog box. Click on the **Font** tab, if necessary. In the Font Style list box, select the font **Times New Roman**. Then compare your screen to Figure 13.19. Notice the sample text displayed in the Preview box.

Figure 13.19
Modifying a style in the Font dialog box

5. Click on **OK** to close the Font dialog box and return to the Modify Style dialog box.

6. Click on **Format** (to open the Format drop-down menu) and choose **Paragraph** to open the Paragraph dialog box. Click on the *Indent and Spacing* tab, if necessary.

7. Under the Spacing option, change the *Before* text box to **0 pt** and the *After* text box to **0 pt**. Click on **OK** to return to the Modify Style dialog box.

8. Click on **OK** to return to the Style dialog box. Notice the difference in the sample text displayed in the Character Preview box. In the Description box, the font and spacing is different.

9. Click on **Apply** to close the Style dialog box. Notice that all text with the Subhead style now reflects the changes. Scroll to view all the headings. All of the headings are updated.

10. Save the disk file as **My Style B**.

11. Print the document and compare your printout to Figure 13.20.

12. Close the document.

USING STYLES TO CREATE AN OUTLINE

An outline is a multi-level format that enables you to structure text in an outline format (or hierarchically) just as its name suggests. Each step in the structure represents a different level of the text. For example, this book has different levels starting with the chapter, and then topics, and so on.

Figure 13.20
The completed My Style B document

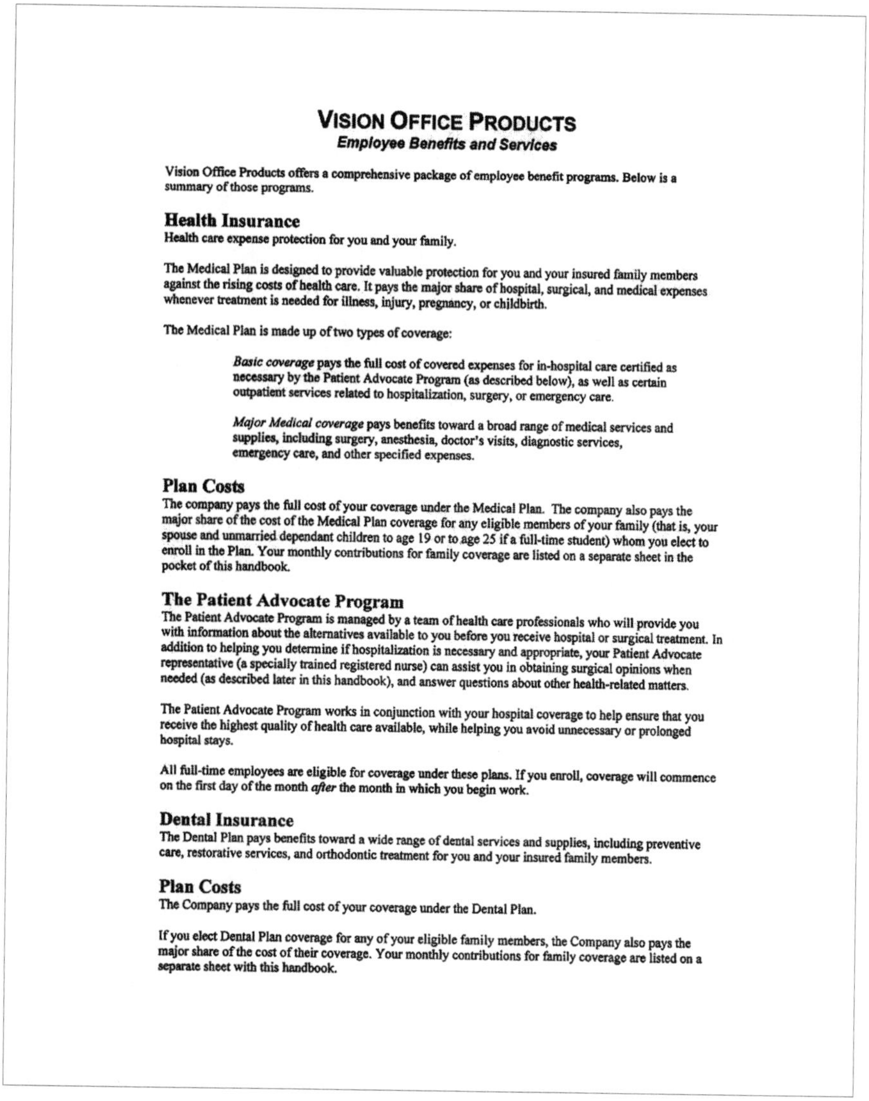

VISION OFFICE PRODUCTS
Employee Benefits and Services

Vision Office Products offers a comprehensive package of employee benefit programs. Below is a summary of those programs.

Health Insurance
Health care expense protection for you and your family.

The Medical Plan is designed to provide valuable protection for you and your insured family members against the rising costs of health care. It pays the major share of hospital, surgical, and medical expenses whenever treatment is needed for illness, injury, pregnancy, or childbirth.

The Medical Plan is made up of two types of coverage:

> *Basic coverage* pays the full cost of covered expenses for in-hospital care certified as necessary by the Patient Advocate Program (as described below), as well as certain outpatient services related to hospitalization, surgery, or emergency care.

> *Major Medical coverage* pays benefits toward a broad range of medical services and supplies, including surgery, anesthesia, doctor's visits, diagnostic services, emergency care, and other specified expenses.

Plan Costs
The company pays the full cost of your coverage under the Medical Plan. The company also pays the major share of the cost of the Medical Plan coverage for any eligible members of your family (that is, your spouse and unmarried dependant children to age 19 or to age 25 if a full-time student) whom you elect to enroll in the Plan. Your monthly contributions for family coverage are listed on a separate sheet in the pocket of this handbook.

The Patient Advocate Program
The Patient Advocate Program is managed by a team of health care professionals who will provide you with information about the alternatives available to you before you receive hospital or surgical treatment. In addition to helping you determine if hospitalization is necessary and appropriate, your Patient Advocate representative (a specially trained registered nurse) can assist you in obtaining surgical opinions when needed (as described later in this handbook), and answer questions about other health-related matters.

The Patient Advocate Program works in conjunction with your hospital coverage to help ensure that you receive the highest quality of health care available, while helping you avoid unnecessary or prolonged hospital stays.

All full-time employees are eligible for coverage under these plans. If you enroll, coverage will commence on the first day of the month *after* the month in which you begin work.

Dental Insurance
The Dental Plan pays benefits toward a wide range of dental services and supplies, including preventive care, restorative services, and orthodontic treatment for you and your insured family members.

Plan Costs
The Company pays the full cost of your coverage under the Dental Plan.

If you elect Dental Plan coverage for any of your eligible family members, the Company also pays the major share of the cost of their coverage. Your monthly contributions for family coverage are listed on a separate sheet with this handbook.

Creating an outline with styles gives you the flexibility to view any combination of topic headings, subheadings, or text. You can quickly assign different formatting to each topic level in an outline, and you can view topic levels with only certain styles applied to them. For example, you might create an outline with Heading 1, Heading 2, and Heading 3 applied to the text. While viewing the topics, you can display only the text with Heading 1 applied to it, rather than all of the text.

To create an outline with styles:

- Apply the appropriate styles to your document.

- Switch to Outline view (choose *View, Outline*). The Outlining toolbar is displayed.

- On the Outlining toolbar, click on the appropriate button. For example, click on the Show Heading 1 button to view only the text with Heading 1 applied.

The following buttons are located on the Outlining toolbar (in the order they appear on the toolbar):

Button	What it does
Promote	Applies the next higher style to the selected text (for example, changes Heading 2 to Heading 1).
Demote	Applies the next lower style to the selected text (for example, changes Heading 1 to Heading 2).
Demote to Body Text	Applies the style associated with body text, such as Normal.
Move Up	Moves selected text up in the outline, one line at a time.
Move Down	Moves selected text down in the outline, one line at a time.
Expand	Expands the outline to show all of the styles.
Collapse	Reduces the outline, one style at a time. (For example, it will collapse the Body text first and then Heading 7, and then Heading 6, and so on.)
Show Headings 1 through Show Headings 7	Works like the Expand and Collapse button, but refers to the corresponding style.
Show All Headings	Will show all headings styles but not body text styles.
Show Formatting	Displays all the formatting associated with the style.

QUICK REFERENCE

In this chapter you learned how to create documents using the templates provided with Word. You also learned how to use existing styles, as well as how to create your own styles and apply them to your documents. Finally, you learned how to modify styles.

Here is a quick reference guide to the Word features introduced in this chapter:

Desired Result	How to Do It
Attach the Normal template to a file	Choose *File, New*. Click on *OK*.
Insert the current date	Position the insertion point where you want the date to appear. Choose *Insert, Date and Time*. Select the desired date format. Click on *OK*.
Insert a file	Activate the destination document window. Place the insertion point at the desired destination. Choose *Insert, File*. Select the name of the file to be inserted. Click on *OK*.
Attach the Fax Wizard to a document	Choose *File, New*. Select *Fax Wizard*. Click on *OK*. Fill in the desired options in the Fax Wizard dialog box, and then click on *Next*. After answering the last step, click on *Finish*.
Apply a style	Place the insertion point in the desired paragraph or select the desired paragraphs. Open the Style drop-down list box and select the desired style.

Desired Result	How to Do It
Create a style	Format a paragraph as desired.
	Select the formatted paragraph.
	Select the style name in the Style list box.
	Type the new style name.
	Press *Enter*.
Modify a style	Select the paragraph containing the desired style.
	Choose *Format, Style*.
	Click on *Modify*.
	To modify a font, click on *Format* and choose *Font*.
	Click on the *Font* tab, if necessary.
	Make the desired modifications.
	Click on *OK*.
	To modify line spacing, click on *Format* and choose *Paragraph*.
	Click on the *Indents and Spacing* tab, if necessary.
	Make the desired modifications.
	Click on *OK*.

In Chapter 14, you will work with Word's Internet features.

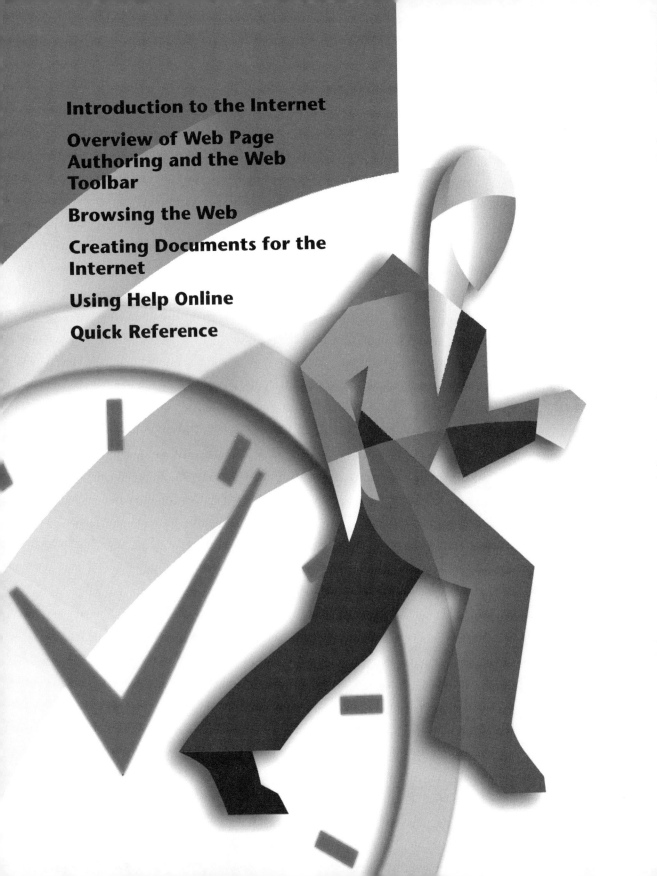

Chapter 14

Introducing the Internet

In Chapters 1 through 13, you learned how to create and format professional looking documents. In this chapter, you'll learn how to create documents for use on the World Wide Web. You'll also learn how to access Microsoft's online features, and how to browse the Web.

When you're done working through this chapter, you will know:

- How to access a browser application, such as Microsoft's Internet Explorer
- How to insert a hyperlink into a document
- How to save a document as an HTML file
- How to access additional Help from Microsoft through the Internet

INTRODUCTION TO THE INTERNET

The Internet is a worldwide network of networks. Each *subnetwork* can consist of a few or a large number of computers.

The *World Wide Web* provides you with access to all kinds of information stored in documents on file servers throughout the world. For example, you can read magazines, order products, download software documentation, or browse a catalog.

You can use a browser application, such as Internet Explorer, to view documents on the World Wide Web. (**Note:** Internet Explorer ships with Microsoft Office 97.)

In order to access the Internet, you will need:

- A computer configured for TCP/IP. TCP/IP is a network *protocol* (or language) that enables computers on a network to communicate with each other.
- To install Internet Explorer or another browser application.
- To install a modem or other network connection.
- An account with an Internet service provider (either through a remote, dial-in computer, or a computer attached directly to a network; for example, at work) through your TCP/IP connection.

Note: If you are missing even one of the components listed above, you may not be able to complete the tasks in this chapter.

The TCP/IP protocol is built into your Windows 95 operating system.

FINDING A SERVICE PROVIDER

These days, service providers are easy to find. Of course, you can contact the big service providers like CompuServe or America Online. Or, you can check the yellow pages of your local phone book, under Internet or World Wide Web, for local service providers.

OVERVIEW OF WEB PAGE AUTHORING AND THE WEB TOOLBAR

Web page authoring and the Web Toolbar are new and innovative features in Word 97. With these features, you can browse the World Wide Web (by launching a browser application) and create and edit Web pages.

Note: Internet Explorer does ship with Microsoft Office 97 (along with other Microsoft products); however, you must install it. For information on installing Internet Explorer, see your Microsoft documentation or onscreen help.

BROWSING THE WEB

Thanks to the wonders of modern technology, you can get to the Web without ever leaving Word. To browse the Web:

- Click on the *Web Toolbar* button (or choose *View, Toolbars, Web*) to open the Web toolbar.

- Select the text in the *Address* text box (or, click on the *Go* button and choose *Open* to open the Open Internet Address dialog box).

- Type the Internet address, such as *http://www.Microsoft.com*.

- Press *Enter*.

- If necessary, specify your service provider (for example, CompuServe, or your Internet account). (Depending on the browser software, you may not be able to complete this chapter.)

- Surf to your heart's content.

If you are not running Word on your computer, please start it now. Close all open documents except for the start-up document—Document 1. Let's browse the Web:

1. Click on ![] (the **Web Toolbar** button).

   The Web toolbar is displayed under the Formatting toolbar. You can use the Web toolbar to launch a Web browser.

2. Click on ![] (the **Start Page** button).

3. Word launches the browser application and displays the Microsoft Office home page (see Figure 14.1). Don't panic if your screen doesn't match Figure 14.1. Companies and people are constantly changing their home pages.

Figure 14.1
The Microsoft Office home page

Once you launch the browser application, you can jump to other Web pages. There are a few ways to move to new locations. You can click on any of the *links* (buttons or highlighted and underlined text) in the document or type the URL (uniform resource locator) address.

Let's spend a few minutes surfing the Internet:

1. Click on any button or link on the Microsoft Office home page. The browser application takes you to the new page. Do this as often as you like.

2. To return to the previous page, move the mouse pointer anywhere on the Web page and click the **right mouse** button and select **Back** from the QuickMenu.

3. In the *Address* or *Location* text box (the name of the text box depends upon the browser application you are using), type **http://www. Microsoft.com** and press **Enter** to move to the Microsoft home page.

   Note: Feel free to type any URL address you'd like to check out. We won't know.

4. When you're done looking at the location you selected, choose **File, Exit** to close the browser application and return to the Word window.

HYPERLINKING TO A WEB PAGE FROM A WORD DOCUMENT

You can create a hyperlink to any Web page on the Internet from any Word document. You can also create a hyperlink to another document or application on your computer or across a network. To create a hyperlink:

- Save the document (if the document is new, Word requires you to save it before creating a hyperlink).

- Select the text or graphic you want to use as a link.

- Choose **Insert, Hyperlink** to open the Insert Hyperlink dialog box.

- In the *Link to File or URL* text box, type a URL address, path and name of a file, or the path and name of an application (or use the Browse button to locate and select the file or application).

- Click on OK.

Note: Using the Named Location In a File (Optional) text box, you can create a hyperlink to a part of a file, such as a bookmark in Word, a named cell in Microsoft Excel, or a named object in Microsoft Access.

Let's create a hyperlink to a document on the Web:

1. Open a new document, if necessary.

2. Type **TestLink** to create the text for our hyperlink.

3. Save the document as **My Test Link**.

4. Select the text *TestLink*.

5. Choose **Insert, Hyperlink** (or click on the Insert Hyperlink button) to open the Insert Hyperlink dialog box (See Figure 14.2).

6. In the *Link to File or URL* text box, type the URL address of a page you'd like to link to (we'll use http://www.Microsoft.com). You can also create a link to a specific file or application on your computer or across a network.

7. Click on **OK**. Note that the text changes color and is underlined. This indicates that it is now an active link.

8. Save the document.

Now, let's try the link:

1. Click on the link. If everything goes well, the browser application should open to the page you choose to link to.

Figure 14.2
The Insert Hyperlink dialog box

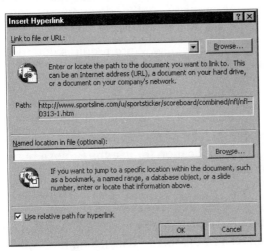

2. Choose **File, Exit** to close the browser application and return to My Test Link.

3. Observe the text *TestLink*. The text has changed colors to indicate that the hyperlink has been used.

4. Save and close the document.

CREATING DOCUMENTS FOR THE INTERNET

You can use Word's Internet features to create a document and put it on a Web-enabled file server where anyone can view it on the World Wide Web. Check with your Internet service provider for help advertising your home page. (What good is a home page if no one knows it's there!)

Let's create a simple Web page:

1. Open VOP Home Page.

2. Observe the document. This document includes four lines of text with simple character and paragraph formats applied. From this document we will create the Vision Office Products home page for the World Wide Web.

3. Choose **File, Save As HTML** to open the Save As HTML dialog box. The Internet uses HTML (Hypertext Markup Language). If you are planning to publish the file to the Internet, you'll need to save your document as an

HTML (Hypertext Markup Language) file. Word adds the codes necessary for your document to be used on the Internet. By saving a document as an HTML file, it will be recognized by the browser.

4. In the *File Name* text box, type **My VOP Home Page**. Observe the *Save As Type* drop-down list box; it is set to *HTML document*.

5. Click on **Save**. Observe My VOP Home Page and compare it to Figure 14.3.

Figure 14.3
My VOP Home Page saved as an HTML document

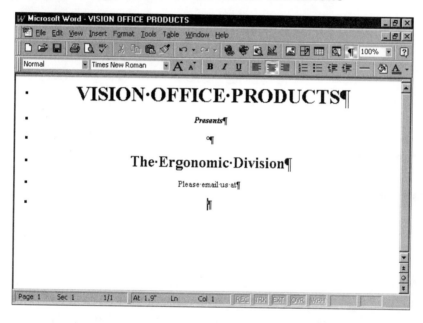

6. Place the insertion point in the blank paragraph under *Please email us at*.

7. Choose **Insert, Hyperlink** (or click on the Insert Hyperlink button). In the *Link to File or URL* text box, type **ergdiv@vop.com**.

8. Click on **OK**. The document now includes a hyperlink to an e-mail address.

9. Click on [icon] (the **Web Page Preview** button).

10. The browser application will open and display the document as it would appear on the Internet. (If you are prompted to save the changes, click on *OK.)*

11. Observe the My VOP Home Page displayed on the browser application and compare it to Figure 14.4.

Figure 14.4
My VOP Home Page displayed on a browser application

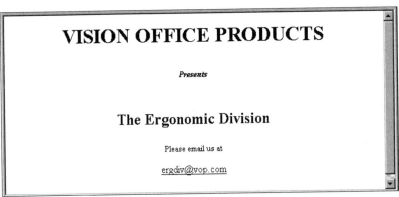

12. Close the browser application (choose File, Exit) to return to My VOP Home Page.

USING HELP ONLINE

One of the best things about Microsoft's Internet access is that you can get help online by going to one of Microsoft's many web sites. To go to one of Microsoft's web sites:

- Choose *Help, Microsoft on the Web* to open a drop-down menu of ten Microsoft web sites (each concerning a broad-based topic).

- Choose a topic. The browser application will open with the topic web site displayed.

- Read the information and follow the links.

In addition to online help, Microsoft also offers other support through the Internet, such as utilities, updates, information, and clip art, among others.

With My VOP Home Page still open, let's try the Web Tutorial:

1. Choose **Help, Microsoft on the Web**. Observe the ten web site options available in the drop-down menu (note the topics listed in the menu; you might view them later).

2. Choose **Web Tutorial** to open the browser application to Microsoft's *Web Tutorial* site.

3. Read the information displayed on screen and follow the appropriate links to view the entire (or part of the) tutorial.

4. When you have finished with the Web Tutorial, close the browser application to return to My VOP Home Page.

5. Click on the **Web Toolbar** button to close the toolbar (close any other extraneous toolbars that might be open).

6. Save and close the document.

Let's exit from Word:

1. Choose **File, Exit** to close Word.

2. Close Windows.

QUICK REFERENCE

In this chapter, you learned how to surf the Internet, how to create a hyperlink, how to save a document as an HTML file, and how to access Help online.

Here's a quick reference guide to the Word features introduced in this chapter:

Desired Result	How to Do It
Browse the Web from Word	Click on the *Web Toolbar* button.
	Select the text in the *Address* text box.
	Type the Internet address of your choice.
	Press *Enter.*
Move to a location in a browser application	Click on any button or link.
	Or, in the Address (or Location) text box, type the URL address and press *Enter.*
Close a browser application	Choose *File, Exit.*

Desired Result	**How to Do It**
Link a Web page to a Word document	Save the document.
	Select the text or graphic to use as a link.
	Choose *Insert, Hyperlink*.
	In the *Link to File or URL* text box, type the URL address.
	Click on *OK*.
Link a Word document to another file or another application	Save the document.
	Select the text or graphic to use as a link.
	Choose *Insert, Hyperlink*.
	In the *Link to File or URL* text box, type the name and path of the file or application.
	Or, use the Browse button to locate and select the file or application.
	Click on *OK*.
Save a document as an HTML file	Choose *File, Save As HTML*.
	In the *File Name* text box, type the name of the document.
	Verify that the *Save as Type* drop-down list box is set to *HTML Document*.
	Click on *Save*.
Use Help online	Choose *Help, Microsoft on the Web* to display the drop-down menu.
	Choose a topic web site.

Congratulations! You have now learned how to use many of Word's features. You are now prepared to take all that you've learned and apply it to your own documents. Remember, to master the skills that you've acquired, you must supply the most important ingredient—practice. Only through practice will you be able to get beyond the techniques themselves. Good luck!

Appendix A
Installation

This appendix contains instructions for installing Word 97 for Windows on your computer and for selecting a printer for use with Word.

BEFORE YOU BEGIN INSTALLING

Please read through the following two sections before beginning the installation procedure.

PROTECTING YOUR ORIGINAL INSTALLATION DISKS

Word comes with a CD-ROM or several floppy disks that you'll need to install the program on your computer. Before you begin, you should protect your original installation disks from accidental erasure. When a disk is protected, its data can be read, but not modified.

To protect a 3 1/2-inch disk:

• Slide the plastic locking button in the corner of the disk to its uppermost position.

REQUIRED HARD-DISK SPACE

You need to have at least 55MB (55,000,000 bytes) of free hard-disk space to install Word 97 for Windows. If you do not have this much free space, you will have to delete enough files from your hard disk to bring the total free space up to 55MB. For help in doing this, please refer to your Windows manual.

Note: Remember to back up (copy to a floppy disk) any files that you wish to preserve before deleting them from your hard disk.

INSTALLING WORD ON YOUR COMPUTER

Follow these steps to install Word 97 for Windows:

1. Start Windows. (If you have not already installed Windows 95 or Windows NT on your system, please do so now; for help, see your Windows 95 or Windows NT reference manual.)

2. Insert the installation disk labeled **Setup** in the appropriate drive. If you are installing Word from a network, you will be prompted for the drive and folder later in the installation process.

3. In the taskbar, click on **Start**, point to **Settings**, and choose **Control Panel**.

4. Click on the **Add/Remove Programs** icon, and verify that the Install/Uninstall tab is active.

5. Click on the **Install** button to begin the installation.

6. Follow the onscreen instructions to complete the installation. Here are some guidelines:

   • For help understanding the contents of an installation dialog box, click on its *Help* button.

   • In general, accept all installation defaults (by clicking on *Continue* or *OK*).

   • When prompted to select an installation option, choose either *Typical* or *Custom* to install Word. The *Typical* option installs the basic Office 97 or Word setup, which will still give you access to many features. The *Custom* option allows you to install the Word components of your choice. The hard-disk space required for each component is listed next to it. (**Note:** Do not choose the Compact option, as doing so will prevent you from completing the exercises in this book!)

   • If you discover that you don't have enough free hard-disk space to install the option of your dreams, either exit the installation procedure, free up some space on your hard disk and repeat the installation, or try life without it.

7. When the installation is complete, you are returned to Windows. To start Word, click on **Start**, point to **Programs**, and click on **Microsoft Word**. If you've installed Microsoft Office, you might need to click on **Microsoft Office** in the Program menu, and then click on **Microsoft Word**.

SELECTING A PRINTER FOR USE WITH WORD

Before you can print from Word, you must select a printer. To do so, follow these steps:

1. Start Word 97 for Windows.

2. Choose **File, Print** from the menu to open the Print dialog box.

3. In the Print dialog box, click on the **Printer** button. The Print Setup dialog box is opened, displaying a list of the printers that are currently installed on your system.

4. If your printer appears on the list (you may have to scroll), select it and click on **Set as Default Printer**. You can now use this printer with Word.

5. If your printer does not appear on the list (even after scrolling), install the printer on your system. (For instructions, refer to your Windows documentation.) Then repeat this printer-selection procedure from step 1.

6. Click on **Close** to close the Print Setup dialog box, and click on **Close** (do not click on OK) to close the Print dialog box.

Note: The printed examples shown in this book were all printed on a PostScript laser printer. Your printouts may differ somewhat, depending on which printer you are using. Printer choice also affects how text appears on your screen. If you are using a non-PostScript printer, your screen typestyles and sizes may differ from those shown in this book's figures.

Appendix B
Keystroke Reference

This appendix lists the keystrokes that you can use to issue Word commands.

INSERTION POINTER MOVEMENT

Move	Key/Key Combination
One character to left	Left Arrow
One character to right	Right Arrow
One line up	Up Arrow
One line down	Down Arrow
One word to left	Ctrl+Left Arrow
One word to right	Ctrl+Right Arrow
To end of line	End
To start of line	Home
Down one screen	Pg Dn
Up one screen	Pg Up

Move	Key/Key Combination
To start of document	Ctrl+Home
To end of document	Ctrl+End
To any page of document	F5
Back to last insertion point location	Shift+F5

TEXT SELECTION

Select	Key/Key Combination
Left character	Shift+Left Arrow
Right character	Shift+Right Arrow
Previous line	Shift+Up Arrow
Next line	Shift+Down Arrow
Extend selection	F8
Shrink selection	Shift+F8
Column	Ctrl+Shift

TEXT ENTRY AND FORMATTING

Format	Key/Key Combination
Start new paragraph	Enter
Start new line	Shift+Enter
Insert hard page break	Ctrl+Enter
Insert column break	Ctrl+Shift+Enter
Insert normal hyphen	Hyphen
Insert optional hyphen	Ctrl+Hyphen
Insert hard hyphen	Ctrl+Shift+Hyphen
Insert hard space	Ctrl+Shift+Spacebar

TEXT EDITING

Edit	Key/Key Combination
Move selected text	F2
Copy selected text	Shift+F2
Delete character to right	Del
Delete character to left	Backspace
Delete word to right	Ctrl+Del
Delete word to left	Ctrl+Backspace

FONT FORMATTING

Format	Key/Key Combination
Increase point size	Ctrl+]
Decrease point size	Ctrl+[
Change point size	Ctrl+Shift+P
Change case	Shift+F3
Remove formatting	Ctrl+Spacebar
Capitalize	Ctrl+Shift+A
Capitalize (small caps)	Ctrl+Shift+K
Bold	Ctrl+B
Underline	Ctrl+U
Underline words, but not spaces	Ctrl+Shift+W
Double underline	Ctrl+Shift+D
Enlarge font	Ctrl+Shift+>
Shrink font	Ctrl+Shift+<
Change font	Ctrl+Shift+F
Hidden text	Ctrl+Shift+H
Italic	Ctrl+I

Format	Key/Key Combination
Subscript	Ctrl+Equal sign (=)
Superscript	Ctrl+Plus sign (+)

PARAGRAPH FORMATTING

Format	Key/Key Combination
Single-space lines	Ctrl+1
Double-space lines	Ctrl+2
11/2-space lines	Ctrl+5
Center lines	Ctrl+E
Left-align lines	Ctrl+L
Right-align lines	Ctrl+R
Justify lines	Ctrl+J
Remove paragraph formatting	Ctrl+Q

FILE AND WINDOW MANAGEMENT

Format	Key/Key Combination
Save As	F12 or Alt+F2
Save	Ctrl+S
Open	Ctrl+O
Close document window	Ctrl+F4
Restore document window	Ctrl+F5
Maximize document window	Ctrl+F10
Close Word window	Alt+F4
Restore Word window	Alt+F5
Maximize Word window	Alt+F10
Next window	Ctrl+F6 or Alt+F6

Format	Key/Key Combination
Previous window	Ctrl+Shift+F6 or Alt+Shift+F6
Next pane	F6
Previous pane	Shift+F6

MISCELLANEOUS

Function	Key/Key Combination
Help	F1
Help pointer	Shift+F1
AutoText	F3
Repeat command	F4
Repeat Find/Go To	Shift+F4
Insert bookmark	Ctrl+Shift+F5
Spelling checker	F7
Thesaurus	Shift+F7
Menu	F10
Print	Ctrl+Shift+F12
Insert date field	Alt+Shift+D
Insert time field	Alt+Shift+T
Insert page number field	Alt+Shift+P
Update fields	F9

Index